DEATH OF A U-BOAT

On July 7 the submarine spent almost the whole day on the bottom. By midafternoon the air was so foul that the men were laboring to breathe. Lieutenant Degen decided to chance it and surface. He came to periscope depth and looked around. He saw nothing. He surfaced, and as the conning tower came out of the water, the men began pouring up, and as the decks cleared, they were out, taking great gulps of fresh air. But then out of the sun came an American Lockheed Hudson bomber, of No. 59 Squadron, on antisubmarine patrol. The lookout saw it very late. Degen hustled the men back down and crash-dived. The bomber was on them, and the first depth charge fell just twenty-five feet short. The second and third were right on target, in the stern, and tore open the pressure hull. In a minute water was pouring into the control room, and she was going down...

• • • •

"Hoyt brings to life the story of the underwater battles and shows how these submarines affected the political, strategic and ideological outcome of the war."

—*The Retired Officer*

Also by Edwin P. Hoyt

The U-Boat Wars
U-Boats Offshore: When Hitler Struck America
Submarines at War: The History of the American Silent Service
Sunk by the Bismarck
War in the Deep: Pacific Submarine Action in World War II
The Lonely Ships: The Life and Death of the U.S. Asiatic Fleet
How They Won the War in the Pacific: Nimitz and His Admirals
To the Marianas
Guadalcanal
The Glory of the Solomons
The Battle of Leyte Gulf
Blue Skies and Blood: The Battle of the Coral Sea
The Men of the Gambier Bay
Raider 16
Storm Over the Gilberts
Raider Battalion
Merrill's Marauders
The Invasion Before Normandy
The Pusan Perimeter
On to the Yalu
The Bloody Road to Panmunjom
Airborne: The History of American Parachute Forces
Kamikazes

ATTENTION SCHOOLS AND CORPORATIONS

WARNER books are available at quantity discounts with bulk purchase for educational, business, or sales promotional use. For information, please write to: SPECIAL SALES DEPARTMENT, WARNER BOOKS, 666 FIFTH AVENUE, NEW YORK, N.Y. 10103

ARE THERE WARNER BOOKS YOU WANT BUT CANNOT FIND IN YOUR LOCAL STORES?

You can get any WARNER BOOKS title in print. Simply send title and retail price, plus 50c per order and 50c per copy to cover mailing and handling costs for each book desired. New York State and California residents add applicable sales tax. Enclose check or money order only, no cash please, to: WARNER BOOKS, P.O. BOX 690, NEW YORK, N.Y. 10019

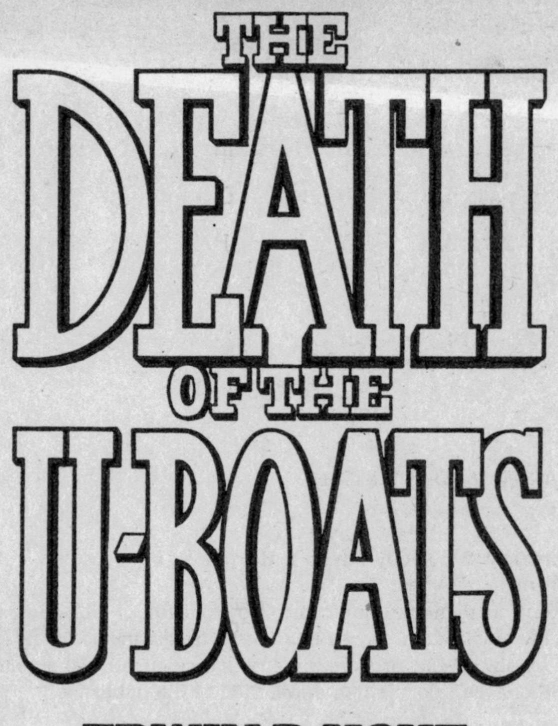

EDWIN P. HOYT

A Warner Communications Company

WARNER BOOKS EDITION

Copyright © 1988 by Edwin P. Hoyt
All rights reserved.
Except as permitted under the Copyright Act of 1976, no part of this publication may be reproduced or distributed in any form or by any means, or stored in a data base or retrieval system, without the prior written permission of the publisher.

This Warner Books Edition is published by arrangement with McGraw-Hill Book Company.

Cover art courtesy of Edwin P. Hoyt
Cover design by Don Puckey

Warner Books, Inc.
666 Fifth Avenue
New York, N.Y. 10103

A Warner Communications Company

Printed in the United States of America

First Warner Books Printing: June, 1989

10 9 8 7 6 5 4 3 2 1

Contents

Maps

A Noble Proposal: The London Submarine Agreement of 1936

In the 1930s, Britain, Japan, the United States, and the other maritime powers labored long, if unsuccessfully, to try to end the armaments race among nations, which in those days was manifested largely in terms of naval power. The British, in particular, sought the outlawing of the submarine as a weapon of warfare. The Japanese and the Americans did not see it that way. So the naval talks failed.

After Adolf Hitler came to power in 1933, Germany secretly began to throw off the armament limitations forced on her by the Treaty of Versailles. The next year twenty-four U-boats were completed. In 1935 Hitler repudiated the Treaty of Versailles, and the British were persuaded to work out the Anglo-German Naval Agreement, which allowed Germany a new submarine force and surface fleet. The British knew that the Germans were already building submarines. They faced two alternatives: stop the Germans by force, or negotiate control. The politicians were unwilling to stop the Germans, so the technicians tried to control them. The price exacted by the British was a limitation on submarine warfare; this was the London Submarine Agreement of 1936.

It proclaimed:

> The following arrangements are accepted as rules established in International Law.
>
> 1. In their actions regarding merchant ships, the

> submarines must conform to the rules of International Law which control surface warships.
>
> 2. In particular, except in the case of persistent refusal to stop after a proper demand, or active resistance in boarding, a warship, whether it be a surface vessel or a submarine, may not sink or make incapable of navigation a merchant ship without having first placed the passengers, crew and ship's papers in a safe place. In this sense, the ship's life boats are not considered to be a safe place because the safety of the passengers and crew cannot be assured; account must be taken of the state of the sea, atmospheric conditions, by the proximity of land, or the presence of another ship which would be prepared to take them aboard.

(Thus, if no other ship was nearby, the submarine would have to take the passengers aboard and guarantee their safety, or leave the ship alone. In effect, since a typical U-boat usually carried a crew of about thirty-five, and those small numbers strained the resources of the boat, even using the "hot bunk" system of two men to one bed, any but the very smallest vessel encountered on the high seas would have to be let go.)

1
Shadow of Terror

September 1, 1939. Poland was attacked by Hitler's troops. During the morning the British government ordered mobilization of all armed forces. Prime Minister Neville Chamberlain began to reorganize his government for war. He offered a seat in the War Cabinet and the position of First Lord of the Admiralty to Winston Churchill, an independent who had been extremely critical of Britain's defense policies for years. Churchill, who had held the post briefly in the First World War, accepted immediately.

"Winston is back." The word was flashed from Whitehall to the British Royal Navy around the world. And at six o'clock on the afternoon of September 2, three days before he was officially anointed, Churchill took over. For the next two days and nights there was precious little sleep for the new First Lord of the Admiralty. He had to meet a whole new contingent of men: Sir Dudley Pound, the First Sea Lord, was then a stranger; Churchill had been extremely critical of Pound's activities in parliamentary debate in the past. Now Churchill the politician and Pound the professional had to forge a working alliance.

Churchill and Admiral Pound agreed among themselves that the submarine would be the great menace at sea. But not just yet. Britain's anti-U-boat warfare system was elementary. Churchill learned within twenty-four hours that the Admiralty estimated the U-boat force at sixty vessels (only four off the actual mark of fifty-six). Fortunately, that number could not carry out a total blockade. There would be losses, Churchill said, but they would not in the beginning be conclusive. He had time.

But not as much time as he thought, before the losses started.

Hitler's sea war machine was far better prepared than anyone outside Germany recognized. All through the war the U-boat men complained that they operated with a skeleton force; this was true only in terms of their own expectations. Illegally, they began the war with a U-boat force as large as that of Britain, although it was supposed to be only half as large. The greatest advantage, however, was that as aggressor they could choose the battlegrounds. Admirals Raeder and Doenitz kept talking in the 1930s about five more years to build the fleet, but Hitler was not that patient. In 1938 he was completely ready for war. When he prepared to go to Munich in September 1938, to negotiate away from his potential adversaries the independence of Czechoslovakia, Hitler was prepared to fight. Commodore Doenitz's submarines were ready. Nearly sixty U-boat commanders were summoned to Doenitz's headquarters in Wilhelmshaven. There, standing on a dais before the rows of officers hunched on their folding chairs, Doenitz told them they were now to go to sea.

"Before leaving here you will be issued with sealed envelopes containing secret orders, and I must impress upon you that the seals are not to be broken until you receive signals from me indicating that hostilities have been declared. . . . Every operational submarine must be at battle stations within the next three days."

The enormous activity at Wilhelmshaven and Kiel was bound to be noticed, so it was covered by an official announcement that the German navy was setting out to conduct fleet exercises in the Baltic. Actually, twenty-five submarines sailed into the North Sea and formed a ring around Britain as Hitler's train moved toward Munich. Three days later Hitler had secured what he wanted by threat alone, and Doenitz called his "boys" home.

But by August 1939 the top commanders of the Wehrmacht, the Luftwaffe, and the German navy all knew that war would break out in two weeks. On August 19 Commodore Doenitz again deployed most of his operational U-boats in the waters around Britain. The smallest boats, 250-ton coastal submarines, were confined to the North Sea, but not twenty-six ocean-going submarines. Twenty of these were at action stations around the British Isles and in the British sea lanes.

Just after 11 A.M., German time, Berlin warned the U-boat command that Britain and France had declared war on Germany. Ten minutes later Commodore Doenitz sent his first war orders to the U-boat commanders surrounding Britain:

> BATTLE INSTRUCTIONS FOR THE U-BOAT ARM OF THE NAVY ARE NOW IN FORCE. TROOPSHIPS AND MERCHANT SHIPS CARRYING MILITARY EQUIPMENT TO BE ATTACKED IN ACCORDANCE WITH PRIZE REGULATIONS OF THE HAGUE CONVENTION. ENEMY CONVOYS TO BE ATTACKED WITHOUT WARNING ONLY ON CONDITION THAT ALL PASSENGER LINERS CARRYING PASSENGERS ARE ALLOWED TO PROCEED IN SAFETY. THESE VESSELS ARE IMMUNE FROM ATTACK EVEN IN CONVOY.
>
> DOENITZ.

As that message moved through the air, the Donaldson liner *Athenia* was on the high sea off Ireland. She had set sail from Glasgow on September 1 on the first leg of a transatlantic voyage to New York.

She had stopped off at Liverpool for passengers and did not leave Liverpool harbor until 4:30 on the afternoon of September 2.

At eleven o'clock on the morning of September 3, the captain received a message from the Admiralty in London announcing that war had been declared by His Majesty's Government against Nazi Germany. The word was passed to the crew and passengers. No one worried a great deal. The officers knew that they were protected by the London Submarine Agreement of 1936, as Commodore Doenitz had indicated to his captains. Following the horror of the "unrestricted submarine warfare" of World War I, the surprise sinking of merchant vessels had been outlawed for all time. Germany had agreed that merchant vessels had to be stopped by a surfaced submarine, which would then search for contraband. If the vessel was a ship of an enemy power it could be taken as a prize or sunk, but the safety of crew and passengers had to be secured. For all practical purposes that meant the ship would have to be allowed to continue on her way, because the submarine would have no way of dealing with the thousand people involved.

By evening on September 3 the *Athenia* was well out at sea, alone on the Atlantic. The first call to dinner sounded just after 7 P.M., and Captain James Cook left his bridge and moved into the first class dining saloon. As was the custom of the transatlantic liners, the captain entertained favored passengers at his own table.

At dinner the captain told a few of his best stories and settled down to his food. Suddenly, a little after 7:30 he heard an explosion on the port side of the ship. An officer rushed down from the bridge, and the captain asked if the watertight doors had been closed. Then he excused himself and checked to his own satisfaction. He also gave the emergency alarm and ordered the wireless officer to send out an SOS giving the course, speed, and position of the ship.

In a few moments the *Athenia* took a list of about six degrees to port. Soon all the lights went out. That meant the electrical system had failed. Closing the watertight doors had not solved the problem. The captain knew that his ship was about to sink. He ordered the "Abandon Ship" signal sounded, and the crew turned to to man the boats.

The chief officer, Mr. Copeland, walked around the deck checking on the crew, passengers, and boats. Walking on the port side of the boat deck, suddenly he saw a submarine, about a half mile away. He watched it for about two minutes. Then it disappeared.

The boat drill procedure called for getting the passengers and crew off the ship in an orderly fashion. The starboard boats, however, gave some difficulty; the explosion had occurred on the port side, and because of the list the starboard boats tended to slide down and jam up against the ship. But they were worked down, and eventually all were launched. In less than an hour, twenty-seven lifeboats were in the water.

There was no problem with the port boats. Soon virtually all of the passengers who had come on deck were in the boats, along with the crewmen assigned to man them. The senior staff of the ship stayed aboard, along with four passengers who refused to go into the boats. But all the other passengers who had presented themselves and the crewmen needed to man the boats were off the ship by 9 P.M. The captain himself went down into the steerage where the explosion had occurred. All he saw were 112 dead, blackened bodies, the result of the explosion in the space between the main hatches and the main hold, which had been converted to cheap accommodation for passengers, some of them students, some of them refugees from Europe.

The captain personally checked every body to be sure no living persons were left aboard. He then instructed the chief wireless officer to be sure that every crewman got into a lifeboat. Finally, as far as the captain knew, all living persons were accounted for, and the staff got into the boats. The captain thought he was the last man to leave the ship.

Fortunately for the passengers and crew of the *Athenia*, they were close to the British Isles, and it was not many hours before several ships arrived on the scene. The steamer *Knute Nelson* was the first. The steamer *Southern Cross* came up and so did the destroyers HMS *Electra* and HMS *Escort*. By 10 A.M. on September 4 all the survivors had been picked up and transferred into the vessels. Now the chief officer checked the passenger records and could account for all but one woman. During the disembarkation she had fallen down a companionway, cut her lip badly, and had suffered a concussion. She was unconscious. At that time the chief officer had taken her to the sick bay. The ship's doctor had given her a shot and stitched up her damaged lip. Later the nurse had told him that she could not manage the woman by herself. Chief Officer Copeland had then sent two crew members to take the woman off, but for some reason they had failed to do so.

Copeland hurried up to the bridge of the destroyer *Electra* and told his story. The captain gave him a boat, and

Copeland then went over to the *Athenia* with a boatswain and an ablebodied seaman. It was now about 10:30 in the morning. The woman was still unconscious. The boatswain and the seaman carried her down into the boat. The chief officer stopped to look at the No. 5 hatch and saw that the bulkheads were in dangerous condition. He did not believe the ship could last much longer. They all went back to the destroyer and had scarcely gotten aboard again when the *Athenia* sank. It was 11 A.M.

The submarine that Chief Officer Copeland had seen off the port side of the *Athenia* was the *U-30*, sailing under Oberleutnant Fritz-Julius Lemp. Lemp was a round-faced, stocky officer, in his middle twenties. These U-boat skippers were almost all young, it was a demanding and exhausting trade. But their youth belied the naval experience Doenitz demanded before he chose a submarine captain. Lemp had plenty of training behind him in sailing ships and steam vessels before he had been accepted for U-boat duty, and more training to make him eligible for command.

Lemp's ship of war was a Typle VII Atlantic U-boat, capable of a voyage of 6,200 miles on the surface at a cruising speed of ten knots, able to make sixteen knots in a pinch, and about seven knots under water. The *U-30* carried five torpedo tubes, three forward and two aft, a 4-inch gun for surface fighting and an Oerlikon antiaircraft gun.

Lemp had sailed from the submarine base at Wilhelmshaven on the morning of August 22, traveled up through the North Sea close to the Arctic Circle, and then around the northern tip of the British Isles, and down to his patrol area west of Liverpool.

At 1:30 on the afternoon of September 3, at his submarine command post in a wooden house on the Totem Weg on the Saxon plain near Wilhelmshaven, Commodore Doenitz received the word that Britain had declared war. Here in this old seat of the German navy was the headquarters of the most powerful submarine force in the world. Its spacious inner harbor had been especially designed and built for submarines. Commodore Doenitz closeted himself with his charts and graphs of the waters of the North Sea, English Channel, and Atlantic approaches to England. Later in the afternoon he went out to the Neuende Naval Radio Station in Wilhelmshaven, which was soon to become the nerve center of his U-boat fleet. There he conferred with Admiral Boehm, commander in chief of the fleet, and Admiral Saalwechter, commander of Naval Group West. They discussed Naval Directive No. 1, from the *Oberkommando der Wehrmacht*—the supreme command of Germany's armed forces. It called for the submarines to wage the *guerre de course*—raiding war—against England.

At 5:15 P.M. Doenitz coded the message about liners and ordered it sent to all U-boats then at sea.

As noted, Doenitz's message to his submarine skippers was punctilious in its adherence to international law. But fresh in Lieutenant Lemp's mind was his last briefing from Doenitz, just before he had set sail on this voyage. Doenitz had been musing over the past, those years of World War I when he had been a young U-boat officer. Almost absently he had expounded at length on the danger a U-boat captain might face, as Doenitz had, from British auxiliary cruisers. In the last war, Doenitz had reminded the young officer, the British had been exceedingly swift and adept in arming fast passenger vessels, which then took after German ships. An auxiliary cruiser could mean the end of a captain. As it turned out it was unfortunate that Doenitz had chosen Lieutenant Lemp for this discourse, because Lemp was an impressionable young man, and his commodore's admonition had stuck with him.

That first day of war, as the shadows of evening began to lower, and Skipper Lemp stood on the bridge of his surfaced U-boat, he saw off to starboard a very large ship approaching him. He called Lieutenant Peter Hinsch up for a look. Hinsch was the gunnery officer, and he would be in charge if they decided to use the 4-inch gun to stop the vessel.

But, dared they operate that way? If the ship was an armed merchant cruiser, it might have one or more guns of its own and the speed with which to ram the submarine fatally.

So Lemp decided that the vessel approaching was indeed a merchant cruiser, and thus subject to attack. He took the *U-30* down and started his approach to torpedo the enemy.

He fired three torpedoes, and then a fourth that stuck in the tube. One of those first three torpedoes struck the *Athenia*, while Lieutenant Lemp and his crew struggled to free the fourth torpedo—which they finally did.

Lieutenant Lemp brought the *U-30* to the surface, and his radio operator received the SOS of the stricken ship. A look at the Lloyd's Register told Lemp the awful truth: he had miscalculated, and in his first encounter he had broken the laws of war. The ship was a passenger liner; it must be carrying men, women, and children. Since it was the *Athenia*, and on the U.S. run, some of these passengers would have to be Americans.

And so it was. Not only passengers, but 28 of the 112 dead were Americans. Lieutenant Lemp did not then know the figures, he knew that he had committed a grievous error, but there was no way for Lemp to recognize the ramifications of what he had done. Winston Churchill, First Lord of the Admiralty, had never believed the Germans would abide by the London Submarine Agreement of 1936. The first German act of war at sea against a passenger liner had convinced Churchill beyond all argument that his intuition was correct. From that moment forward, as far as he was concerned, the London treaty was so much paper. He began his plans to fight off the German submarine menace, and the very first thing was to begin arming merchant ships so they could fight back.

Late on the afternoon of September 4 the world learned that a German submarine had torpedoed a British passenger liner carrying neutral citizens. Commodore Doenitz knew nothing about this except what he learned from the BBC because Lieutenant Lemp was prudently maintaining radio silence. The first reaction of OKW, the high command, was to deny that any German vessel had been responsible. But *Athenia* Chief Officer Copeland had seen the U-boat and so had others. In Washington, President Franklin Roosevelt and the State Department took the most serious view. Ambassador Joseph Kennedy was dispatched to Ireland to interview survivors and try to get to the bottom of the case.

The Germans decided to bluff. They denied everything. They claimed that the *Athenia* had been sunk by British destroyers, on the specific order of Winston Churchill, to make the Germans look bad. They began assembling "proof." A Norwegian mechanic aboard the *Knute Nelson* had taken a picture of the *Athenia* with a British destroyer alongside. This was "proof," claimed the Germans, that the destroyer had sunk her.

Gustav Anderson, a travel agent from Illinois, went home to the United States to file an affidavit with the State Department to the effect that the *Athenia* had been carrying a cargo of guns for Canadian defenses. He said his informant was Chief Officer Copeland. He also said Copeland told him the *Athenia* was to be fitted out as a raider as soon as she reached North America. Copeland denied making any such statements. Another American passenger, Helen MacDonald, indicated that a British submarine had been responsible. Propagandist Josef Goebbels took up the theme that the sinking had been a British plot, and the airwaves around the world resounded with German charges that the British were the foul fiends who had done the job. The propaganda continued for more than a month; it was a year from the date of the sinking before the U.S. government established what the State Department called "a strong presumption" that the Germans had sunk the ship. Even then the controversy continued in America until the United States entered the war.

While the story for world consumption was that the British had sunk the *Athenia*, inside the German naval establishment the story was quite different. On the very afternoon of September 4 Commodore Doenitz sent out a general message to his U-boat commanders:

"Existing orders for mercantile warfare remain in force."

Before midnight Hitler had been informed of the dreadful truth. He was furious; one stupid U-boat commander threatened to bring the United States into this war as another had helped to do with the sinking of the *Lusitania* in 1915. The Fuehrer acted immediately. Out from the OKW went a new order:

"By order of the Fuehrer passenger ships until further notice will not be attacked *even if in convoy.*"

That order must have made Lieutenant Lemp quiver in his

seaboots, for it could not help but indicate to him how angry the high command must be with his breach of discipline. And that was true, for Hitler threatened the most dire consequences for the unfortunate U-boat commander. Lemp was lucky to be still at sea. Doenitz sympathized with the young officer's problem and had very little confidence in a U-boat war conducted on the lines laid down in 1936, but in September it was still too early for Doenitz to say so. What had to be done first was to build a case for abandonment of the restrictions. Doenitz set out to do just this. Meanwhile the twenty other captains of Doenitz's Type VII oceangoing U-boats were creating serious problems for the British, within the rules of war established in 1936.

At eleven o'clock on the morning of September 5 the British *Royal Sceptre* was steaming off the Spanish coast en route from Buenos Aires to Belfast. Chief Officer Norman Hartley was on the bridge, since he and the captain shared watches, and the captain was the asleep. The ship's third mate was on watch with Hartley, the second mate was off duty.

At that moment a submarine surfaced 500 yards abaft the port beam. Hartley put the ship about, stern to the enemy, and began to run to evade capture. The submarine opened fire, quite within the rule of warfare, and the ship did not stop. At first the fire straddled the ship, but then it began hitting, and one shot blew away the radio aerial.

The captain came on deck, and just seconds afterwards a shot burst in his bathroom. He ordered the ship abandoned. The chief engineer stopped the engines and the crew began to get into the two lifeboats. The chief officer went to his stateroom and got his overcoat and then climbed down into the port boat, which was his station. He got down into the boat just as another shell hit the ship. That shell struck near the captain's boat as it was being lowered and killed him.

The submarine ceased fire and slid up close to the boats. The German captain told the chief officer to go back and rescue two men still left aboard the *Royal Sceptre*.

The submarine approached the other boat and asked for the captain. The officer was told that the captain was dead. The submarine then went alongside the chief officer's boat and the U-boat captain asked the first officer if the crew had food.

"Yes, plenty," said Officer Hartley.

"Water?"

"Yes, thank you."

The submarine moved away, then came back again.

"Have you any wounded?"

"We are all quite well here, thank you."

"Have you any cigarettes?"

"No."

"You can go back to the ship and get some if you wish."

"No thank you," said Hartley. "I am safer here where I am."

The submarine then moved off again. At about noon it reappeared six hundred feet from the ship and fired a torpedo into her. She sank less than four minutes later.

The submarine captain again came alongside the boats.

"I am going to send assistance to you," the skipper told Hartley. And he pointed to the direction from which the assistance would come. Then he went off for good.

At about 6 P.M., sure enough, smoke appeared on the horizon in the direction the German captain had indicated. It was the steamer *Browning*, which picked up the survivors of the *Royal Sceptre*. Only then did Chief Officer Hartley learn that many of the men in the other boat had been badly wounded by that shell that killed the captain.

The survivors were landed at Bahia, Brazil. Their ship had been sunk by the *U-48*, and the officer who had spoken to them in clear, if heavily accented, English, was Lieutenant Commander Herbert Schultze. In the next few days he would also sink the 5,000-ton ships *Winkleigh* and *Firby*. Obeying all the laws of war, he had still dealt the British a heavy blow.

2
Reaction

On September 6 the *U-38* surfaced to capture the 7,200-ton British steamer *Manaar.* Something new had been added. Winston Churchill had come to the Admiralty determined to combat the submarines from the outset of war, and one of his first acts had been to order 150 British merchantmen equipped with deck guns (only 150 because that was the supply of guns available; if Churchill could have wished them aboard, every merchantman would immediately have been armed).

The *Manaar*'s gun was mounted aft and her captain chose to fight. The commander of *U-38*, Lieutenant Commander Heinrich Liebe, found he had a tiger by the tail and was now engaged in a deadly battle. The *U-38* managed to sink the *Manaar*, but Liebe was shaken by the experience. He reported the "unfair" incident to Commodore Doenitz, who put it into the file of British breaches of the Submarine Warfare Agreement for future reference.

The Lemp sinking of the *Athenia* was consigned by Hitler to the secrecy file. Lemp continued on patrol, reporting nothing to Wilhelmshaven. Of course, Doenitz was not fooled. He had divided the world's waters into a system of grid squares, and the movements of his U-boats were very carefully delineated on the big chart in his operations room. There was only one U-boat in position to have sunk the *Athenia*. What was to be done about Lemp's breach of orders remained to be seen. Meanwhile he continued on patrol. On September 11 the *U-30* sank the SS *Blairlogie*, and went on.

* * *

Doenitz shared all Churchill's misgivings about the attempt to control the natural proclivities of the submarine, the hunter of the deep. The great strength of the submarine was its ability to track its enemy secretly, and secretly to attack. It seemed ridiculous to sacrifice these advantages. Every indication that the British were not abiding by the Submarine Agreement was seized by Doenitz for his file. His own radio operators heard SOS broadcasts in which British ships under submarine attack were heard to be giving the information about attack, the coordinates of the attack, and the course and speed of the ship and the submarine.

At the moment, moved by Hitler's anger over Lemp's audacious act, the U-boat corps was behaving with the utmost punctility. Captains Schultze, Kretschmer, and all the rest came to the surface alongside their prey, sent boats to board, and let ships go when there was any question. Kretschmer, in *U-23*, came home from his first patrol to protest the restrictions. He told Doenitz that he had stopped a Swedish steamer carrying timber to Newcastle. Did it not seem stupid to let a cargo of timber go to Britain to be used to shore up the mines so British miners could get coal for British steel mills to make weapons to kill German soldiers?

Doenitz agreed. But unlike his eager young U-boat commanders, Doenitz was willing to wait, pile up the evidence of British perfidy, and then take the case to the Fuehrer.

Doenitz had no illusions about the nature of this battle of the U-boats against England. If the Germans were to triumph, they were going to have to use their weapons to the utmost. Anything that happened in these early days of the war was skirmish. The battle was yet to come.

As the Lemp sinking of the *Athenia* indicated, Commodore Doenitz was very wary of Q-ships, to the point of paranoia. These were ordinary merchant vessels that had been fitted out as warships with heavy guns concealed behind false bulkheads, heavy plating, antiaircraft guns, and manned by Royal Navy crews. They also carried depth charges. Their mission was to lure enemy submarines into surface attack. The submarine would come up to capture the innocent-looking merchantman, and down would come the false bulkheads, out would flash the big guns, and down to the bottom would go the U-boat. This was Doenitz's nightmare, and he had passed it along to all his bright young captains before the end of the first week of war.

Churchill not only had the constant worry of the U-boats surrounding England on his mind, but in the first days of the war he had to settle on a base for the Home Fleet. He traveled north to look over Scapa Flow in Northern Scotland's Orkney Islands, which had been proposed by the Admiralty as the new fleet base. He noted then the terrible paucity of destroyers, so scarce that the battleship *Nelson* came out of Loch Ewe without a destroyer escort, a dangerous and unprecedented movement.

The British also had learned a major lesson about the use of aircraft carriers; the fleet carrier was much too vulnerable to submarine attack to be allowed to operate in anything less than an attack force. Carriers were withdrawn from antisubmarine service and would not again be used in that role until the development of the special escort carrier later in the war.

On September 19, patrolling off the Butt of Lewis, Johannes Franz's 500-ton *U-27* ran afoul of seven British destroyers in an antisubmarine formation. She fired two torpedoes, both of which exploded prematurely. Guided by the superweapon developed between the wars, the sounding device called Asdic, the British destroyers then zeroed in on the *U-27*. The first pattern fired by HMS *Fortune* was without effect, but the second pattern of five depth charges damaged one propeller and bent the shaft. Water began to come in through the stern. Franz brought her up to periscope depth, and then saw four destroyers around him, all using searchlights on the water. He went down to 393 feet, which was a feat in itself. He then tried to shake off his pursuers. But they would not shake. At 2:12 in the morning the *Fortune* found the submarine four miles from the first position, and the destroyer attacked again. This time the five depth charges damaged the *U-27* badly. The stern was full of water and rivets popped loose all over the boat. She listed 30 degrees to port. Water was coming down the conning tower. Finally only enough air pressure was left to blow the boat and surface. She did at 2:41. Twenty men jumped overboard. The *Fortune* turned to ram, and then opened fire, but ceased when her skipper saw that the U-boat was not fighting back. He ordered the captain to stop and abandon ship. At 3:15 all the men were taken off. The *Fortune*'s engineer officer went across to the submarine to see if it would be possible to salvage her, but it was not. She went down stern first at 3:50.

Lieutenant Lemp went home to Germany. He was lucky enough to have held out at sea until September 27. By the time Lemp was ashore, what had seemed a criminal act on September 3 was being justified in Berlin by evidence that the British were ignoring the Submarine Agreement of 1936. Lemp was hustled off to Berlin under arrest, and he told his story. The high command (*Oberkommando der Wehrmacht*) believed what it wanted to believe, that he had sunk the *Athenia* by mistake, but OKW never admitted this to the world. On Lemp's return to submarine headquarters at Wilhelmshaven he was kept for one day and given a book of the silhouettes of British merchant ships to study. Then it was back to duty, for Doenitz was really not angry with him. The German press reported that Lemp had been granted the great favor of an audience with Hitler and had received the Iron Cross, Second Class. If the British wondered why the sinking of but two merchantmen would occasion an audience with the all-highest, no one raised the issue. It was many months before the world knew that Lieutenant Lemp had sunk the *Athenia*.

3

The Real War Begins

Only one month after the outbreak of the war, the London Submarine Agreement of 1936 was recognized by both sides to be dead. The Germans had lost two U-boats, but (quite unlike the pattern that would develop later) most of the crews of *U-27* and *U-39* were rescued to become prisoners of war in England. First Lord of the Admiralty Winston Churchill was doing all he could to strengthen Britain's antisubmarine war; Commodore Doenitz was pleading for speed and a higher priority for U-boat construction. Neither man was totally successful: the Royal Navy was still "battle fleet" oriented. Since the days of Lord Nelson Britain's power on the sea had been assured by her ships of the line, now become battleships and battle cruisers. The fact was that not since Jutland, in 1916, had there been even the suspicion of a battle fleet encounter between British and German navies. In this war it would be the same; one minor scrape at Dogger Bank would be the closest. In fact, the German naval high command, while preserving the fiction and many of the trappings of the old High Seas Fleet concept in which Kaiser Wilhelm had dreamed of besting his cousin George V of England in a great sea battle, had returned to a much more sensible German concept: the raider fleet. The new German battleships and pocket battleships were designed to be used as raiders on the high seas. Admiral Raeder had suggested that the U-boat fleet would also be of supreme importance in bringing England to her knees. But just now, Hitler's priorities were concentrated on the land war machine.

So Commodore Doenitz, who had hoped that the outbreak of war would bring him unlimited resources, was disappointed. In those years when Germany's naval abilities lay fallow, Doenitz had dreamed many dreams. One of them involved a new approach to submarine warfare—the wolf pack attack. He had practiced this technique in the years since 1935 and was now certain that it would be enormously effective. With the new U-boat now developed, the 500-ton Type VII Atlantic boat, Doenitz had the weapon that could do the job. The problem was that he did not have enough Type VII boats to carry out pack warfare. He engineered a major coup on October 14, 1939, in the sinking of the British battleship *Royal Oak* inside Scapa Flow, Churchill's new fleet naval base. The propaganda value was enormous; Hitler was pleased, and he honored the submarine skipper,

Guenther Prien of *U-47*, with a medal and Commodore Doenitz with a promotion to rear admiral. At the ceremonies, Admiral Doenitz managed to wring from the Fuehrer a reluctant promise for a bigger submarine building program. But as with all things that irritated the German leader, the building program languished. Admiral Doenitz found himself fighting the war with his handful of submarines, which were not nearly so effective as they ought to have been.

If Doenitz had been given what he had been promised in 1936, according to German naval historian Juergen Rohwer, he would have been able to keep fifteen U-boats constantly in the area west of England. In fact, in these first months of war, he was able to maintain only about five boats in this vital area. The 250-ton boats were too small to venture into the Atlantic, where the action was already perceived to be. Also, Doenitz had other problems. The submersible was the boat of those days. (A true submarine was designed to remain under water all the time; a submersible was a diving boat that depended on surfacing for survival.) The difficulty of keeping the submersible boats seaworthy was enormous, and it meant that Doenitz was always operating with but a fraction of his U-boat force at sea. In the first few days of the war the admiral's most trusted captains came back from initial operations to report on torpedo failure. It was true. The magnetic exploder of the German torpedo was faulty and cost many a captain a "miss" when he was certain he should have sunk a ship. In these early days, despite the publicity already given the U-boat war, courtesy of Lieutenant Lemp, the most effective aspect of U-boat operations was the one the captains liked least: minelaying. Of course, mines were a double-edged weapon. British mines in the Strait of Dover cost the Germans their next two submarines, Lieutenant von der Ropp's *U-12* and Lieutenant Barten's *U-40*. The difference was that part of Barten's crew was saved but von der Ropp's went to the bottom, the first U-boat sinking of the war to bear the cryptic note: no survivors. It was October 8, 1939.

The capture of three U-boats proved to be of inestimable value to the British in learning about the plans and operations of their enemy at Wilhelmshaven. British intelligence was superb in its techniques of questioning. As a matter of form, all prisoners were questioned, but the officers in charge knew that only limited value could be found in that sort of questioning. Admiral Doenitz's U-boat captains had been carefully trained never to reveal information about their trade to the enemy, and the younger officers and crewmen were given the same sort of instruction. But, as the British knew, there were always weak links. Their problem was to find them. Very early in the game the intelligence officers devised a technique designed to extract maximum information. Over several periods of questioning, the attitudes of various officers and men were examined carefully. The Nazis, of course, had to be discarded immediately. Their propagandistic approach to the war was very effective; the British believed scarcely anything the Nazis said.

Once an officer or a man had been found to be amenable to discussion of the war, he could be used with others. The idea was to stimulate "discussion" among prisoners. To do this, after the initial or shock questioning, the men were led into talk about all sorts of matters, girl friends, social habits, and their likes and dislikes. With some who had large egos or felt buoyed up by such conversation, the results were satisfactory in the highest degree, and these men could be used to help question others. In the beginning, a British military man was often inserted into the "cages" in the guise of a prisoner of war. He had to be authentic in language and culture, of course; he might actually be a German or an Austrian; so many refugees had taken root in Britain in 1939 that cultural management was no real problem. These "plants" often elicited remarkable information from the enemy. The technique was so solid that it was used throughout the war. Some POWs, trusted by their captors, were used time and again in the questioning of new men. The result was a constantly growing body of information about the enemy, which was of inestimable value in the Royal Navy's fight against Admiral Doenitz's U-boats.

The surfacing of a U-boat was also a great opportunity. The Royal Navy destroyermen had been instructed that one of their responsibilities was to get a man aboard a surfaced U-boat as soon as possible, to go below and bring back anything of value he could find, particularly secret papers.

The great coup would be the capture of a damanged U-boat before the crew could scuttle it. So far the British had not been that lucky, but from one of the captured boats they had extracted the order book, in which the U-boat captain saved all the orders from Doenitz. An examination of this series of documents told the antisubmarine warfare command a great deal about the high state of morale and discipline within the U-boat corps and something about what sort of war could be expected in these early days.

WAR ORDER NO. 151

> . . . In the first place, attack and keep on attacking; do not let yourself be shaken off; if the boat is temporarily forced away or driven under water, follow up in the general direction of the convoy, try to get in touch again, and once more ATTACK! . . .

This order encapsulated Doenitz's entire approach to the war. From the moment of application to the *U-Boot-Waffe*, an officer came under the personal command of Admiral Doenitz. His primary concern was for the fitness of the U-boat men, first moral and mental, and then physical. When war broke out, Doenitz had developed a highly effective force. In the five years since the rejuvenation of the *Kriegsmarine*, he had picked and trained until the *U-Boot-Waffe* represented the cream of the German navy. And these young men followed their admiral's instructions.

> . . . Report as soon as possible . . . and between attacks, send further reports to enable contact to be maintained . . .

From the outset, the young captains learned that they were the eyes, ears, and fingers of the U-boat force, but that Admiral Doenitz was the brains. Throughout the war tight control of German submarine activity would be maintained by U-boat headquarters, whether it was in Wilhelmshaven, Lorient, or Berlin.

One of the cardinal sins of a U-boat captain was to waste fuel, for Germany entered the war with a shortage of petroleum that was never more than half-alleviated by the Rumanian oil fields. Part of the reason for Hitler's drive to the East was to secure oil for his war machine. U-boat skippers were warned never to consume any more fuel than necessary; with one exception:

WAR ORDER NO. 152

> . . . When attacking, no regard need be paid to fuel consumption provided that the return voyage is not endangered . . .

Admiral Doenitz's concern about Q-ships never ceased. He talked about the danger in meetings. In this order he warned that the U-boat must be extremely careful in approaching its prey. The deck gun, while it had its uses, was not the primary weapon:

> . . . The sinking of the vessel is invariably to be by torpedo . . .

WAR ORDER NO. 153

> . . . On every occasion of using gunfire it must be borne in mind that nearly all enemy ships are armed and that neutral markings afford no proof of the actual neutral nationality of a steamer. Remain therefore a good distance away . . .

Above all, the skipper must be aggressive. Doenitz could forgive many breaches of normal naval discipline to the captain who remembered:

WAR ORDER NO. 154

> . . . Never yield to self-deception: I will not attack now or will not continue the attack tenaciously because I hope later on to find something else elsewhere. One has what one has! . . .

Before that first month of war was out the U-boat captains knew how slender were their resources and how much responsibility was placed on each of them. Everything depended on nerve, on the development of that "sixth sense" that warns of danger and opportunity.

> . . . If war on commerce is being waged in accordance with the Prize regulations observe caution in holding up ships. . . . The near zone is the danger zone. Upon this rests the hope of submarine traps.
> . . . at night . . . keep your nerve . . . remain on the surface, evade the enemy on the surface, if necessary go around in a circle, passing astern of the enemy. . . . Fire from a position before the beam and at short range. . . . Do not take trouble about the steamer's boat. Weather conditions and distance from land are immaterial. Think only of your own boat. . . . We must be hard in this war. The enemy started the war in order to destroy us, and it is this issue, nothing less, that is at stake.

All of these orders were signed: DOENITZ

So there was no doubt, even from the beginning, about Doenitz's intentions or the character of the German U-boat enemy.

Unknown to the public of the world at the time was another battle, far less heroic in every way, but far more vital to the survival of Britain on the one hand, and Admiral Doenitz's success in cutting the British sea lifeline to the New World on the other. It was told in the story of a convoy, just one convoy of scores that were massing and moving in and out of England.

The U-boat was Lieutenant Commander Alexander Gelhaar's *U-45*.

The convoy was KJF3, Jamaica-Liverpool. Actually, by Admiralty definition it was not a convoy at all, but a conglomeration of four ships, the British *Karamea* and *Lochavon* and the French *Oregon* and *Bretagne*.

Captain C. E. Ratkins of the *Lochavon* had not wanted to travel in any sort of grouping. He was an independent British sea captain of the old school. His ship made sixteen knots and he felt much safer traveling alone. He had come in from San Francisco, and he had already been delayed for two days at Cristobal, in Panama Canal Zone, following a submarine sighting report, and then he had been sent up to Kingston on a route just fifteen miles east of the steamer lane, which did not make a great deal of sense to him either.

When he had arrived in Jamaica early in October the naval control service officer had been most mysterious. No, he could not tell the captain when they would sail, or with whom he would sail. No, he could not sail alone. Admiralty instructions were very precise on this.

The captain had gone to a bar on the waterfront and there he had learned all about his sailing. He would sail on Friday—the fast convoys sailed on Fridays, the slow convoys sailed on Tuesdays.

When Captain Ratkins went back to beard the port officer with this disturbing report of lax security, he was told that he was going to be "commodore," in charge of the convoy. It was a thirteen-knot convoy. No, there would be no escort. No air cover. No surface craft. Nothing. Later that day he discovered that two of his ships could make only twelve knots, and this meant a cruising average of something under eleven knots, in an Atlantic full of submarines. From the beginning, Captain Ratkins was not a happy man.

He sent a messenger to the French ships to tell the captains they would absolutely have to keep up, and, knowing French owners, he said they would have to sacrifice their boilers if need be, otherwise it might be the ships.

The voyage started out well enough. They made the average speed, just under eleven knots, zigzagging. They cleared the Bahamas. They slowed at night to ten knots. The *Karamea* was in the lead, the *Lochavon* was next in line, then came the *Oregon*, and finally the *Bretagne*.

All went well on October 12 as they neared the submarine operational area. On the thirteenth they were especially watchful, moving at maximum speed until dark. Nothing happened. When it was dark, Captain Ratkins's ship sent a message to the others, telling them to cease zigzagging and slow down. They would resume the zigzag pattern and speed up at 5 A.M.

The night passed uneventfully. The captain had decided to

resume the zigzag half an hour early, and the word was passing down the line by Aldis lamp when suddenly the *Lochavon* was struck on the port side at No. 2 hatch by a torpedo. As ordered, the convoy went on, leaving the stricken ship to her fate. Captain Ratkins immedately ordered his men into the boats. The wireless operator sent out an SOS signal and gave the ship's position; this was picked up by radio stations at Land's End and Valencia, and was rebroadcast. The captain put his papers into a weighted bag, threw it overboard, and watched it sink. Then, from a boat, he watched his ship sink, too.

Half an hour after the men took to the boats a destroyer came steaming up, but did not even slow. Her bridge sent a message by signal lamp: "Sorry, cannot stop, will be back later." The destroyer sped off in the direction of the convoy. Shortly afterward, Captain Ratkins heard what he thought were depth charges exploding. Actually what he heard was the submarine's vicious surprise assault on the *Bretagne*, in violation of all those rules of war laid down in the London Submarine Agreement. On September 30 Hitler had unleashed the U-boat force against France, whose ships had been held sacrosanct earlier in accord with the Fuehrer's hope that France could be persuaded out of the war. Except for Lemp's sinking of the *Athenia* Gelhaar's attack on the *Bretagne* was the first such surprise attack in the war.

Commander Edward Templeton Grayston (RNR, Retired) was the captain of the *Karamea* and vice commodore of the convoy. He spent the night of October 13–14 on the bridge. At four o'clock he went into his cabin and, without undressing, lay down on the settee. The bridge was left to his chief officer, Moffatt, and the fourth officer and two cadets.

At 4:25 the chief officer saw an explosion about the *Lochavon*, and then they all heard seven short blasts and one long blast on the *Lochavon*'s whistle. That was the convoy's emergency signal.

Commander Grayston rushed out of his cabin to the bridge. The first officer had already given the order "hard aport." He turned to the captain.

"There she is, sir," he said. "There's the bastard." The

captain then saw the *U-45*—how could he miss it? Gelhaar had passed his bow within ten feet and was not more than twenty-five feet away at that moment. The chief officer of the *Karamea* had tried—and failed—to ram the U-boat. The submarine was having maneuvering difficulties and had surfaced right abeam of the British ship.

Three minutes later the lookout on the forecastle saw a torpedo pass down the starboard side of the ship, and miss. The submarine seemed to have overcome its difficulties, and it made off toward the *Bretagne*, the last ship in the line.

By this time Commander Grayston had given the order "full speed ahead" and turned away from the submarine. When the ship had gone three miles he saw gun flashes and the first shell bursting on the forecastle of the *Bretagne*. Lieutenant Commander Gelhaar was disobeying his admiral's instructions, opening the attack with his deck gun.

The men of the *Karamea* saw five more shells strike the *Bretagne* in rapid succession, and then a torpedo hit the French ship, raising a column of water 100 feet into the air.

The submarine surfaced, and Commander Grayston saw that its bow wave was pointing in his direction. He checked the crew to be sure that every man had a life belt, and he warned them to get the boats ready just in case.

The commander went back to the bridge.

"Do you think we should zigzag, sir?" asked the chief officer.

"Yes," said the captain, for he had no idea how many submarines might be in the area. Zigzagging during daylight was standard procedure anyhow.

Much to Skipper Gelhaar's delight, the *Karamea* zigzagged for an hour. It became apparent to the captain that this was a terrible mistake, for the submarine was chasing them, and if they had gone at full speed of sixteen knots they would have gotten away.

The *U-45* followed them for four hours. There were no escorts in sight, so Gelhaar stayed on the surface, where his speed was greater than that of the zigzagging steamer. When the submarine came up to within five miles it began shelling. The captain steered toward every spout, without slacking speed. The U-boat fired thirty shells, but only one near miss caused any damage.

All this while the *Karamea* was sending a steady stream of messages to shore stations, reporting on the attack.

The captain had the men put food into the boats, and he got the gold bullion out of the safe and brought several valuable show dogs that belonged to Viscount Galway out of the kennel. He told the crew that the ship had to continue to run for it. They had no gun, and they had seen what happened to the *Bretagne*—that crew never had a chance, for the U-boat had shelled her unmercifully and then torpedoed her with the crew aboard. He had not seen a man get off before she went down.

The captain of the submarine would certainly remember that the *Karamea* had tried to ram, and he would not show them any mercy either, the commander told his men.

At eight o'clock in the morning the commander estimated that he had about three hours left before Gelhaar's U-boat caught up and could torpedo him. But there was nothing to do but run and wait.

The messages kept going out in a steady stream of dots and dashes. The fourth officer kept recalculating their position to be sure they were sending correct information.

The captain wandered around the bridge, watching the submarine and listening to the near misses, some of them as close as twenty-five feet from the hull.

He went into his cabin and picked up his wife's photograph, his razor, and a few other small things and laid them out on his bunk, just in case there would be a chance to take to the boats. He lit a cigarette and started back for the bridge. As he passed his calendar he noted that it still said October 13, and he tore off the page to set things right.

Back on the bridge he wedged himself into the after corner on the starboard side and watched the submarine through his binoculars. She was gaining on him, slowly but steadily. Into his mind came Lydell's hymn, "Abide With Me," and he found himself humming it.

The submarine continued to gain. There was no doubt about it.

Commander Grayston walked back to the center of the bridge where the chief officer was standing.

"Well, Moffatt, I think we can reconcile ourselves to the end. May we go clean out."

"Oh, sir, for the sight of destroyer or a plane..."

"Yes, that would be... Well, thank God anyhow for the navy."

The steward came up with tea and the commander took a cup.

"How's my hand?" he asked the chief officer.

"Steady."

"Much better than my tummy," said the captain.

He went back to his cabin and got another cigarette from a tin of fifty. As he was lighting up he recalled that the crew was still operating under the no-smoking restrictions. And what did that rule matter now?

He went back to the bridge and had the word passed that everybody could smoke all he wished. He went back to the cabin and stubbed out his cigarette. Immediately he lit up another.

The third officer came to his day cabin door. He realized suddenly that this young man—scarcely more than a boy—was a lieutenant in the naval reserve—submarines. It seemed funny.

Then, before the captain and crew of the *Karamea* could notice, Lieutenant Commander Gelhaar's sound men caught the whishing of fast screws, which meant the approach of a destroyer. Down went the gun crew of *U-45*, and down went the skipper, and down went the submarine.

"The submarine has vanished," said the third officer. "I see a destroyer astern."

"Owen, I could almost kiss you. Shake my hand."

They shook hands solemnly.

The destroyer began signaling by lamp, and the commander had his signalman respond. The destroyer put on speed and flashed by and was gone. Commander Grayston kept course and full speed till 1 P.M. and then changed to 110 degrees to clear the Irish coast and then turned to 90 degrees for the Bristol Channel. They were home—safe.

And also safe, because he had the good sense to break off the action against the *Karamea* before it was too late, was Lieutenant Commander Alexander Gelhaar in *U-45*. He had accomplished quite a feat for a young captain on his first war patrol: two ships and 19,000 tons sunk. But his luck ran out at the end of the patrol, and the *U-45* was sunk by the destroyers HMS *Inglefield*, HMS *Ivanhoe*, and HMS *Icarus* off the Western Approaches.

4

Seven Boats Lost

The British, in their incurable optimism, believed that they had sunk half a dozen U-boats in September 1939, but they would soon learn to take a dimmer view and demand much more complete evidence of sinking.

The weapons were fairly matched that fall. The German Type VII was the most effective submarine in existence, with the possible exception of the Japanese I-boat, but in Britain, no one had to worry about I-boats then. In their concern with designing a most effective killing weapon, the Germans had devoted less attention to defensive measures. The British were far ahead in this regard with their Asdic sounding device. All the Germans had for protection was the hydrophone, developed in World War I. Thus those British destroyers had been able to zero in on the U-boats, much to the surprise of the captains. *U-39* and *U-27* had been the victims of Asdic. As noted, von der Ropp's *U-12* and Barten's *U-40* had both been destroyed by protective mines laid in the English Channel by British ships and planes.

This early in the war neither side had yet given serious consideration to the combination of sea and air weapons. The British did call on aircraft for coastal patrol, but these aircraft were very limited in range, and the bombs they carried were completely unsuitable for use against submerging submarines. The way was open for Doenitz's use of the wolf pack, but in September he still did not have enough Type VII U-boats to set loose the packs. Nor had any progress been made on matching up long-range aircraft with U-boats. The Germans had magnificent aircraft for the purpose, the Focke-Wulff bomber, but these and other effective aircraft were under the tight control of Reichsmarshall Hermann Goering, and the navy's wishes were very low on his list. So, in September and October 1939, Doenitz had to be content with his own resources. As the new Type VII boats came forth, he sent them out individually to see what they could do. One of the early Type VIIs was Lieutenant Commander Werner Lott's *U-35*.

After dark on September 8 the *U-35* sailed from Wilhelmshaven on her first war cruise. Why after dark? Because just four days earlier British planes had bombed the harbor at Wilhelmshaven with special attention to submarines. The raid had been a splendid failure; the U-boat men watched as several British bombers came in low, bombed, and were then splashed into the sea by the German antiaircraft gunners. But one failure did not mean that the next raid would be so ineffectual, and Doenitz had suspended daylight sailings temporarily.

Commander Lott's orders were to pass through the Dover Straits. At dusk on September 9 the *U-35* was very nearly sunk by a British submarine. (Lott's first encounter with Asdic: he saw three torpedoes and was luckily able to comb the tracks and avoid disaster. He tried to ram the submarine, but failed.)

On September 10 the *U-35* traveled north, and 180 miles west of Aberdeen she was attacked by an aircraft that dropped three bombs. The bombs were close enough to break several light bulbs. Had the British possessed proper bombs or air-dropped depth charges, the *U-35*'s career would have ended right there. So much for the boasts of the earliest submarine commanders that they were not worried about British aircraft. Thereafter Commander Lott kept a sharp eye out for aircraft.

Moving through the North Sea was slow going because Lott remained submerged during the daylight hours. Again, aircraft were keeping him down and slowing his voyage. The *U-35* passed through the Fair Island Channel on the night of September 16. On September 18 she sank two trawlers by gunfire, the *Lord Minto* and the *Arlita*. The survivors were put aboard the trawler *Nancy Haig*. No matter what Admiral Doenitz's orders said about abandoning victims to the sea, most of these submarine skippers at this stage of the war did their best to observe the rules of humanity.

Also on September 18 the *U-35* sighted the trawler *Alvis* and stopped her. If Lott sank her, where would the crewmen go? He contented himself with sending men to dismantle the wireless and destroy the fishing gear. He gave the captain of the *Alvis* a bottle of gin and told him to go home to Fleetwood and stay there.

The *U-35* now headed for the Western Approaches. On September 21 she attacked Convoy OA7 and fired two torpedoes. The first failed to sink the steamer *Inanda*, one of the leading ships. The second damaged the *Teakwood*, in the rear of the convoy, and she had to return to England for repairs. Commander Lott was then attacked by a British destroyer that dropped only one depth charge (because, said the escort captain, contact was doubtful). That depth charge was so accurately placed that it knocked out one of Lott's periscopes and put the blower system out of action. The *U-35* bottomed out at 420 feet, far deeper than any engineer had promised the vessel would survive. Down there repairs were made, although the valves began to leak from the pressure.

With the boat back in order, Lott took her into the English Channel. He cruised off Cherbourg and Le Havre. He saw the big liner *Aquitania*, which was traveling alone, and could have torpedoed her, but he was under orders to ignore all passenger ships. On October 1 between the Ushant Channel and Land's End he came upon the Belgian steamer *Suzon*, and he stopped her with gunfire; then when the crew had abandoned ship, he torpedoed her.

On October 3 Commander Lott sighted the Greek ship *Diamantis*, which was traveling in extremely heavy seas. He fired a round which fell ahead of the steamer, and the crew panicked and got into the single boat and cut the falls that supported the boat. The boat capsized in the rough water, and *U-35*'s men spent an hour rescuing the Greek sailors, again in complete violation of Admiral Doenitz's orders.

Those Greeks, said Commander Lott, were great eaters. He recalled that they had such fine appetites that at the end of the voyage he and his men nearly ran out of food altogether.

He sank the *Diamantis* then, although it took him three torpedoes. He hung around the coast, submerged, and on October 4 with great trepidation about being caught in shallow water, he landed the Greeks in Dingle Bay, using a collapsible boat. What Doenitz thought of that was obvious, but Lott was an independent sort, and just then the German high command was on its very best behavior so Lott could get away with it.

After these unusual adventures in romantic warfare, Captain Lott then headed home for Germany, traveling through such rotten weather all the way that the boat was delayed time and again. When they pulled into harbor they had one hour's fuel left. Lott reported to Admiral Doenitz on his torpedo failures and his successes, but not on his humanitarian gestures. He also told the story of the repairs made at a depth of more than 400 feet in an oozing boat on a rolling bottom. The engineer got an Iron Cross for that. The *U-35* then went up to Hamburg for her annual refit. This would occupy her until the middle of November, and the crew had leave.

Lott's success, his report on the ineffectuality of the British aircraft attacks, and similar reports from U-boat skippers working the east coast of Britain persuaded Doenitz that even with his minimal force of Type VII boats he might hazard a venture with the wolf pack technique. He had three boats available, Commander Werner Hartmann's *U-37*, Lieutenant Herbert Sohler's *U-46*, and Lieutenant Commander Herbert Schultze's *U-48*. He sent them out.

He also dispatched Lieutenant Rolf Dau's *U-42* to sail independently. On September 30 Skipper Dau left Wilhelmshaven on the first war cruise of the Type VII *U-42*. His distination was the Western Approaches, which he reached on October 13. At 7:30 that morning Dau sighted the British steamer *Stonepool*, part of outbound convoy OB 17d, which had sailed from Liverpool on October 9 to America.

The arrangement for the convoy had been as usual: it was to have escort until it passed the Western Approaches. Then the escorts would turn back, and the convoy would be on its own.

The escorts, HMS *Imogen* and HMS *Ilex*, had turned away, leaving the convoy at dark on October 12. But at 7:15 that night they heard distress calls from the French tanker *Emile Miguet*, announcing that she had been attacked by a submarine 200 miles southwest of Cape Clear. The two destroyers sped to the area. The next morning, when the *U-42* suddenly surfaced to assail the *Stonepool*, Captain A. White ordered his wireless operator to begin sending the SOS call. The two destroyers heard. They were only 110 miles northeast of the steamer's position.

The lookouts on the bridge of the *Stonepool* watched, fascinated, as the submarine's periscope became a conning tower, and then the deck of the U-boat splashed to the surface and men came running out of the conning tower to man the 4-inch gun. The U-boat was three miles off the ship's port beam. Skipper Dau's gun crew fired a warning shot, which landed about 200 yards ahead of the merchant ship. Captain White then turned hard to starboard, for his ship was carrying a gun and he intended to use it. When Skipper Dau saw what Captain White was up to he began firing for effect. But so did the *Stonepool* with her stern gun. After ten minutes the *Stonepool*'s shots were coming too close for the U-boat's comfort. Dau took the boat down in a crash dive and fired a torpedo. It misfired. Instead of firing another, Skipper Dau surfaced to pick up the gun crew he had abandoned in the crash dive. Then Dau dived again and began to work his way around to get ahead of the *Stonepool* so that he could sink her. Like so many of Doenitz's captains at this point, Dau had lost much of his faith in the torpedoes he was using, and he preferred to work with his deck gun. This is what he planned to do.

HMS *Imogen* and HMS *Ilex* joined up with the *Stonepool* at 3:40 in the afternoon. When Captain White indicated what had happened the two destroyer skippers were certain that they had not seen the last of this particular U-boat. They moved out on both sides of the *Stonepool* and headed north, the direction in which the U-boat was last seen.

At dark, Captain White caught sight of the U-boat on the horizon. She was lying on the surface, waiting. Lieutenant Commander P. L. Saumarez ordered flank speed on the *Ilex* and opened fire as he ran toward the surfaced *U-42*. Commander E. B. L. Stevens followed in the *Imogen*. Skipper Dau took his boat down.

Half an hour later the ships reached the area where the submarine had dived and began to search, using their Asdic. At 7:18 Saumarez reported that he must have overrun the U-boat. Just then, *Imogen* had a contact. Six minutes later the *Ilex* had a contact, too.

As the destroyers swept the area with their Asdic sounding gear, Skipper Dau left the conning tower and went into the control room. He put on headphones and listened. Through the hydrophones he could hear the ping-ping-ping, coming from both sides, so he knew he was being hunted by two destroyers. He ordered several alterations of course, but the destroyers caught them and followed. Finally Dau took the boat as deep as he dared and stopped the electric motors. He hoped thus to evade attack. If he could hold out, perhaps the enemy would go away.

But guided by the Asdic transmissions, Lieutenant Commander Saumarez was already attacking. At 7:27 the *Ilex* dropped five depth charges, set to explode at 250, 300, and 350 feet. The fifth charge, set for the greatest depth, did the job. It exploded just off the stern of the U-boat and the boat began to flood. The submarine slipped down to a 45-degree angle, with the stern down.

The destroyer propeller noises were going away. As often happened, the firing of a pattern of depth charges knocked out the Asdic temporarily. The British ships had lost contact with the U-boat after the *Ilex*'s attack.

The men in the middle of the U-boat closed the watertight doors. Skipper Dau ordered everybody in the middle and front of the boat to move toward the bow, to help regain trim. The angle was too steep and they slid back down against the transverse bulkheads. He tried to blow the after tanks, but they had split open. He blew the central and forward tanks. The submarine began to rise. Dau wanted to stop her at periscope depth, but he no longer had control of the stricken boat, and she came up, up, up. At 7:30 she burst out of the water like a cork.

The destroyers turned immediately and opened fire. The *Ilex* prepared to ram. Lieutenant Commander Saumarez saw that the U-boat was out of control, and no real danger to him, and he slowed the *Ilex* to diminish damage to the ship. She was doing six knots when she struck the submarine just behind the engine room. The bow broke the plating. Skipper Dau ordered all tanks blown and told his men it was time to abandon ship.

One by one, seventeen men came out of the submarine, that was all. The U-boat men forward and aft were lost to the sea when the watertight compartment in the control room area were shut on them. Only seventeen men survived, including Skipper Dau and his first lieutenant.

On the eastern shore of England, in the North Sea, the battle continued unabated, the little 250-ton boats defending themselves against trawlers, aircraft, and the occasional destroyer that could be spared from fleet work. The fact was that Britain's naval building program in the past few years had been all wrong for the sort of warfare that was developing. Churchill was putting an end to the emphasis on construction of cruisers and heavy destroyers just now, in favor of a new class of ships, not very fast (about fifteen to seventeen knots), small, maneuverable, cheap, and quick to build for employment as convoy escorts in the war against the U-boats.

But the British did not have those vessels now, and they suffered a serious shortage of any sort of craft available for escort duty. They were commandeering the yachts of the nobility and the merely wealthy for this task, so serious was the need.

Many of the 250-ton U-boats were put to minelaying still. Lieutenant Otto Kretschmer in *U-23* was sent to the Scapa Flow area on October 1. So confident was he of the inability of the British to mount a successful air attack that he traveled on the surface during most of the three-day journey. On station at Pentland Firth he attacked the coastal steamer *Glen Farg*, firing first with his deck gun, which was nothing more than a machine gun. The *Glen Farg* sent out calls for assistance, but there were no warships in the area available for submarine search. Without hurry, in spite of the fact that he was just off the enemy's main fleet base, Lieutenant Kretschmer then torpedoed the ship.

That was the way it went. Easy.

In that sense, the results of the first wolf pack, which on October 14 attacked convoy HG 3, homeward bound from Gibraltar, were not that much better than the results of U-boats operating alone. The three U-boats of the pack sank three ships in that convoy. There was an enormous expanse of western sea to be covered and, despite Hitler's promise, the U-boats were not coming off the ways as they should. Reluctantly, Doenitz abandoned the wolf pack technique temporarily, until the promises made him about U-boat delivery should be carried out. Just now in October Doenitz had reason to be cautious. He had lost two boats in September (*U-39* and *U-27*), which was acceptable. But in October the toll rose. On October 8, *U-12* was sunk by a mine, on October 13, *U-40* and *U-42* were lost, on October 14, *U-45* was sunk, and on October 24, Lieutenant Wellner's *U-16* was lost. Wellner had begun the war unluckily, starting out from Germany but encountering mechanical troubles that sent him back to port before a shot was fired. Between September 13 and 29 the *U-16* was in dry dock, her electrical system under repair, then he had gone out again to the Scapa Flow area. He was the man who had persuaded Doenitz that the attack on Scapa Flow was possible, but Prien had gotten the job. Poor unlucky Wellner. On October 24 he had been cruising in the Portland area when he was attacked by the trawlers HMS *Puffin* and HMS *Cayton Wyke*. In the struggle the *U-16* ran aground and had to be abandoned by the defeated crew. So by month's end Admiral Doenitz had lost seven U-boats, more than twice as many as he could afford to lose.

On the other side, as October ended, the British were well pleased with the results of their antisubmarine warfare—too well pleased in fact. Winston Churchill, in particular, radiated optimism. He and Admiral Pound journeyed to the French navy headquarters near Paris to consult with their allies. Churchill told the French that the U-boat attack on merchant shipping "has been controlled by the Anglo-

French antisubmarine craft.'' Part of the reason for this statement, of course, was to encourage the French, lest they falter in the joint effort. But part of the reason was that Churchill believed it. The statistics showed submarine sinkings doubled in October and British ship sinkings halved. Moreover, most of the ships sunk had succumbed to mines. In September and October a dozen merchant ships were sunk by magnetic mines laid by the 250-ton U-boats. At the moment the problem was a vexing one because the British had not yet secured one of the German mines and thus did not know precisely how to combat them. Half a dozen vessels entering the Thames estuary ran into mines. But in the third week of November the British did find a magnetic mine in a mudflat, disassembled it, and soon were on the road to a remedy. It was ''degaussing,'' the process of demagnetization of a ship's steel hull by passing an electric current around it through a cable. After degaussing a ship's hull was immune to the magnetic mine unless it struck one by accident. ''Degaussing'' would become an integral procedure in the movement of all ships across the seas.

October, then, was a worrisome time for Admiral Doenitz and a moment of brightness for the British. Then came November, and change. The third week of November saw the slump of Winston Churchill's brave hope that the Royal Navy had taken the starch out of the U-boat campaign. The navy's antisubmarine warfare division had to announce that after an interval of three weeks U-boat activity in the Western Approaches had again become a threat. Those three weeks of inactivity, of course, and the slowing before that, had been the direct result of Admiral Doenitz's foray with the wolf pack. But now at the end of November, Doenitz was sending his boats out to the old places, and they were sinking ships. Between November 16 and December 1, the U-boats sank twenty-four merchant vessels. Several captains, notably von Dresky, concentrated on trawlers, because the British were using more and more of them as antisubmarine patrol vessels. Von Dresky's *U-33* alone sank five trawlers, and then went on to sink two larger ships, including the 13,000-ton *Sussex*.

Despite such successes, Admiral Doenitz was having

problems about which the British then knew nothing at all. They were torpedo difficulties such as those of Commander Lott, problems about which all those young captains had been complaining steadily.

The German torpedo of 1939 had been developed at the end of World War I. It was designed to explode automatically beneath the steel bottom of a ship, where it would do the most damage. The technical experts were so pleased with themselves that they ignored certain troubling factors. One of these was the magnetic firing pistol, which often malfunctioned. Sometimes the torpedo would explode prematurely. Sometimes it would not explode at all. Sometimes it exploded at the end of its run. Almost always the magnetic torpedo ran deep, which meant that the magnetic feature might not be activated. Sometimes the torpedoes failed to explode even on direct contact.

Doenitz reported each torpedo failure to the technical experts and waited for the answers. As the number of U-boat attacks increased so did the failures and the excuses. The first excuse of the technicians was always to blame the submarine captain's shooting. But as the reports continued to come in Doenitz realized this did not hold true. Sometimes, yes. Always, no.

Doenitz was becoming more strident in his demands for answers, but he was not getting them. For each failure the "experts" had a remedy and an excuse. These all sufficed during peacetime to convince the submariners that all would be well.

But now that war had come and the submariners were firing those magnetic torpedoes and too many of them were reporting misses, it was obvious that something serious was wrong.*

---

*The failure of the German magnetic torpedo had its ironies. At the end of World War I, when the spoils of Germany's war machine were divided up among the Allies, the United States secured plans and samples of the German magnetic mine and magnetic tropedo, which they then developed independently. Out of this came the Mark XIV torpedo with the Mark VI exploder, based on the German design. These were the torpedoes with which the United States entered World War II. They had almost precisely

By the end of November 1939, any mention of the London Submarine Agreement of 1936 at higher headquarters in Wilhelmshaven or London had become little more than a charade. Both governments were pursuing policies that were directly in violation of the agreement. This was not surprising, since neither the attackers nor the defenders found it sensible to follow rules devised in an entirely different time. The U-boats were now torpedoing Allied vessels without warning, and also neutral ships. The British said this was part of a fright campaign to convince neutrals that it was too dangerous to try to trade with Britain. The submarine war had become a different sort of war, not yet altogether savage—as this story of Lieutenant Commander Gustaf Adolf Mugler's *U-41* shows—but different.

Early in November Mugler moved out for his second war patrol in the *U-41*. His patrol area was along the Iberian coast, his targets would be ships bound home to England from Gibraltar or elsewhere in the south.

On his way around the northern tip of the British Isles, on November 12 Mugler picked off the 275-ton trawler *Cresswell*. She was too small to waste a torpedo on her, so he sank her with gunfire. That same day he found the 11,000-ton Norwegian motor tanker *Arne Kjoede*. In line with Doenitz's new policy, Skipper Mugler gave no warning. His torpedoes came out of the dark water with a dreadful suddenness, and the tanker burst into flame.

Mugler's next target was the British steamer *Darino*.

She was a 1,325-ton ship, with grey hull, buff upper works and a green funnel. She could hardly look less like a Q-ship, and she was not one. She was one of those typical small British freighters that coursed the waters of the world. She had left Oporto for Liverpool on November 18 with a cargo of wine, cork, and sardines. The *Darino* was traveling alone because there was no option. Her skipper kept her zigzagging during the daylight hours and even until 1 A.M. because it was a bright, moonlight night.

---

the same faults as the German torpedoes. Doenitz corrected his torpedoes after a major scandal and court-martial of four officers in 1942. It took the Americans until 1944 to correct theirs.

The moon went down before 2 A.M. Chief Officer J. H. Casson, who had the bridge, put the ship on a straight course for the rest of the night. He had just done so at 2 A.M. when he saw a torpedo heading toward the ship's starboard beam. It struck as he watched, and the ship immediately began to sink by the stern. The after boat davits were blown sky-high and landed on the boats, putting them out of commission. The masts came down with a clatter. The wireless room was wrecked so not a single message was sent out.

Casson and a number of other men were blown overboard. The ship went down in six minutes, and a number of men were trapped inside. Casson and the other survivors were swimming about amidst the wreckage for forty-five minutes, wondering how they would survive. Suddenly the submarine appeared about 500 yards away. Lieutenant Commander Mugler raised a megaphone.

"I will wait for you," he said.

The men swam toward the submarine and most, but not all, made it. The crew threw out lifebuoys and pulled the men on board. Eleven men were picked up, which meant that sixteen were lost. Casson knew that three engineers and a cabin boy had gone down with the ship. But the captain and eleven men were lost in the water.

Mugler's men took the Englishmen below. The Germans took off their wet clothes and stuffed the men into warm bunks. Some of the U-boat men turned out of their own bunks so the survivors could have them.

The crew fed their captives breakfast: dark bread, sausage, coffee, and tinned milk. Later they were given lunch: boiled pototoes, tinned meat, red cabbage, and a blancmange for dessert.

After picking up the survivors, Mugler traveled along the surface. It was only a short while before he took the boat down. All below were told to be quiet, they were shadowing a convoy. But Mugler had no luck, and it was not long before the engine noise above subsided.

The Englishmen stayed aboard the submarine for about ten hours. They were given the run of the ship and spoke to many of the officers and men in English. There was the usual talk about why England and Germany were at war.

"Are seamen in England conscripted?" asked Captain Mugler.

"No," said Chief Officer Casson.

"If they were, I would have made you prisoners of war," said the U-boat captain. As it was, he would find a neutral vessel and put them aboard. He had rescued seven seamen from the other tanker and had done the same for them. (He did not say the tanker was Norwegian.)

The U-boat men made no effort to conceal anything from Casson and his seamen. The British watched the loading of one of the torpedo tubes, and they got a view of the magnetic exploder, a silvery cylinder of two different diameters, the smaller one screwing into the torpedo, and the larger part sticking out about twelve inches. In front of this was a small, two-bladed propeller about six inches in diameter.

At about 2:30 P.M. on Sunday, November 19, Captain Mugler sighted a steamer and ascertained that she was Italian, the *Katarina Gerolomich*. (Italy was still neutral in the war.) He stopped the ship and transferred the British survivors aboard. He warned the captain of the ship not to send any wireless transmissions for a while. During all this he made sure that the British went up through the conning tower and remained on the bridge. If they had to dive, he said, he did not want to leave them in the water.

After the transfer the U-boat crew lined up along the rails and took pictures of the ship and their ex-captives. Everyone was laughing and cheering, and the British and the Germans waved to each other as the submarine picked up speed and moved away, soon fading out of sight.

So the war was not always what it seemed. Captain Mugler had a copy of Doenitz's standing orders that told him to ignore enemy survivors in the water or in boats. But he chose the humanitarian way. But how long could he keep this up in a war where the attitudes of those in command were changing so very rapidly?

The fact was (which the Americans recognized without a whimper in 1941) that none of the old chivalry of war could apply to the submarine if it was to be effective. The submarine was like a nightstalker, its success depended on surprise, speed, and ruthlessness. Those who would counter the submarine had to use any weapon they could. Those were the lines that were being drawn at the end of 1939.

5
The Real War

In the last months of 1939 Admiral Doenitz's U-boats were most effective as minelayers. The mines sank as many ships as did the submarine torpedoes, overall about 160,000 tons in the month of December. The torpedoes were so faulty that they created a real morale problem among the young captains. Prien had gone out on patrol that fall, after his enormous success at Scapa Flow, and had miserable results. He sighted the cruiser *Norfolk*, tracked her, and fired torpedoes. One exploded and for a moment he thought he had sunk the warship, but the torpedo had blown up in the wake of the cruiser and did no harm. Like bulldogs, the British destroyers came after the submarine, and *U-47* was subjected to a depth charge attack that shook her up very badly. Prien came home disconsolate, complaining that a submarine captain could not fight "with a wooden gun." Kretschmer came in after one of his ptarols to the Shetland Islands to report that he had expended three torpedoes on a 1,000-ton coastal steamer. Why? because the first two damned torpedoes didn't work, that was why. But the most devastating experience of the period was that of Lieutenant Commander Wilhelm Zahn. *U-56* caught a battle squadron in formation off Loch Ewe: the battleship HMS *Nelson*, in company with the battleships *Rodney* and *Hood*, and a ring of destroyers. With great daring, Zahn approached and put three torpedoes into the *Nelson*. None of them exploded! Zahn returned to Wilhelmshaven so distressed that Doenitz had to remove him from command and put him ashore. By the end of the year Doenitz estimated conservatively that his captains were missing at least 25 percent of the time because of defective torpedoes. Probably, he believed, the incidence of failure from that cause was higher.

As 1939 drew to its end, British air surveillance improved, and Doenitz ordered his daring captains to submerge at the sight of any aircraft. The *Nordsee Enten* (North Sea Ducks), as the 250-ton boats were known in the U-boat service, continued to lay mines and attack coastal craft, but with meager success. Doenitz was beginning his new concentration of activity in the Western Approaches. He had available thirty-two *Nordsee Enten*, about thirty 500-ton boats, and fifteen of the 750-ton Atlantic boats, plus one 1,100-ton U-boat, a type still largely experimental. He would have liked to have had heavy concentration on the 750-ton boats at this time, but the construction emphasis was on the 500-ton boats, really neither fish nor fowl; they were overstrong for the minelaying in the North Sea and did not have the seagoing capacity for the far Atlantic.

But as Doenitz so often reminded his skippers, he had to fight with what he had against the enemy, while fighting against the military bureaucracy to secure more U-boats. "One has what one has."

Toward the end of November 1939, First Lord of the Admiralty Winston Churchill allowed himself to grow somewhat complacent about the prospects of the naval war. On November 29, the warships *Kingston, Kashmir,* and *Icarus* sank Lieutenant Lott's *U-35*, 120 miles east of the Shetland Islands. The captain and first officers were among the seventeen men rescued from the submarine, and they joined the growing ranks of POW Camp No. 1, a British prison camp established especially for submariners. Yes, said Churchill, he had been right again; they were getting a handle on the U-boats.

By the end of November, the British had sunk nine of Admiral Doenitz's U-boats, but that month the submarines had sunk another twenty-one ships. Fortunately, from the British point of view, they were all small ships, aggregating 55,000 tons. Churchill, then, looked on the sea war with equanimity.

The First Lord was put off by a change in German naval strategy. In November the U-boats sank twenty-one merchant ships, seventeen of them British. In December they sank thirty-nine merchant ships, but twenty-two of them were neutrals. The sinking of neutrals represented a major change, as did the method: the submarine commanders now had total authority to fire on darkened ships, zigzagging ships, ships that used their wireless, any vessels that seemed to them suspicious.

Because of the torpedo problem, the most effective work of the German submarines during December 1939 was still minelaying. The German navy switched its emphasis from the Thames estuary to the narrow channels off the Norfolk coast, through which the east coast convoys had to pass. That month mines took thirty-three merchant ships.

The emphasis on minelaying showed in another way: Doenitz was not risking many boats in the Western Approaches, partly because of the torpedo problem. Consequently he lost only one U-boat in December, Lieutenant Wilhelm Froehlich's *U-36*, on her second patrol. And this loss was really due to Froehlich's carelessness. Doenitz had warned his captains time and again to exercise "suspicion and caution while under way; when there is nothing to attack, continue sharp lookout."

Froehlich had failed the test. The *U-36* was on the surface on December 4 when she was sighted by the British submarine HMS *Salmon*, which put a torpedo into her. Froehlich paid for the error, he and his crew of twenty-nine men went to the bottom.

In January Winston Churchill was still ebullient about the sea war prospects. The British were making wild claims about submarine sinkings, attributing the lack of activity in the Atlantic to a shortage of German boats. Doenitz was pleased to let the enemy think that way.

In January, the torpedo problem was still not solved, but some captains were resolving it personally but cutting out the magnetic exploder feature of their torpedoes, and relying entirely on impact. This posed difficulties because the use of the magnetic exploder presupposed putting the torpedo beneath the vessel. The captains were aware of the torpedo deficiencies despite the continued denials of the technicians that there could be anything wrong with the weapons. Each captain had to solve the problem in his own way.

At the end of 1939, Admiral Doenitz had enough U-boats to lay out a more aggressive campaign for the coming year, and the vessels began moving out, through the German Bight and up through the Kattegat and Skagerrak, across the North Sea, and around Scotland into the Atlantic.

The little 250-tonners did not cross around, for the most part, but stayed in the North Sea. One of their tasks was to try to find the British fleet, which after Prien's attack on Scapa Flow had deserted that anchorage to move around to the other side of the British Isles. Otto Kretschmer's *U-23* spent countless days at that task, searching in vain the inlets of the Shetland Islands. Out of this search came a new tactic developed by Kretschmer: one night at Inganes Bay he came across a big tanker anchored in a small channel, guarded by a pair of patrol boats. He tried to find a way in at periscope depth, but the water was too shallow for maneuvering. He surfaced, moved in at high speed, attacked with a torpedo, made a 180-degree turn, and raced back out to sea and safety before the British inside knew what was happening. Audacity had gained the day.

The larger ocean submarines did not stop in the North Sea but crossed around for the hunting grounds of the Atlantic. One such was Lieutenant Commander Werner Heidel's *U-55*.

The *U-55* was a new oceangoing boat; the production of 250-ton boats had ended, and Doenitz was looking to bigger and more powerful submarines to carry the war to the farthest reaches of the British Empire. As these new submarines came out, Doenitz rewarded the most skillful captains of the little boats by transferring them to the more important commands. Lieutenant Heidel got *U-55* as a reward for his successful cruise in *U-7* in September, when he had achieved the remarkable feat of sinking three merchant ships.

The *U-55* was laid down in the Germania Yard at Kiel on November 2, 1938. She was commissioned in October 1939, one of the first of those new Type VII boats. For two months Lieutenant Heidel worked up his ship and trained his men. By mid-January he was ready to go out.

The *U-55* passed out through the Kiel Canal behind an icebreaker in the third week of January. She then proceeded into the North Sea, where she sank the steamers *Tekla* and

Andalusia. Off the Firth of Moray Heidel also sank the British destroyer *Exmouth*. But these were incidental matters; she was moving toward the Western Approaches as part of Admiral Doenitz's submarine force that was to reinvigorate the Atlantic campaign. In fact, the *Tekla* and the *Andalusia* were both small vessels, under 1,500 tons, and Lieutenant Heidel feared he would have some explaining to do because by the time he reached the Western Approaches on January 24 the *U-55* had expended nine of her fourteen torpedoes. Only a dozen torpedoes could be stowed below, so someone had the bright idea that a watertight container on deck could carry another pair, thus increasing the power of the U-boat by almost 15 percent. It was a nice theory, but not very practical for the North Atlantic in January. Doenitz knew the dangers, and he had issued orders that the shifting of torpedoes was to be undertaken only in out-of-the-way areas when the vessel was not in danger from the enemy, but he had said nothing about the weather. Lieutenant Heidel would have loved dearly to move those two torpedoes down below to his forward stowage, but there was not a chance. The water in the North Atlantic was so rough that the U-boat crew could not work on deck.

On January 29, surfacing at night, Lieutenant Heidel received word by radio from Doenitz's headquarters that a convoy had been sighted by other U-boats and was headed his way.

At one o'clock on the morning of January 30 up came the Southend part of Gibraltar-bound convoy OA 80G with a single escort, the sloop HMS *Fowey*. This particular convoy had been divided into three parts, the other two from Portsmouth and from Liverpool. Because of the exceedingly bad weather, the Southend section had missed contact with the Portsmouth section on January 29, and Commander H. B. Ellison, captain of the *Fowey*, spent most of the day trying to find those vessels. He was not successful. Pushed by a fierce following wind, the Southend section headed for the rendezvous point where they were supposed to meet the Liverpool section at nine o'clock that morning. The weather was so heavy that several of the ships began having trouble steering close enough to the compass to keep in line. The convoy opened up. It was about 100 miles southwest of Land's End.

Lieutenant Heidel sighted the convoy shortly after 1 A.M. and dived. He moved behind the convoy and surfaced. In the driving sea and wind no one in the convoy noticed his presence. Two of the ships, the British tanker *Vaclite* and the steamer *Beaverbrae*, had fallen astern of the convoy. Lieutenant Heidel chose the tanker, and he was able to move up to within 300 yards of her on the surface. At 1:38 he put a torpedo into her. The *Vaclite* sent up two red rockets, but in the fury of the storm no one in the convoy saw them except the *Beaverbrae*. Her watchkeepers had also heard a dull thud, but that was all. They saw no submarine. They did not see the tanker sink. No one else even suspected what was happening. The two ships were too far behind and the storm too intense.

The *Beaverbrae* then put on full speed to catch up with the convoy, but it took her captain two and a half hours to come up to a point where he could make a visual signal announcing what he had seen. He did not know that a ship had been torpedoed, though he suspected it.

The convoy commander counted noses and then tried to raise the *Vaclite*. He failed. In the meantime, Lieutenant Heidel had moved the *U-55* around in front of the convoy, where he waited.

At 9:50 in the morning the weather had abated enough so that the convoy commander ordered the zigzag maneuver to begin. But the ships began running into heavy fog, and the convoy soon fell out of line. The zigzagging was stopped at 10:20.

Half an hour later Commander Ellison made contact with the U-boat, broad on the starboard bow, approximately 2,000 yards ahead. But the fog was too intense to see the vessel. He had to wait.

At 11 A.M. Lieutenant Heidel torpedoed the Greek freighter *Karamiai*, which was third ship in the starboard column. Also hampered by the fog, Lieutenant Heidel had shot down the throat of the convoy and had been lucky enough to hit the Greek ship. The *Fowey* sped across the convoy, and soon she had a contact on her port bow, but then lost it when she altered course at high speed to chase. Two minutes later a lookout spotted the periscope of *U-55* on the starboard bow, and Commander Ellison again changed course to run an attack pattern of five depth charges.

Lieutenant Heidel had not seen the escort, and he dipped down, then reappeared only 300 yards ahead, this time keeping the periscope up for half a minute. In that half minute the range closed from 300 to 150 yards.

Commander Ellison had been running with his depth charges set at 500 feet, expecting the U-boat to dive fast and deep. But there was no time for Heidel to get anywhere near that depth, and as he fired the depth charges, Commander Ellison knew it. They exploded well beneath the U-boat, Ellison estimated 200 feet below, the Germans said more like 65 feet below.

Commander Ellison turned about and made another run, but the Asdic had lost contact. He called Coastal Command, and a Sunderland flying boat from 228 Squadron was sent to help in the search for the submarine. Two destroyers were also despatched.

The five deep depth charges did not sink the *U-55*, and Lieutenant Heidel got away. But he soon discovered that he was far from safe. The explosions had caused the boat to take in about fifteen tons of water. She was sluggish, and the air supply had been diminished seriously. Heidel estimated that he had suffered so much damage that he had to surface, and once on the surface, see what repairs could be made.

When the Sunderland flying boat came over, the pilot found the area almost completely closed in by clouds that hung down to the surface, but the pilot found a hole, and came down, and below he saw the *U-55* on the surface, moving at about ten knots, with her gun crews on deck. The Sunderland attacked and dropped a bomb. The *U-55* returned gunfire but made no move to submerge. The Sunderland pilot then radioed the position of the submarine.

Heidel submerged again. At 1:30 the destroyers *Whitshed* and *Ardent* joined the chase.

At about two o'clock the *Whitshed* had a contact. Commander E. R. Conder brought the destroyer in and dropped one depth charge set for 250 feet. It did more damage to the boat, and Heidel surfaced once more, this time in the teeth of his enemies. At 2:20 the *Fowey* sighted the U-boat on the surface again and opened fire from 4,000 yards. The fog closed in, and the *Fowey* continued to fire, but only intermittently, and without inflicting any damage on the *U-55*.

The French destroyer *Valmy* came up, for she was about to take over responsibility for the protection of the convoy. She also opened fire. The *U-55* returned the fire, but the breach block on the deck gun jammed, and that ended her firing.

At that, Skipper Heidel decided the time had come to scuttle his ship lest it fall into the hands of the enemy. He gave the orders to abandon ship and asked for volunteers to open the valves. The first lieutenant and the engineer officer volunteered and the three went below. After a time the first lieutenant and the engineer came up, but the captain never appeared. He had stayed behind intentionally, to go down with his ship, in the old tradition of the German naval service.

The others clung to a raft until the Allied destroyers came along. Then they were rescued. Forty-one members of Lieutenant Heidel's crew were saved and joined the men of *U-35* and those other lucky ones in the prison camps.

When the *U-55* failed to report in after her attack on the convoy, Doenitz suspected, and when the silence lasted several days, he knew. He had developed high hopes for Lieutenant Heidel. It was another of the "painless losses" he had learned to expect in this hard war.

6
Doenitz Bears Down

At the end of six months of war, the German U-boat commander who pays any attention to International Law is the exception. Neutral ships as well as belligerents have, for some time in the past, been sunk without warning. There appear to be two objects in this policy, to frighten neutrals away from English ports, and to decrease the world tonnage, since this will work to the Allied disadvantage.

—British Naval Intelligence Report,
U-Boat Offensive, January 1940.

British naval intelligence was quite right in its assessment of the first object of Admiral Doenitz's submarine command in the winter of 1940, although in the second, the British gave Doenitz credit for a long-range program that was quite beyond his resources.

As the year turned and the winter gales of January swept across the North Atlantic, Admiral Doenitz had begun to show the British that their estimate of the sea war had been seriously in error. Production had been ordered stopped on the 250-ton "canoes" and Doenitz's eyes were on the 750-ton Type VII boat for the future. Besides Heidel's *U-55* several other U-boats appeared in the Atlantic in the second and third weeks of January, although they confined themselves to attacking single ships and laying mines. They laid mines on the approaches to Liverpool, and these accounted for the sinking of two British ships. It was not glamorous work, but it was effective. Two other mines sank British ships off Falmouth harbor and off Swansea. Two submarines were known to have laid mines in the Bristol Channel.

February began badly for Doenitz. The command post at Wilhelmshaven was still calling up *U-55* when the word came that Lieutenant Frahm's little *U-15* had been rammed in operations in the Baltic and sunk. Most of the crew was rescued, but another boat was lost; fortunately for Doenitz's plans it was one of the little ones, for the plans called for exerting maximum effort against the Western Approaches.

It was evident that something was stirring in Norway. The Germans increased their naval traffic significantly, although most of it was carried on the inshore route, so British submarines and destroyers had little chance to intercept it. At this time, the British decoding experts were hard at work at Bletchley Park, the site of the Ultra radio intelligence center, where the British would read the German secret codes for all branches of the service during much of the war. But in January and February 1940, British decoding experts had a long way to go in spite of their possession of the Enigma coding machine that had been turned over to them by the Poles.

So by no means could the British be certain of what was happening either in the Atlantic or on the far shores of the North Sea.

In the British cabinet, Winston Churchill was arguing that the Germans certainly planned to assault Norway, and he was gaining support for his plan of a preemptive attack to prevent the Germans from gaining control of that country. But at the same time the German plan for invasion was in the works; the Germans were already moving on land and at sea to do just what Churchill feared. That plan included the use of most of Admiral Doenitz's available forces.

Doenitz, however, was not in on the secret. He was going his own way. At the beginning of February Doenitz sent eight boats into the Atlantic to work the Western Approaches. First to arrive was Lieutenant Mugler's *U-41*. She attacked Convoy OB 84 bound for North America. On February 5 she sank the Dutch tanker *Ceronia* and the British merchant ship *Beaverburn*. But the British captain of the destroyer *Antelope* was on his toes. He was the sole guardian of the convoy at that moment, yet he broke off and went after *U-41*, and sent her to the bottom. Thus ended the career of one of Doenitz's bright young captains, after three patrols and six ships.

Hartmann, Schultze, and Lemp were the next to arrive in the Western Approaches that month. They were all eager to perform for fame and Fatherland. Among the submarine commanders, at the end of January von Dresky led in sinkings with twelve. Next was Schultze with eleven. Then along came Habekost with nine, Hartmann and Rollmann each with eight, and Juerst, von Klot-Heydenfeldt, and Schepke with seven. Habekost had the additional honor of damaging the battleship *Nelson*, and bad boy Lemp nearly sank the battleship *Barham*.

The number twelve, however, was not von Dresky's lucky one. He was still on patrol on February 12, mining the River Clyde on orders, when he was surprised by HMS *Gleaner.* The *U-33* was attacked, damaged, scuttled, and the crew, including Lieutenant von Dresky, made prisoners of war.

The U-boats sank nine ships in the following week, all vessels that were trying to make the run west independently.

Harald Grosse arrived in the *U-53*, and soon there were seven boats working the Western Approaches. Grosse's appearance was a symbol of Admiral Doenitz's efficiency and ruthlessness in management of the U-boat command. The earlier skipper of the *U-53* had been Lieutenant Heinicke, but one patrol had convinced the admiral that Heinicke did not have the stuff that made a successful U-boat captain; he was moved ashore and the new man given his chance. Needless to say this system put the new captains on their mettle from the first moment. Grosse came in eager to prove his worth.

On February 11 he sank the 400-ton Norwegian motor ship *Snestad*, and the 8,000-ton British tanker *Imperial Transport*. Next day he sank the 4,000-ton Swedish freighter *Dalaroe*. On February 13 he sank the 1,000-ton Swedish freighter *Norma* and on the fourteenth, the Danish merchantman *Martin Goldschmidt*. On February 18 he sank the 2,100-ton Spanish freighter *Banderas*. That was six ships in twelve days; in a single patrol Harald Grosse was rivaling all the others. And then, on February 23, Harald Grosse encountered the destroyer *Gurkha*, and his career came to a sudden, watery end.

In the North Sea on February 18, Lieutenant Commander Otto Kretschmer in the *U-23* continued his remarkable exploits by sinking the British destroyer *Daring*.

Sinking a warship gave a captain a special place in the skippers' club, and now Kretschmer had joined up. The fact made more difference to Hitler and Admiral Raeder than it did to Admiral Doenitz, for Doenitz knew what the game was really about: the starvation of England and the number of merchant tons sunk. That was his way of looking at success. His problem now and throughout the war was to convince the naval and Nazi hierarchies to give him the resources he needed. Then, he insisted, he could win the war for them.

Kretschmer's triumph was Churchill's tragedy. Only five members of the crew of the *Daring* were picked up, and although eleven destroyers combed the area seeking vengeance against the U-boat, Kretschmer got away clean.

But there was the other side of the coin . . .

The British had learned from POW interrogations at least some of the routes the German submarines used when they approached the northern tip of the Scottish Isles, and they had done some appropriate mining of their own. On February 14 Lieutenant Kutschmann's *U-54* was sunk by a mine in the North Sea. She went down swiftly with all hands. Doenitz had not the slightest idea of what had happened to her, and would not have until after the war. Eventually the British found the wreckage.

On February 17, while Kretschmer was approaching the scene of his triumph, Junior Lieutenant Guenther Lorentz began his voyage in a much improved version of the discontinued 250-ton "canoe"—the *U-63*. Her keel had been laid in the last months of peace, and she had been completed in December. Trials in the Baltic lasted six weeks, and then the *U-63* had moved down to Heligoland via the Kiel Canal. She arrived there on February 1 for a two-week workup in which the new young skipper and his crew were supposed to get the feel of the boat. Unfortunately the weather was so bad that they had only eight days of operations, and even then felt constrained to return to harbor every evening.

On February 16, the *U-63* took on her war load: four electric torpedoes. These were the standard of the U-boat service. Their great value, as learned too late by the survivors of the *Daring*, was that they left no wake, and when fired by the new method of ''surgeless discharge'' gave not the slightest hint of their coming. Their grievous fault was in the magnetic proximity fuse, but, of course, Junior Lieutenant Lorentz knew nothing about that.

Four torpedoes were not many, and that was one of the major reasons that Admiral Doenitz had asked for discontinuation of the production of these small vessels. A brave skipper and a trained crew of twenty-four men could be used much more effectively in one of the big boats that carried eighteen torpedoes. But for a short haul in the North Sea, the ''canoe'' could still be effective, and as he so often observed to his subordinates, Doenitz, too, had to make do with what was available.

On February 17 at one o'clock in the afternoon, Skipper Lorentz took his boat to sea. He cleared the German Bight, and then dived since he was coming into waters where British danger lurked. When night came he surfaced, charged batteries and stayed on the surface, sending and receiving radio messages, until daylight.

Thus the *U-63* proceeded to her operational area, fifty miles east of the Orkneys. She arrived on station on February 20. Kretschmer was still in the area; on February 22 he sank the 5,000-ton British steamer *Loch Maddy* at 70 degrees 20 minutes, in the Orkneys area. But the patrol areas had been carefully plotted on the big chart in Doenitz's office, and they did not overlap. Not even Doenitz had thought of teaming up the ''canoes'' for wolf pack attack.

Doenitz's intelligence service, from the outset of the war, had been superb. He had agents all over Norway and the continent. On the night of February 23 Doenitz's headquarters warned Skipper Lorentz to expect a convoy coming through his area, bound from Bergen to Methil. Lorentz began to search.

He searched all day on February 24 and found nothing. But at evening, shortly after dark, he sighted a lone steamer. He went after her. The chase lasted just an hour and a half, and then the *U-63* fired a single torpedo, and the ship sank. No trouble there. With a full boat, and a very tiny one at that, it was easy for Lieutenant Lorentz to remember Doenitz's standing orders against stopping to help survivors; he did not even pause. Some of the swimmers were picked up later by a British destroyer.

Lorentz went on, on the surface, and reported his sinking to headquarters. About an hour later he was surprised by a British plane that came out of nowhere and bombed. Lorentz got down in time; the bombs were far short anyhow. It was a cheap lesson.

He tracked a small shadow of a ship. At a few minutes before midnight he surfaced and fired a torpedo. It misfired. Only then did he realize that the target vessel was too small to warrant the expenditure of another shot; it was not even worth the first one. He had only two torpedoes left.

Lorentz headed to the east, and at about 2 A.M. on February 25 he found convoy HN 14, and he began stalking. The convoy was escorted. He saw two destroyers. It was hard to get within firing range, for the convoy zigged and zagged and the escorts sped up and down the perimeter, crossing bow and stern. But a few minutes before midnight a chance came. The escorts were out of the way at the other end of the convoy, and the *U-63* surfaced and fired another torpedo. It misfired. Lieutenant Lorentz was learning about torpedo troubles. He now had one torpedo left. He made a new approach on another ship, and as he was ready to fire, his diesel engine began acting up. The chance was missed.

He submerged, tagged along close by the convoy, and waited for a new chance. One of the escorting destroyers came up nearby in a tour of the convoy perimeter.

From the German point of view, one of the great assets of the "canoes" was their virtual invisibility if submerged to periscope depth in anything but a mirror sea. This destroyer came by within 400 yards of the *U-63*, and no one aboard the ship turned a hair. Skipper Lorentz put his boat in line for a shot. Then, from the torpedo officer came the word that the men had not reloaded. By the time they could get the torpedo into the tube, the destroyer had whizzed by at twenty knots, and the chance was gone. So much for a new crew on its first patrol.

The *U-63* was then spotted by one of its own kind, the British submarine *Narwhal*. It was an indication of the desperate need for escort vessels that the Royal Navy would so employ a submarine. But these new Norway ore convoys were deemed vital; already Kretschmer had knocked off the *Daring* when she was escorting the first ore convoy, and every precaution had to be taken.

The *Narwhal* immediately warned the surface escorts, HMS *Escapade* and HMS *Escort*. And from general patrol duty up came HMS *Inglefield* and HMS *Imogen*. The convoy was turned over to the British submarine for protection while the ships went after the U-boat.

At eight o'clock in the morning four escorts were whipping the water around the convoy. Lieutenant Lorentz took the *U-63* down, and down and down some more. The fathometer read more than 100 meters—395 feet. The *U-63* was 65 feet below her safe depth. And as the engineers had warned, trouble began. She started taking water through her diesel exhaust valves.* The water got in and doused the electric motors. An enormous cloud of chlorine erupted, but was controlled. Lorentz brought the boat up to 160 feet.

The *Escapade* was the first vessel to make contact, but her Asdic coughed at the wrong moment, and she lost touch. Half an hour later the *Escort* made another contact at 1,800 yards. She began to close at fifteen knots, found the target moving to starboard, and steered 20 degrees to the right to intercept. Seven minutes later she fired a pattern of five depth charges, two to explode at 150 feet, two at 250 feet, and one at 350 feet.

Down below, the charges began going off. The boat shook, and the lights flickered. But that was all.

---

*One of the deficiencies of German submarines lamented by Admiral Doenitz was that their valves faced the wrong way, so that instead of sealing the valves, outer water pressure had a tendency to open them.

The firing had cost the *Escort* her Asdic contact. The escorts then started a search pattern, forming up abreast and combing the area. At nine o'clock the *Imogen* made contact again. It was not a very good contact, for the U-boat was lying with its stern to the line of search. The Asdic showed that *Imogen* was moving down on the target and was only 500 yards off. Then the Asdic failed her and contact was lost.

The ships formed up again in a search line, steamed for half an hour, turned about and steamed back. Thirteen minutes later, the skipper of *Imogen* saw something dead ahead . . .

Lieutenant Lorentz had been having more than his share of difficulties. The boat had taken hundreds of gallons of water, and the electric motors had been damaged enough to short out. It was extremely difficult to hold any depth position. Lorentz had to pump and blow at the same time to retain trim, and when he reduced speed to cut the noise, the boat headed down toward the bottom. The pumps then quit discharging because the motors could not handle the pressure. He brought her back to 195 feet, and the motors began to sputter. The boat went down again toward the 300-foot mark.

Lieutenant Lorentz looked at his compressed air indicators and discovered he had only 225 pounds left in the bottles. The boat was growing heavier every moment as she shipped more water. There was only one solution, he had this last chance to surface. So he fed in the air and turned up the planes and took the boat up, and up she went like a porpoise after air. He stood in the conning tower and opened the hatch, and was immediately popped out the top and over the side like a champagne cork blown by an amateur. His men leaped out and hauled him back aboard, and that is where they were when the *Imogen*'s captain came up.

As the British escorts sighted the surfaced submarine they all opened fire with their guns. But it was not necessary, for the *U-63* was already filling with water, and by the time they arrived she was sinking. They rescued the three officers and twenty-two enlisted men of the crew and these, too, went to join the happy warriors in the prison camps, whose lives had been so miraculously given back to them.

Happy warriors? Lorentz and his men complained all the way back to England, about the food, their treatment, and one another. Lorentz charged that the British sailors had stolen all his belongings (quite possible since British sailors were souvenir hunters like German sailors). The Nazis complained about the non-Nazis. The enlisted men complained that the skipper was incompetent, and Lorentz complained that the crew were incompetent. The worst quarrel was between the engineer officer and torpedo officer on the one side and Lorentz on the other; Lorentz was bitter at the loss of the chance to sink a destroyer because the torpedo officer had not been ready with that last torpedo. They had failed him, he charged. But the other two said the failure was entirely the captain's because of his incompetent handling of the boat.

From the record it does not seem that the captain was unskilled. Skipper Lorentz had a very difficult job, bringing the *U-63* up and down like a cork, and the fact that he had managed to keep the boat together as long as he did was quite remarkable. But then, the German engineers built very good U-boats.

The British did not really care much who triumphed in this war of wordy acrimony. They had sunk another U-boat and taken another crew that would never again make trouble for honest British seamen. They dismissed the whole debate as a quarrel among Nazis. "The officers and crew of *U-63* showed, on the whole, the usual Nazi mentality." Their good words were reserved for the petty officers, who, they observed, "were much less rabid than the younger seamen."

The failure of *U-63* to report again brought a note of sadness to the Doenitz command post, but no pause in activity. Such tragedy had to be expected as part of the price of success. By month's end the bad news had been repeated several times: seven boats were lost that month, it was the highest loss of any month of the war so far. But to counter that statistic, those eight Type VII oceangoing boats and half a dozen of the smaller boats operating in the North Sea gave a good account of themselves that month. They sank fifty-two ships, the highest total yet, and in the shortest month of the year. It was not satisfactory, the loss ratio of submarines to ships sunk was entirely too high, and that would have to be remedied. But the new Type VII boats had proved their worth, and Doenitz was looking forward to the day when he would have enough of them to put to sea his wolf packs.

7

The Golden Age Begins

From the point of view of the U-boat force there was only one good thing to be said for the Norway campaign of the spring of 1940: it brought about an end to the torpedo problem. Early in March, Hitler had ordered Doenitz to stop whatever he was doing—which was gearing up for the Battle of the Atlantic—and concentrate his U-boats around Norway to support the German invasion, and prevent British counterinvasion. Doenitz did as he was told. He began with reconnaissance: on March 3 Lieutenant Lemp's *U-30* moved up the Norwegian coast, poking into the fjords and spying out the defenses at periscope depth. So did other submarines. As a result, by the end of the month Germans had a good picture of the shore defenses and the number and sort of warships and merchant ships that used the various fjords. The reconnaissance finished, Doenitz put together a U-boat force of thirty-one vessels to support the military action. They were to be disposed in three defensive lines, which would prevent the British fleet from interfering. Fourteen U-boats were sent to Narvik, Bergen, Trondheim, and Stavanger. Thirteen more were assigned to three groups that would attack the British Home Fleet if it tried to move in force. Four U-boats patrolled the Skagerrak to protect German lines of communication from British naval attack. OKW envisaged a great sea battle in which the submarines would triumph over the British fleet.

It did not work out that way. A large number of the submarines had at least one shot at a British warship, but the torpedoes functioned at their absolute worst. The British counted twenty U-boat attacks on major warships, twenty *failed* attacks. The battleship *Warspite* alone was attacked four different times without success. Seven cruisers were attacked and seven destroyers, all without success. Of ten attacks on military transports only one succeeded. Prien got one ship but had so many misfires it was hard to believe. The story was the same for nearly every U-boat captain and worse for some. Almost unnoticed by the Germans was one development that month that presaged a very unpleasant future for the U-boats. It involved an airplane.

The 500-ton boat *U-31* was laid down on April 1, 1936, and finished on December 28 of that year at the Deschinag shipyard in Bremen. She went on two cruises into Spanish waters in 1937, a part of Hitler's effort to shore up the Franco revolution. Lieutenant Habekost, her skipper, had taken her out in September, as noted, and had sunk three ships. She was back in Wilhelmshaven on October 2. On her second war cruise in October, she was laying mines and produced nothing at all. She was back in port again by November 1. The third war cruise redeemed all; Habekost sank four ships, and one of the mines he had laid in Loch Ewe damaged the battleship *Nelson*. After that cruise the *U-31* went into dry dock for a refit, and all the crew had leave until February.

The *U-31* was undergoing trials in Schillig Bay in the Heligoland Bight in the second week of March. March 11 was the day the U-boat war changed again. That morning British Bomber Command ordered up a reconnaissance mission by several Blenheim bombers of the Heligoland Bight. One of the aircraft came in at about 3,500 feet, flying between two layers of clouds. When the pilot reached the Schillig Roads area, he brought the plane down to 2,500 feet. Bursting out of the clouds that way, he surprised Skipper Habekost and the crew.

The bomber moved in to attack, camera clicking at the same time. Skipper Habekost ordered a crash dive, and five seconds later the boat was starting down. But the Blenheim was atop the U-boat then and dropped four 250-pound bombs. The pilot scored one or two direct hits. He circled and a minute later took a third photo, which showed oil and air bubbles rising to the surface.

Inside the *U-31* the diving horn was still sounding when the first bomb hit alongside the deck gun on the starboard side. It wrecked the gun and tore a hole in the outer plating. The boat went down, leaving the chief quartermaster and one seaman on the surface. The second bomb created such a concussion that it caused the compressed air bottles to explode and broke the pipes, so that the boat's pressure rose so high that it killed every man in a matter of seconds. The boat sank to the bottom in fifty feet of water. The abandoned quartermaster and the abandoned seaman were no better off. They drowned before rescue could arrive.

So the war against the U-boats entered a new phase. The British learned that an aircraft could indeed sink a U-boat, even an oceangoing U-boat, singlehanded, if using the right weapons. Twenty-pound bombs were not going to do the job but 250-pound bombs could.

Lieutenant Mathes's *U-44* was sunk by HMS *Fortune* on March 20 in Vest Fjord. Five submarines were sunk in April: *U-64*, in Hersangs Fjord, by planes of 700 Squadron and HMS *Warspite*; Lieutenant Deeck's *U-1* was sunk by the British submarine *Porpoise*; *U-49* by HMS *Fearless*. *U-22* went down when she hit a mine. *U-50* was off the Shetlands when she encountered HMS *Amazon* and HMS *Witherington*, and they sank her.

The Norway campaign ended satisfactorily for Hitler, another conquest, but it came very close to destroying the U-boat service. The boats were withdrawn, and officers and men moped dismally about the bases, complaining that they had no weapons. Admiral Doenitz made a personal inspection tour of the bases to try to build up morale. Equally important, the captains finally convinced the command, and the command finally forced a thorough investigation of the torpedo magnetic exploders, which proved that the weapons were faulty. Several heads rolled, and a crash program of improvement began. The captains relearned the use of the weapon, which was more or less adequate if fired directly at the target at shallow settings.

May 1940 brought two new developments in the U-boat campaign, one positive, and one negative: Admiral Doenitz finally had enough 500-ton and 750-ton boats in hand to undertake the wolf pack campaign. Winston Churchill became Prime Minister of England, thus putting into command the most implacable and prescient enemy of the U-boats.

Before Doenitz could launch his renewed offensive, he had to reestablish the self-confidence of the U-boat corps. He did this by detaching his operations officer, Lieutenant Commander Victor Oehrn, for a cruise in the *U-37*. Oehrn sank eleven ships, totaling 47,000 tons, using the standard electric torpedo, but eliminating the magnetic warhead. His performance convinced both the admiral and the U-boat captains that their weapons would do the job.

By June 1, then, the submarine command at Wilhelmshaven was prepared to carry the war against Britain in the Atlantic. A number of new boats had undergone their trials and were ready, among them Lieutenant Kretschmer's *U-99*. He had been given this 500-ton boat as a reward for his exceptional exploits in the *U-23*: nine patrols in which he had laid hundreds of mines from the Firth of Forth to the Shetland Islands, eight merchant ships and one destroyer sunk.

Even as Doenitz planned the "spring offensive" the war changed enormously in his favor. The capture of Norway and Denmark meant that the U-boats had easy access to the North Sea and to emergency ports all along the Norwegian coast. Bergen and several other ports would be developed into U-boat harbors. Once Hitler had secured his flank with the capture of Norway, he moved swiftly to knock France and England out of the war. The French had spent years and millions of francs to fortify the ground between themselves and Germany; the Germans swept easily around the north of all this concrete bastionry, down through Belgium to the sea, and drove for Paris. By the end of May they had apparently trapped the British Expeditionary Army against the sea, but in a remarkable display of daring and perseverance the people of Britain turned to and rescued their army at Dunkirk. Still, by June 15, the Germans were in Paris, France was out of the war, and the channel coast and Bay of Biscay ports were now available to the U-boats as harbors. This would extend the U-boat range much farther into the Atlantic; now Type VII boats, at least, could cross over to the American side. It would be a number of months before the French ports would be properly equipped to handle U-boats, but immediately they were available as fueling stations and ports of refuge. One of the great German advantages, now that the British were learning to use their aircraft, was the extension of their operational area beyond the range of the shore-based planes.

At the end of the first week in June, Admiral Doenitz was launching the offensive. Lemp sailed from Wilhelmshaven in *U-30* on June 8, proceeded up the North Sea through the Fair Isle Channel and into the operational zone between the North Channel, west of Ireland, south to St. George's Channel.

On June 10, Prien's *U-47* sailed from Germany to the Southwestern Approaches. He went as far south as Spain; he sank ten ships and claimed 66,000 tons on his return. Other boats fanned out to cover the other approaches to Britain. The record was indicative of what was happening. Kretschmer's *U-99* sailed on June 17 and was very nearly sunk by a scout bomber from the battle cruiser *Scharnhorst*. The plane's first bomb broke the lens of the attack periscope and jammed the scope; both compasses were knocked out. Kretschmer escaped, but he had to scurry for the Norwegian coast, and after stopping off at Bergen he headed back to Wilhelmshaven and three days of repairs before starting out again.

But that near miss was, literally, the worst that happened to Doenitz's U-boat force that June. Not a single submarine was lost. The U-boats were having the most successful cruises of the war so far. One tragedy did mar the results: among the ships sunk by Prien, without warning, now, in obedience to orders, was the *Arandora Star*, which had been carrying German and Italian internees to safety. The loss of German lives was high. But the loss to Britain was staggering: the U-boats sank sixty-four ships that month, for a total of more than 260,000 tons. Besides Prien, the heroes of the hour were Lieutenant Engelbert Endrass in the *U-46*, with six ships sunk, and Lieutenant Hans Jenisch in *U-32*, with five ships. Altogether, Doenitz's captains compiled a real record: they sank ships on twenty-six days of the month. By far the majority of these ships were traveling alone. The British were using convoys, but the convoy system had not been perfected, largely because of the shortage of escort craft. Because of this shortage, the British were operating under a false premise that was very helpful to Doenitz and his captains: a number of destroyers were being used on regional patrol. They covered designated "trouble" areas in a designated pattern. Their effectiveness was extremely limited, nothing at all sunk in June, for example. Much more effective was the British countermining of certain areas, such as the East Coast Barrage, which extended from the Thames to the Moray Firth. These minefields would cost the Germans a number of submarines.

In June, the British were building escort craft furiously. Sixty-seven destroyers were under construction, ninety-two corvettes and sloops, forty-three trawlers, and two hundred motor launches. But under construction did not mean available, and Doenitz had many things going for him this month. Not the least, apparently, was the entry of Italy into the war on the German side, which put the staggering number of a hundred more submarines into action for the Axis! The future looked bleak indeed for Britain, with the German high command planning Operation Sealion, the invasion of England, and with Doenitz now controlling the French coast from Dunkirk, around the channel, south along the Bay of Biscay to Hendaye on the Spanish border, with open access into mid-Atlantic.

On June 23, Admiral Doenitz boarded a Junkers bomber and was flown to Lorient to establish forward U-boat headquarters there. And there, the admiral presided over the beginning of the Golden Age of the U-boats. Immediately he ordered the building of U-boat facilities at the port in the area called Keroman and began arrangements for the build-

ng of the famous reinforced concrete U-boat pens, so well
uilt by the Todt Organization that when the Allies finally
aptured Lorient in 1944 they discovered that not one of the
housands of bombs rained down on that facility had ever
enetrated into the pens. The garrison was housed in hotels
nd in the music academy of the city. The command post
vas located in the prefecture offices, which Doenitz took
ver. The officers' mess was there, too. The key was
)oenitz's operations room with his big chart of the waters of
he Western world all marked off in its square grids. Behind
vas the "museum" where pictures and statistics showing
he history of the U-boat force were maintained. He made it
rule to see his heroes off to war, the men standing at
ttention in their fatigue uniforms aboard the departing
J-boat, Doenitz reviewing them, and then giving the cap-
ain that hearty handclasp to speed him on his way. A
riumphant return, accompanied by a patrol craft into har-
or, meant a brass band and any number of dignitaries and
lowers, and then, once the boat was safely put up, the
lrinking and the singing began.

The officers in these days stayed at the Beau Sejour or
ne of the other leading hotels, and the men at a second-
lass hotel such as the Pigeon Blanc. Sometimes the boats
vere in port for only a few days, the need to relieve the
tress was immediate and powerful, and Lorient quickly
cquired a reputation as a wild and woolly haven for these
igers of the sea. In July Doenitz set up his central commu-
iications office in Paris, but Lorient was the headquarters of
he Battle of the Atlantic.

The luck of June could not hold, as everyone at Doenitz's
eadquarters knew. Only July 3, Lieutenant Scherlinger's
J-26 was caught by a combination air-sea attack. A Royal
ustralian Air Force plane and HMS *Gladiolus* combined
fforts to sink her in mid-Atlantic. Fortunately most of the
rew were saved. Not so with Lieutenant Loof's brand-new
J-122. She went out and simply disappeared, whether
ictim of attack or an accident no one knew.

Still, a loss of two boats for 267,000 tons of shipping was
iot a bad exchange for Doenitz, one he could live with very
iicely, particularly since the new boats were coming faster

now. The Italians began to add to the sinkings, and the breaking of the British merchant code helped Doenitz's staff move U-boats into the paths of the convoys. No one had yet adopted Kretschmer's night surface attack technique, but he was still using it with great success. He was awarded the Knight's Cross of the Iron Cross, joining Prien, Herbert Schultze, Otto Schubart, and Wilhelm Rollmann; they were the five leading captains of the U-boat service that summer.

By this time, the summer of 1940, three names dominated the list of the U-boat captains: Prien, Schepke, and Kretschmer. They were the lions of the force, and the terrors of the convoys. By September, Admiral Doenitz had his wolf packs working, and they were accomplishing all he could have expected: the sinkings for the month of September came to just under 300,000 tons, a new record. From Hitler's point of view, the summer of 1940 was most unsatisfactory. Operation Sealion, the invasion of England, depended on control of the air above the English Channel, a matter that Hermann Goering had virtually dismissed as everything but a fait accompli. But the fact was that in the summer battles in the air, the Spitfires and Hurricanes of the RAF turned back the German attackers with such heavy losses that Operation Sealion was abandoned. There would be no early end to the war. It was going to be fought to a finish.

All the more reason, then, that Admiral Doenitz's U-boats must block off Britain's supply of war materials from the Americas and destroy Britain's communications with the Mediterranean.

The U-boats continued to hold the upper hand during the late summer and fall. Doenitz lost three boats in August, but all of them had to be regarded as fluke losses: Lieutenant Beduhn's *U-25* struck a British mine west of the Inner Hebrides; Lieutenant Knorr's *U-51* was spotted by the British submarine *Cachalot* while on the surface fifty miles west of Belle Isle (a foolish place to be, as Knorr discovered too late). Lieutenant von Kloth's *U-102* fell victim to another of those strange mysteries of the sea. She set out from Germany and was not heard from after she entered the North Sea. Probably, she, too, hit a mine.

Three submarines for one month's work; the results were

still not bad considering the improvement in delivery of new boats. September was much better, only Kuehl's *U-57* was lost, rammed by a Norwegian freighter in the Baltic. The British defenses, the escorts and aircraft, seemed to have been completely eclipsed by the U-boats, even though with the arrival of the new corvettes off the ways the number of convoys was increasing. So was the German working of the convoys, and some captains were beginning to adopt Kretschmer's night surface attack. In September Doenitz's captains took sixty ships from the convoys, another fifteen that were sailing independently, and the Italians sank three ships in the south.

One of the U-boats operating alone in October was the *U-31*, which had been sunk in Schillig Roads back in March by a British bomber, going down with all hands.

The *U-31* had been raised eight days after her sinking. When the salvage vessel brought her to the surface, and they moved her to Wilhelmshaven, they opened the conning tower hatch. The men were greeted with the sad reminder of the lot of the unlucky U-boat man. All the officers and men of the unfortunate *U-31* were jammed together in the conning tower. Officers and men were buried in the Heroes Cemetery (Heldenfriedhof) in Wilhelmshaven, and Kapitaenleutnant Hans Habekost was given a fine obituary by the Hamburg newspapers.

The *U-31* was fitted with the new Radio Direction Finding (RDF) equipment. This new RDF equipment was another factor in the increasing success of the U-boats; the capture of Norway and France had made it possible for Doenitz's radio experts to set up triangulations to locate convoys within the German grid system. The new RDF was now becoming standard in the U-boat fleet, and all new boats were equipped with it.

The 500-ton *U-31* was recommissioned in August 1940. Lieutenant Wilfried Prellberg was given the ship. He was an experienced U-boat man, with service under Doenitz since 1937. He had been with Lieutenant Rollmann on several cruises in the *U-34* before given his chance with his own boat. He took the *U-31* into the Baltic for trials and a workup and then returned to Wilhelmshaven. After the usual briefing by Admiral Doenitz, Prellberg set out on his first patrol on September 14. He had with him four officers, four chief petty officers, eleven petty officers and twenty-five seamen. He was not going to be involved in a wolf pack, not on his first patrol.

The *U-31* was carrying eleven torpedoes, most of them the air-driven type A, a sort that had replaced many of the unreliable electric torpedoes. The *U-31* sank a 50-ton sailing vessel by gunfire and then the unescorted Norwegian steamer *Vestvard*, which was carrying a cargo of lumber. Skipper Prellberg had a hard time with her, using up three torpedoes. But his failure was not unique; in the summer Kretschmer had used three torpedoes to sink another lumber ship. Sometimes, even for the most skillful captains, nothing seemed to go right. Prellberg was having some difficulty in getting acclimated; he spent the rest of his torpedoes without sinking another ship. On the morning of October 8, on the surface in the high sea, the *U-31* was surprised by the British submarine *Trident*, which fired six torpedoes at her. The *Trident* then opened fire with her gun and claimed hits on the conning tower. Prellberg barely managed to dive the U-boat in time to escape another torpedo. The conning tower closed behind him just as the U-boat slid beneath the surface. Prellberg sank down with a sigh of relief, it was the nearest escape he had ever known. The boat was out of trim, and the torpedo men tried to get their tubes ready to fight back, but the boat went bumping down to the bottom. Skipper Prellberg decided that discretion was the best part of valor, and he remained down there, while the *Trident* waited up above. Finally the British submarine, having made no contact for fifty minutes, went on its way.

Prellberg moved then, and finally went into Lorient, to berth on the Scorff River opposite Jenisch's *U-32*. Several of the other boats out that month on individual cruises had better luck. Jenisch, Liebe, Moehle, and Oehrn all found ships without the help of RDF. They and the wolf packs had made of October 1940 the worst month of the war yet for British shipping. In the four months since June, the U-boats had taken 144 unescorted vessels and 73 ships out of convoys. Doenitz had lost only six U-boats in this period, and only two of those were sunk while attacking convoys.

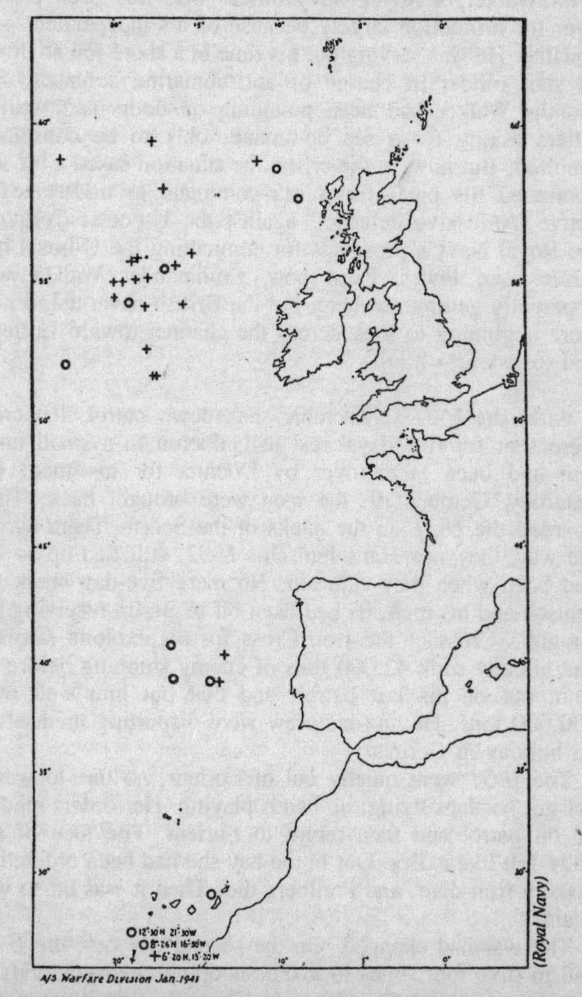

In the early months of the war the battle of the U-boats was fought around the Western Approaches to Britain, shown here.

The British were virtually frantic. Something had to be done.

No one realized that fact more than Commander Frederic John Walker, a Royal Navy officer who had been passed over for promotion largely because of his independent personality. He was serving out his time in a shore job at Dover as staff officer in charge of antisubmarine defenses. For months Walker had been pounding on doors and writing letters asking for a sea command, only to be constantly rebuffed. But now, in the crisis, the situation eased a bit. He continued his pleas for a sea command to undertake an active "offensive defense" against the U-boats. Certainly the Royal Navy's prospects for combatting the U-boats had never been lower. Even now, Commander Walker was apparently getting nowhere, but the British naval authorities were beginning to look across the channel toward Lorient, and to listen to him.

After the *U-31*'s miserable shakedown patrol, the crew were sent for five days' rest to Quiberon to a small hotel that had been taken over by Doenitz for his men. On Saturday, October 19, the men were brought back. They boarded the *U-31* on the banks of the Scorff. There across the way, they saw Hans Jenisch's *U-32*, still tied up as she had been when they came in. No mere five-day break for Jenisch and his men, he had been off in Berlin receiving the Knight's Cross of the Iron Cross for his exploits. Jenisch had already sunk 42,000 tons of enemy shipping before he went out on his last patrol, and that put him well over 100,000 tons. He and his crew were disporting themselves on holiday in Germany.

The *U-31* went quietly out of Lorient, no one to watch her go, no flags flying, no bands playing. Her orders read to go on patrol and then return to Lorient. The men of the *U-31* felt like exiles. Out in the bay she had been ordered to make a trim dive, and Prellberg did. Then it was off to war again.

The war had changed. On the second day out, the *U-31* had to dive four times to avoid snooping enemy aircraft in the area south of St. George's Channel. Where were the planes coming from? The British Coastal Command was finally getting organized.

Bad weather set in, and the men could not decide which was preferable: good weather and enemy air attack, or bad weather and the knocking about that kept the boat submerged for most of the next day and a half.

On October 28 came action at last! Through the periscope Lieutenant Prellberg sighted a 6,000-ton steamer, and he attacked. One torpedo went out, and then another, and a third. Only then did someone notice that the target was not moving. She was the derelict British steamer *Matina,* torpedoed three days earlier and claimed by Lieutenant Kuhnke's *U-28*. All Prellberg had done was waste three torpedoes to get credit for a coup de grace.

The crew of the *U-31* did not have much confidence in their captain in the beginning, and what had occurred on the first patrol did not help. Now their morale was at a new low.

At sea, the *U-31* wallowed in sloppy weather.

Such weather dogged her, she traveled submerged at periscope depth during the night of October 31 to reduce the banging about. When Lieutenant Prellberg brought her to the surface that evening, he found he had a visibility of 100 yards.

Creeping about on the surface, Prellberg came upon a freighter and fired two more torpedoes. Both missed. He wanted to move west, but the hydrophone operator said he heard destroyer propeller sounds. Prellberg submerged and stayed down.

On the morning of November 2, the *U-31* came to the surface. Prellberg had to ventilate the boat. Visibility was seven miles. The sea was relatively calm with a Force 3 wind. Nothing was seen around them.

At 10:15 Lieutenant Prellberg was in the wardroom having his breakfast. The officer of the deck reported an enemy vessel to port. Prellberg told him to take her down, and he switched to silent running. The U-boat began creeping ahead. The hydrophone operator was listening intently. He spoke up: destroyer sounds to starboard. Prellberg took the boat down to 180 feet.

* * *

The destroyer was HMS *Antelope*, an escort of Convoy OB 237 bound outward from Liverpool. The convoy had not yet lost a ship, and the captain of the *Antelope* wanted to keep it that way. At 10:25 an Asdic contact was announced, a minute later it was identified as a U-boat. The captain attacked, dropping six depth charges set at from 150 to 350 feet.

Down below when the charges exploded the lights went out in *U-31*.

Up above the explosions cost the *Antelope* her Asdic contact. An antisubmarine sweep was organized with HMS *Achates*. Then the *Achates*'s Asdic also failed. But at 11:03 the *Antelope* regained contact. Range 1,800 yards, speed six knots.

The *Antelope* made another attack with six depth charges.

Down below, *U-31* was zigzagging carefully. The six charges missed well to port. The rear hydroplane jammed, but the worst result was an enormous noise and vibration that frightened the men in the boat.

Prellberg now began to exercise more than a little skill in his efforts to escape. He had gotten this boat because he had been Wilhelm Rollmann's executive officer in *U-34*. He had been in combat since the opening day of the war, and Rollmann had recommended him for vigor and bravery. At this point Prellberg exhibited both qualities. He turned to make a wide detour of the area. But the skipper of the *Antelope* also turned, and after losing contact made a circular sweep that caught up with the U-boat eight minutes later, 1,500 yards off. The captain of the *Antelope* held the contact but did not attack. He was waiting for the *Achates* to make her repairs so they could attack together. But the *Achates* was slow, and the captain of *Antelope* decided to go in, and to let *Achates* follow when she could.

The *U-31* had come up to 30 feet and altered course and speed frequently. She had just made a turn when the *Antelope* moved in on her attack, and the turn threw off the Asdic. Nothing but "woolly" echoes could be heard aboard the destroyer. A new all-around sweep was made at 12:05, but there was no contact.

The *Antelope*'s skipper stood on his bridge and considered the possibilities. The U-boat had made a sharp turn to the northwest and had speeded up. He had to assume that she was heading northwest at high speed, trying to escape. So he took that gamble. He ordered up *sixteen* knots from engineering and headed northwest, figuring that the U-boat had moved out at eight knots, then after about twenty minutes reduced to four knots. But when he reached the position, there was no contact. He backtracked, and at 1:30 that afternoon he made contact on the line to the old position where he had fixed the U-boat before. She was moving along 150 feet deep, and was 2,500 yards dead ahead. The captain of the *Antelope* ordered a pattern of six charges, set from 250 to 500 feet, and fired.

The shallow depth charges must have landed very nearly on top of the submarine, which had gone down to about 200 feet. She was pushed down by the stern, and began sinking fast. Lieutenant Prellberg ordered full ahead on both electric motors, but the submarine kept sinking by the stern. He sent all men forward, but it did not help. She was down by the stern 15 degrees and still sinking.

Prellberg said he thought they ought to surface.

It would be suicidal said the engineer officer. The destroyer was almost directly above.

One by one the instruments failed. All that was left was the depth gauge.

The *U-31* dropped faster now. She hit 312 feet, and the after torpedo tube and the diesel air shaft filled with water. A large bubble escaped and rose to the surface.

The *Antelope* moved toward the bubble and regained Asdic contact. The U-boat appeared to be moving very slowly. The operator heard bubbling noises, as though the tanks were being blown.

At 1:41 the *Antelope* moved in for a fourth depth charge attack.

When the charges exploded down below, the U-boat suffered more damage. A compressed air bottle smashed, and the air escaped with a bubbling noise, the valves leaked, and the quartermaster told the captain that they were leaving a trail of oil that had to rise to the surface. The trim problem became critical, and despite the advice of the engineer officer, the captain decided to surface.

Better a live prisoner of war than a dead hero, Prellberg said.

* * *

At 1:50 the *U-31* popped up just astern of the *Antelope*. The guns on the after part of the ship opened up and fired until it was evident that the Germans were abandoning their ship.

As Lieutenant Prellberg prepared to abandon, he fixed the wheel to turn to port, and left the motors running at a speed of four knots. Then he went up the conning tower and out on deck to the surface control station.

The skipper of the *Antelope* sent his whaler to board the ship, stop her and take possession. But the speed of the U-boat was too great for the whaler and the crew could not catch up. The *Antelope* then opened fire to stop the U-boat. The 4.7-inch guns fired twenty-three rounds, but all missed in the heavy swell.

The captain of the *Antelope* tried to lay the destroyer alongside the U-boat to board. But Lieutenant Prellberg turned the boat sharply to port, rammed the destroyer as she was maneuvering, and was pushed under. The conning tower filled with water, and the U-boat went to the bottom as Prellberg leaped off and swam away. Whatever might be said of his remarks about dead heroes, Prellberg had accomplished an astonishingly daring feat in destroying his U-boat so that she could not be captured by the enemy. Soon enough he was picked up by the *Antelope* and so were forty-two other officers and men. Only two men were lost. Lieutenant Prellberg had performed better under the pressure of attack than he ever did as a hunter; he had saved most of his crew and made sure the enemy could have no joy or information from his ship.

Thus, in one week, the British had scored coups against the U-boats, after a very long drought. The Prime Minister and everyone down the line could be very pleased, but as they all knew the problem was far from solved. Doenitz's new techniques demanded new answers. Vice Admiral Sir Hugh Binney, chairman of a special Admiralty committee to study the U-boat problem, reported that all seagoing anti-submarine vessels should be employed with convoys. The convoy escorts were bagging the game. The problem at the moment was that a speed of sixteen knots, which was top for many vessels, was not enough for anti-U-boat warfare.

Thus the real impetus of the Admiralty had to be to get faster vessels into the line. A group of fifty U.S. destroyers secured from the United States that fall in the first Lend-Lease arrangement would help. Most of them could make twenty knots. But soon the Flower-class corvettes would be joining the fleet. That would be a great help, said the admiral. Another change must be to bring specialist antisubmarine officers into the fleet, to work with convoys, rather than keeping them at home in training jobs.

Naval precedent had to go by the boards, said the admiral:

"... while I realize that it is undesirable to establish a precedent that certain types of ship can only be commanded by corresponding specialist officers, I feel that an exception might be made in order to try every method of dealing with the present exceptional circumstances and that such officers should be employed in command of groups of corvettes."

Thus were the sinews of war being tightened in Britain even as Admiral Doenitz prepared for new onslaughts with his wolf packs. And thus was Admiral Doenitz's remarkable success offering a new career to Commander Frederic John Walker.

8

Italian Comedy

When the Italians entered the war against Britain in the summer of 1940, their submarine fleet appeared to be so formidable that Prime Minister Churchill considered abandoning the whole eastern Mediterranean and concentrating British resources at Gibraltar. Mussolini had a hundred submarines, eighty of them ready for service at the moment the Italians declared war. This was more than twice as many boats as Doenitz had—four times as many as he was ever able to put to sea at once. Doenitz, then, had hopes that were as high as

Churchill's were low. The Italians immediately offered to join the U-boat war in the Atlantic and sent several boats north to operate out of the new U-boat port at Bordeaux. The Italian submarine service asked that the captains be given one shakedown tour with a U-boat to learn the German ways before they set out. Doenitz was pleased to agree, and the Italian skippers were parceled out among Doenitz's most effective captains. Commander Longobardo of the *Corelli* was assigned to go out with Lieutenant Kretschmer on his August cruise. Kretschmer did not speak Italian, nor did Longobardo speak German, but they were both fluent in English, and that is the language they used for communication of the voyage. Kretschmer was still having troubles with his torpedoes, and, as he put it in his war diary, during the first part of the patrol what he showed Longobardo was "how not to operate a submarine." On a crash dive to escape an aircraft coming in over head, the diving planes had been put too far forward, and the *U-99* refused to respond to the trimming, and the ship plummeted downward until Kretschmer blew the forward ballast tanks. They sank a small Canadian steamer by gunfire, attacked a convoy, and got a solid depth-charging for their pains. They chased the convoy, came up inside it and surfaced so Kretschmer could show off his now famous surface attack technique. But the first torpedo he fired against a freighter leaped out of the water and turned like a porpoise to right angles and leaped back into the water. So did the second. Kretschmer moved in to point-blank range. The third torpedo repeated the performance of the other two, as Commander Longobardo looked on and smiled. But the smile vanished when the Germans on the bridge heard two explosions inside the convoy. Kretschmer had indicated his contempt for the Doenitz doctrine of firing a fan of torpedoes against a convoy, but the effect of his porpoising "fish" was precisely that: he had hit two other ships that he never saw.

The cruise went on without luck for five days. On September 15 the *U-99* sank the Norwegian steamer *Hird*. Two days later, she sank the *Crown Arum* in Britain's North Channel.

Meanwhile, Doenitz had found a convoy and ordered Kretschmer and four other captains to join in a wolf pack attack. He did and sank the *Ivershannon*, then attacked the *Elmbank*. But in spite of two torpedoes, and hundreds of rounds of deck gunfire (Prien, who had no more torpedoes, joined up to fire on the ship), they could not sink the *Elmbank*, for she was carrying a timber cargo below as well as on deck. Eventually the two U-boats went about their business, leaving the *Elmbank* still floating in the middle of a sea of jetsam.

Commander Longobardo returned to Lorient, then, with a complete lesson in German submarine tactics, including some notes on what not to do. Other Italian captains had similar patrols, but none quite so exciting as Longobardo's with Kretschmer. When these "practice" sessions were finished, the Italians then set out on patrol as part of Doenitz's tactical force in the Atlantic.

The Italian submarine promise, however, did not develop in ratio to the number of boats available. In the Mediterranean, the Italians were at sea in August. They also sailed in the Atlantic, but patrolling mostly the Spanish and Portuguese coasts. Commander Leoni in the *Malaspina* sank the 8,400-ton tanker *British Fame* on August 12. Commander Boris's *Dandolo* sank the tanker *Hermes* on August 21, and the steamer *Ilvington Court* on August 26.

In September the Italians sank two Spanish ships, which must have been more of a pain to Generalissimo Franco than it was to the British. In October the Italians sank four ships. And that was all.

The Royal Navy and the merchant shipping operating in the Mediterranean did not seem to have a great deal to worry about from the Italian U-boat fleet. And that fleet was having its difficulties. In June the British sank nine Italian submarines. Two were sunk by Sunderland flying boats from No. 230 Squadron air patrol. In August another Italian boat was sunk by aircraft from the carrier *Eagle*. In September HMAS *Stuart* and a Sunderland flying boat from No. 230 Squadron cooperated in the sinking of still another Italian boat.

And then, in October, came a drama that was a comedy of errors and a lesson to all submarine captains everywhere.

* * *

The Italian submarine *Durbo* was completed by the Odero-Terni-Orlando plant at Spezzia in July 1938. She was a 650-ton boat, with two diesel engines and two electric motors. The *Durbo* could travel 6,700 miles at eight knots; she carried six torpedo tubes, and on deck a 3.9-inch gun and a machine gun.

Her patrol area was around Malta, where she made four cruises between the outbreak of war and the end of September. The *Durbo* claimed to have sunk the French submarine *Morse* on her first patrol, but she sank no surface ships. She had all sorts of mechanical troubles ranging from water in the periscope to leakage in the pressure system. That latter was very common among the Italian boats.

After her fourth cruise the *Durbo* pulled into Messina, Sicily, for some more work, and remained there until the second week of October. She had to wait for torpedoes, and when they came she was rationed to six. Her mission was to attack British convoys off Alboran.

The *Durbo* sailed on October 8. She stayed below during the daytime and surfaced at night. Her captain saw many ships through his periscope, including a British destroyer on October 17. But he did not attack any ships. He was following the adage of the Italian submarine service:

"To destroy a few ships is better than to damage many."

That was not precisely the motto of Admiral Doenitz, or later of Admiral Lockwood of the U.S. Navy Pacific Fleet, but German and American navies never had cost accounting executives as naval leaders. In Rome a torpedo was considered a precious instrument.

As a cautious man, the commander of the *Durbo* noted early on the morning of October 18 that he had an oil leak, and a telltale trickle was staining the surface. He put all available hands to work to remedy the defect. When the light grew bright he took the boat down to 100 feet.

The captain did not know it, but the boat still leaked.

She stayed down all day long. At 5:25 P.M. along came two British patrol aircraft from No. 2 Squadron of the Air Sea Patrol. They spotted the trail of oil and bombed where it ended, and the *Durbo* went down at 200 feet and then down to nearly 400 feet, which was a very long way down indeed.

While she was down deep, along came the destroyers HMS *Firedrake* and HMS *Wrestler.* The aircraft pilots reported on their attacks and gave position. The destroyers arrived in the area at 6 P.M. and almost immediately sighted a large oil patch. In a few minutes the Asdic operator of the *Firedrake* had a contact. The captain ordered the depth charges set at 250 and 350 feet, and they were fired. The result was the emergence of a large air bubble to the surface. Then, amazingly within moments *Firedrake* got her Asdic contact back.

The *Wrestler* attacked with a depth charge pattern set deep. Each destroyer then dropped another pattern of depth charges, and at 6:55 the submarine came popping up. The *Wrestler* opened fire at 500 yards, and the submarine dived. The *Wrestler* dropped another depth charge pattern and this time a large quantity of oil accompanied the air bubble to the top. The *Firedrake* attacked for the third time at 7:02, and then each destroyer attacked once more.

Down below, the *Durbo* was having a terrible time of it. The lights went out. The main shafts bent, and the propellers began to make a whining noise. Water entered the after compartments, and the boat went down by the stern. She reached 300 feet. Then the motors flooded, the after pumps broke down, and chlorine began to rise up in its wispy deadly pattern.

Rome would certainly not have approved the expenditure of nearly fifty depth charges. But London would, for at 7:50 the *Durbo* came popping to the surface like a punch-drunk fighter, less than a mile from each destroyer. Both ships opened fire. One shell hit the conning tower, and the crew was seen coming up on deck as if abandoning ship, so the destroyers stopped shooting.

The *Wrestler* sent an armed whaler alongside, with a sublieutenant in command. His job was to get the papers and keep the captain from scuttling.

A few quick rounds with a Lewis gun persuaded the Italian sailors that they did not want to man their guns. They began calling for help.

The hard-hearted sublieutenant ordered them to swim to the *Wrestler*, a distance of about ten yards. And they jumped off and swam. Meanwhile the sublieutenant caught his Italian counterpart in the conning tower and forced him back down. The latter flatly refused to go below the bottom of the hatch, and the British sublieutenant smelled a rat. He figured that someone had set scuttling charges. He let the Italian go and the officer scurried up and away. The sublieutenant and a petty officer then started to search the submarine.

The bow end was dry. They got into the wardroom and emptied the contents of the cupboards. They got into the wireless office and got the codes. They found lots of books and papers and passed them up and out of the boat.

But in the electric control room aft the water was knee-deep, and it seemed that nothing could be done to stop the water from coming in. A whaler from HMS *Firedrake* came alongside, and more Britons came down to help, but finally they gave up and got out.

And just in time, too.

Someone, indeed, had set scuttling charges and as the two whalers pulled away from the submarine, the charges blew up and the *Durbo* sank in a few seconds.

Aboard the *Wrestler*, it did not take long to discover who had set the scuttling charges. The sublieutenant who had been found in the conning tower hatch was an ardent Fascist, and he offered lectures about the beauties of Fascism and the superiority of the Italian and German races.

The captain of the *Wrestler* looked through the papers captured aboard the *Durbo*. There was a set of the Italian naval codes, and even more interesting at that moment, a chart that showed the *Durbo*'s operating area and that of her companion ship, the *Lafolé*. The information was communicated to higher authority, and on the night of October 19 five British warships made a sweep of the whole area, but did not find the other submarine.

The next day at 3:15 the destroyer force was steering south at 35° 49′ N; 2° 52′ W, when HMS *Gallant* reported a contact on her port side. At the same time HMS *Hotspur*, on her port beam, reported a contact on her starboard side.

It was a nice day for hunting, with a calm sea that displayed periscopes and periscope wakes clearly, no wind, and good visibility. The two destroyers converged on the Asdic contact. At 3:33 a periscope appeared and then the top of the conning tower of a submarine, so close to the two destroyers that neither could open fire. The captain of the submarine realized instantly what had happened, and he dived.

The men were sitting down to mess when the captain ran into the trap. They went to action stations and closed the watertight doors.

Both destroyers dropped depth charges. HMS *Hotspur* then opened out, turned and came back with a deliberate pattern set at 500, 350, and 200 feet. HMS *Gallant* came up and attacked also, twelve minutes later. HMS *Griffin* came up and attacked, too.

Four depth charges exploded very near the submarine, knocking her down to 300 feet. The captain was stunned. Instruments were broken, the rudders damaged, and the high-pressure air system started to break down.

Then all ships lost their Asdic contact. The tiresome pattern of the search line had to be repeated.

Down below, the captain of the *Lafolé* recovered from his minor concussion. He hoped that he had escaped his enemies, but he stayed down and moved slowly to get out of the area. He had to move slowly, the stern glands were leaking so badly they had to be tightened, and the motors turned with great difficulty.

Then HMS *Gallant* regained contact at 4:25. HMS *Hotspur* also had a contact. *Hotspur* attacked first, but the echo became cloudy, so she dropped only one charge set at 500 feet. Then *Gallant* dropped a full pattern.

The destroyers continued the attack. In all they dropped seventy depth charges.

The leakage made it impossible to keep the boat down, and the submarine surfaced between the destroyers.

Aboard the *Gallant* and the *Hotspur* the captains looked for the opening of the conning tower hatch, but it did not come. There was no sign of damage or surrender, so HMS *Hotspur* speeded up and rammed the stern of the boat.

In the submarine the men in the control room found the hatch had jammed. They banged and poked at the hatch, but it would not budge. Then came an enormous shock, as though the submarine had been torpedoed, the hatch sprang open, and the ten men were catapulted only by the built-up air pressure, some falling into the water thirty yards from the boat. A minute later *Lafolé* sank, taking down her captain and thirty-seven of the crew. One officer and nine men were picked up by the HMS *Gallant*.

There was a lesson in this affair for submariners everywhere, one the *Durbo*'s sublieutenant ought to have learned a long time before. It could have been even more important to his fellow submariners than Mussolini's speeches: don't give your charts to another submarine.

In that summer of 1940, when the Italians made good on their promises to Berlin, Admiral Doenitz looked forward to a good deal of help from the Italians in the Battle of the Atlantic. After all, they had twice as many submarines as he did. Now if he could put all this together on the Western Approaches . . .

Doenitz established a real base for the Italians at Bordeaux, and he brought more Italian submarine captains up to Wilhelmshaven to go out with the U-boats on patrol and see how it was done in the northern seas. The Italian submarine crews were given quick courses in German submarine schools. In October, the Italian submarines were brought into action under Doenitz's control on the southern and western edges of the Western Approaches. Doenitz was too canny to expect a lot in the beginning. What he really wanted from the Italians just then was "more eyes." For the British were starting to do a good job of deception in convoy control, changing routes, sailings, and patterns of all sorts. Doenitz regarded his major problem of the moment as finding ships; once found, his captains were having no trouble sinking them.

The Italians were more than willing co-workers. On October 20, Commander Leoni was on the northwest edge of the Western Approaches, where Doenitz hoped he would find an incoming convoy. But Commander Leoni found nothing. Nor did the other Italian submarine commanders do any better in their vigilance.

Not on one single occasion did the Italians succeed in bringing their German allies into contact with the enemy. Their reports were invariably either inaccurate or they came too late; they failed to deliver any attacks of their own or to maintain contact with the enemy. In other cases, too, in which German boats sighting a convoy had summoned other German boats to the locality and had delivered a joint attack, the Italian submarines failed to put in an appearance and took no part.

To prove his point, Doenitz noted that between October 10 and November 30, 1940, the Italian submarines had put in 243 submarine days at sea and sunk only one ship, of 4,866 tons. Meanwhile, said Doenitz, the Germans had put in 378 submarine days at sea and sunk eighty ships amounting to 435,000 tons.

A harsh indictment, Doenitz's, and not entirely accurate. On October 27 Commander Gioacchino Polizzi in the *Nani* sank the 1,583-ton Swedish steamer *Meggie* south of the Western Approaches. On November 9, the *Marconi* sank the 2,734-ton Swedish motor ship *Vingaland* smack in the middle of the joint operational area. Commander Ghiglieri's *Barbarigo* attacked a British destroyer, and missed, but for that matter sometimes German captains missed, too. Commander Bertarelli's *Baracca* was the only boat given credit by Doenitz, for sinking the 4,866-ton steamer *Lilian Moller*. There Doenitz stops. But the next month, December, Commander Crepas's *Argo* attacked and sank the Canadian destroyer *Saguenay* on the edge of the Western Approaches.

In late December 1940 and January 1941, the Italians performed even better. Working west of Ireland, Commander Longobardo in the *Torelli* sank four ships. Commander Longobardo ran up a record that would have made one of Doenitz's own captains proud, and ultimately he was awarded the Iron Cross by Hitler. But Longobardo was the exception.* The Germans just did not appreciate their smiling southern allies for reasons that are not altogether borne out by history. In January 1941, the Axis submarines sank only twenty-three ships, and the Italians accounted for eight of them. Not bad at all.

* * *

---

*Longobardo's submarine eventually was sunk in the eastern Mediterranean. Most of the crew were saved by their British escort attackers, but Longobardo was lost.

The fact was that the Italian skippers serving with the Germans were learning, and fast, considering their differences in approaches to war and to life. What piqued Admiral Doenitz was that he had been unable to get what he wanted from the Italians—information and search, and servile participation in the wolf packs he ran so sternly. It was like the difference between an opera by Wagner and one by Verdi. The Italians could be very brave, even foolhardy, in their daring in undersea warfare. Their attacks with miniature submarines and "underwater chariots" (self-propelled, steerable, torpedoes) on British warships at Alexandria and Gibraltar made some of the most exciting stories of the war. Masters at skindiving, the Italian frogmen mined ship after ship with such success that the British set up special defenses against them. But in the cold, hard game of undersea boat warfare, particularly the coordinated attack controlled tactically by the German submarine master at Paris, they did not seem to have the staying power. Individuals all, the Italians never became very good at the wolf pack approach. The German submarine captain's credo demanded that he keep his ships out of the hands of the enemy at all costs, even if it meant going down with the vessel himself. The Italians had no such stern approach; if the fight was lost, then give up cheerfully and enjoy life as best one might, that was their attitude. Doenitz could not understand his allies and he could not stand their ways. Quietly he began to shuck off the Italians.

9

In Like a Lion, but...

March 1941 came into the Atlantic like a lion raging. Storm followed storm, as it had all winter, but Doenitz's men found the ambience very much to their liking nonetheless.

The U-boat captains called the winter of 1941 "the happy time" for two reasons: (1) Doenitz's possession of the British naval codes and the perfection of the wolf pack technique brought many sinkings to the U-boats, and sinkings meant glory and medals and leave; (2) improved German radio and destroyer detection practices, plus the continued shortage of British convoy escorts and the British inability to employ long-range aircraft against U-boats meant that few boats were attacked successfully. After the capture of Prellberg no more boats were lost in November 1940 until November 23 when HMS *Rhododendron* sank the *U-104* in the Atlantic, and Lieutenant Juerst and his crew went to their deaths at the bottom. Unhappy as was this loss for Doenitz and his staff, it was a small price to pay. Sinkings were very high that fall, to the deep concern of the British and the joy of the Germans. The Nazi propaganda machine was going full blast, and the names of the most successful German captains were becoming household words in Hitler's Europe. Goebbels pulled out all the stops to publicize Prien, Schepke, Kretschmer, Schultze, Schuhart, Rollmann, and Lemp. Fifteen U-boat captains had each sunk more than 100,000 tons of enemy shipping, Goebbels shouted. And all were still afloat, all were still piling up victories. They made it look easy, and their exploits were enormously effective propaganda in Admiral Doenitz's campaign to build the U-boat arm. This was only the beginning, Goebbels said. *Gott strafe England!*

Forgotten were the cold, the danger, the misery of a U-boat patrol in the glory of it all. A man had to volunteer to get into the navy at all, and then found it twice as hard to get into the U-boat corps. Before the war recruits had received twelve months of training; now the training period had been reduced to three months because of Doenitz's need for men to serve in the new boats that were coming off the ways so much more quickly. There was only one exception to this rule: petty officers, the men who ran the crews. Trained men were hard to find, and some petty officers were drafted into the U-boat corps. Some of the more experienced petty officers were now being promoted to become watch officers, so great was the shortage of trained people. So, in the winter of 1941, the opportunity for glory, promotion, and service in the undersea arm was at a new high.

January was marked by a decrease in the number of sinkings. Particularly vicious weather then often made it impossible for Doenitz's captains to find their targets even when the broken codes allowed the admiral to plot the convoy routings. Another reason was the discretion given a convoy commander to change course and speed, discretion often exercised to the full by officers seeking shelter or escape from the terrible storms. In February the total losses of British ships shot up again. There was a new reason: Doenitz had finally managed to get some cooperation out of the Luftwaffe, and combined operations of Goering's Focke-Wulff scout bombers and the U-boats had begun. The result was 290,000 tons of shipping sunk that month.

Out went the captains, one patrol following quickly on the heels of the last. In fact, Doenitz's most successful captains were suffering from fatigue, but there was nothing to be done about it. The admiral still did not have enough boats and superior crews to cover the eastern Atlantic. He never would have enough to suit him.

Something new was being added to the British defenses that winter: an improved HF/DF (High frequency direction finder) radio direction finding system that brought Huffduff stations to the escorts. From the shore stations came warning that a U-boat was in the area of the convoy; from the escort came a line of bearing on the U-boat. The Germans quickly learned of the existence of this new device by which the British could triangulate the broadcasts of a submarine and thus establish its position. Some of the German captains became very wary; one of these was Prien. Doenitz had started a flap by overestimating the accuracy of the new British device, but he had said that by limiting transmissions and making them with new high-speed apparatus this problem could be overcome. Prien was not so sure, and he began to show a reluctance to get on the air, and to stay on it for more than seconds. He went out in February, and in the last week of that month sank five ships in rapid succession. But his reports were so short and so infrequent that Doenitz became annoyed. With so much depending on the skills of his senior captains in this spring of 1940, Doenitz was more than a little upset when he did not hear from Prien at all during the first week of March. He envisaged convoy after convoy going right by Prien as the U-boat spring offensive opened on March 1. But soon enough Doenitz learned that Lieutenant Prien just did not happen to be in the right place when Lieutenant Commander Erich Topp's *U-552* found eastbound convoy HX 109.

Topp radioed to Doenitz, and Doenitz sent in *U-95*, *U-147*, *U-70*, and *U-99*. In rapid succession they sank two ships from that convoy. They claimed many, many more and Radio Berlin began once again to crow about the enormous successes of the U-boat fleet that was driving Britain rapidly to the wall.

Then, on March 6, Prien found outward bound Convoy OB 293. He sent a quick message to Doenitz, and the admiral ordered into action every U-boat capable of reaching the area. Those vessels included Commander Kretschmer's *U-99* and Lieutenant Joachim Matz's *U-70*.

Commander Kretschmer had been out in the *U-99* on his seventh war cruise since February 22. By this time Kretschmer was a national legend in Germany; his exploits topped even those of Prien. Kretschmer had sunk more than 250,000 tons of shipping, and Radio Berlin now called him "the tonnage king."

Kretschmer had with him on this voyage, as first lieutenant of the boat, Lieutenant Hans-Jochen von Knebel-Doberitz, who had been for some time adjutant to Admiral Doenitz, but soon now was to have a U-boat of his own. His cruise with Kretschmer was set up to give him the necessary experience. And so was that of Lieutenant Commander Horst Hesselbarth, another of Doenitz's chosen captains. It was a mark of the admiral's faith in Kretschmer that he would send these men out two at a time with the skipper of *U-99*.

The *U-99* carried the usual load of fourteen torpedoes, two of them on the deck under wraps.

When Kretschmer had the message from Doenitz that night of March 6, he proceeded at full speed on the surface to the coordinates indicated. Early the next morning, astern of the convoy, Kretschmer sighted Prien's *U-47* and tried to make radio contact but was unable to because just then a pair of British destroyers from the convoy came charging down on the *U-99*. That was the moment at which Commander Kretschmer knew that the British now had radio direction finding equipment. He took the boat down; the destroyer *Wolverine* came around and dropped a few depth charges, but obviously failed to maintain the Asdic contact and eventually went away. Lieutenant Commander J. M. Rowland, skipper of the destroyer, was just then in very distinguished company. He had two of Germany's three principal submarine "aces" pinned down for several hours.

The message to join Prien reached Lieutenant Matz in the *U-70* about two o'clock in the morning. A northerly wind was blowing at Force 4 as the U-boat set out on the surface to speed toward the convoy. Matz moved to get ahead of the ships, and after two hours he took the boat down and adjusted the listening gear. Soon the operator heard the sounds of many ship propellers, and he knew the convoy was coming.

Matz brought the boat up and looked around for the largest ship he could find. He attacked the 6,500-ton tanker *Athelbeach* at 4:30. Twenty minutes later he torpedoed the 6,400-ton steamer *Delilian*. Her crew immediately abandoned ship, although she continued to float.

With the attack on the *Delilian*, Lieutenant Matz had emptied his torpedo tubes. He dived to reload the three forward tubes and one rear tube. This process took an hour and ten minutes. She came back up then, but not to the surface. It was six o'clock in the morning, and the light was bright, so Matz remained at periscope depth.

He saw an enormous ship ahead of him. She was the SS *Terje Viken*, a 20,000-ton whaling factory ship that had been converted for war use to a tanker. Matz fired three torpedoes from his bow tubes. All missed. He began to swing the boat around to fire from the stern, but just then Prien came up and fired two torpedoes into the *Terje Viken*. She stayed afloat, although sorely wounded.

Kretschmer's *U-99* arrived on the scene shortly after Prien and Matz had made their attempts. The *Terje Viken* was still making about nine knots, and Kretschmer thought there was good chance she might be salvaged, so he fired another torpedo into her, and then she capsized. Kretschmer saw another crippled ship and went over to investigate. Suddenly one of the convoy escorts appeared, and Kretschmer took the boat down in a crash dive. The escort roamed about on top for several hours, dropping fifty-one depth charges around the *U-99*, all of them set too shallow. But by the time Kretschmer was able to come to the surface, the convoy was out ahead. He saw Prien's *U-47* again as both moved in quite close to the Icelandic shore. They continued to trail the convoy, but Kretschmer lost touch during the night, and then moved off to seek other game.

After the abortive attack on the *Terje Viken*, Matz's *U-70* then attacked the 7,500-ton tanker *Mijdrecht* as she was picking up the crew of the *Delilian*. His torpedo hit her on the starboard side forward of the engine room; she immediately began taking water, and her stern soon dropped nine feet. But she was still moving when her captain saw the feather of a periscope wake two points off the starboard bow. He put the helm over hard, and rammed the *U-70*. The *Mijdrecht* passed completely over the U-boat, which then appeared on the port side, with fifteen feet of the stern sticking up. She was so close the ship's deck gun would not bear, but the captain moved off and tried to shell the submarine. He did not make any hits.

The *U-70* was badly hurt. Her two periscopes were wrecked, and everything on the bridge was smashed. The conning tower was badly dented and the bearing disc was carried away, leaving a tube two inches in diameter, and it was taking water.

Lieutenant Matz then surfaced and took the boat away from the convoy. The crew were able to open the conning tower hatch about halfway, and men came out to plug up the bearing disc hole. Matz then took the boat down to ninety feet to see if the pressure hull had been hurt, and when he found it had not, he surfaced again and made off away from the convoy at high speed.

At 8:15 he was moving along at sixteen knots when one of the new Flower-class corvettes, the *Camellia*, caught sight of his wake and then of the U-boat. The *Camellia* began to chase, and Lieutenant Matz then took the *U-70* down. The corvette came over; just then her Asdic failed, but the captain dropped a pattern of depth charges anyhow by guess.

It was not a very good guess. Down below the men of the *U-70* heard the charges go off but they were far away.

The captain of the *Camellia* then called up another Flower-class corvette, the *Arbutus*, which came up and made an Asdic contact at 9:25. Two minutes later the *Arbutus* fired a pattern of six charges, set at 500, 350, and 250 feet. Ten minutes later she attacked again. The *Camellia*'s Asdic set was still out of order so she was sent back to the convoy to watch over damaged vessels. The *Arbutus* made four more depth charge runs.

Lieutenant Matz had taken the boat down to 262 feet, and at first the depth charges seemed to be far away. He ordered all but the emergency lights turned off to save electricity. The explosions kept coming closer, they damaged the glands, and water began coming into the boat. Four men were detailed to work the hand pump. They pumped during those minutes when depth charges were being dropped, but not in the intervals, fearing that the noise would give them away.

Matz tried to move the boat to escape but the corvette followed. He took the *U-70* down to 280 feet, and then to 300 feet, and stopped the motors. He intended to lie doggo all day and hoped to escape that night.

The increasing load of water began to tell. The boat sank to 360 feet. Matz tried to hold her there, but after half an hour she began to sink again, out of trim. The indicator hand on the depth gauge went to 200 meters (656 feet), which was the limit of the gauge.

Lieutenant Matz tried to trim the boat. The men began to hear ominous cracking sounds. Paint flecked off the bulkheads.

The men were jammed up in the forward compartment, having difficulty holding on because the boat was now at an angle of 45 degrees, down by the stern. Most of the instruments had been smashed, but at least Matz knew that he had about 25 kilograms (60 pounds) of compressed air left, enough for one try to surface. The motors were started, and he managed to trim the boat, by putting them full speed ahead. Then he blew all tanks.

Just then the *Arbutus* came directly over the submarine, dropping charges set at 350 and 500 feet. These exploded directly above the U-boat, but she was so far down that they did no more damage, and she succeeded in surfacing.

When the conning tower hatch was opened, six men at the top were blown completely out of the boat. By the time others scrambled up, the *Arbutus* had opened fire with her 4-inch guns and pom-poms, and the Germans were unable to man their own gun. But they were not trying to fight as the *Arbutus* came up to ram; the corvette captain saw that the men were jumping overboard so he dropped two Carley floats and closed on the U-boat. She was still moving ahead under electric power, but it was not long before she went down. As they came up, the crew had opened the vents. She went down so fast that two officers and eighteen men were lost. The captain and three other officers and twenty-two men survived.

10

The End of the Beginning

March 1941 was a very bad month for Admiral Doenitz. Prien, Kretschmer, and Schepke had gone almost as if with one blow from the enemy. Matz had preceded them, and then, on March 23, HMS *Visenda* had sent Schrott's *U-551* to the bottom with all hands. *U-551* was brand-new. Her designation was a part of the new propaganda campaign to keep the enemy guessing about the number of U-boats Doenitz had to employ. But since she was new, her loss seemed all the more a tragedy, as if losing five boats in a month was not bad enough.

Beyond all this, March was a worse month for Doenitz than he could possibly have known, for this was the month in which Commander Frederic John Walker finally managed to get away from his desk and into a sea command. For months, as noted, he had haunted the Admiralty with requests for sea duty, to no avail. But by March 1941 it was apparent in London that the sea war was going so badly a few straws had to be grasped. And so when Walker appeared in the office of Captain George Creasy, the director of antisubmarine warfare, and Creasy suggested that this officer probably knew more about fighting submarines than anyone afloat, admirals were ready to listen. Commander Walker was given the sloop *Stork* and assigned to Admiral Sir Percy Noble, commander in chief of the Western Approaches. When he reached the command at Liverpool, Walker discovered that he was also senior officer of the new 36th Escort Group, with a command of nine ships. The job was to perfect a command capable of dealing with U-boats, using the best technology available. The Royal Navy now had larger depth charges (one ton), and throwers capable of delivering larger patterns of charges. Surface craft and aircraft now had workable Five-X Radar to detect U-boats on the surface; March had brought the first successful discovery of an enemy submarine by use of this new tool. This was accompanied by intensified use of Huffduff, illumination by starshell and rockets, and the snowflake, a scattering of starshell that illuminated a whole area of the sea. These would be employed to counter the wolf pack night attack, and to coordinate attack on a wolf pack's members by a number of escorts. By summer, several groups such as Walker's were training as the British refined their antisubmarine defenses; with more ships available they planned to go on the attack against the wolf packs.

The Americans were moving steadily into the war of the Atlantic, although the American people did not know it, and most of them then opposed the idea. A representative of the U.S. government sat in on the antisubmarine committee meetings at the Prime Minister's office at 10 Downing Street. His primary responsibility was to obtain information that President Roosevelt could subsequently use to help Britain while at the same time placating the U.S. public and subverting the opposition of the American peace party. The degree of American participation in the Atlantic was indicated by the cooperation of the American naval radio network in the British Huffduff system of triangulating U-boat radio transmissions.

But in April the German spring U-boat campaign was very successful: more 500-ton and 750-ton boats were available, and the losses were again light after March. On April 5 Lieutenant von Hippel's *U-76* was lost and on April 8, Hoppe's *U-65*.

That month, Doenitz also lost Wohlfahrt, who had amassed a considerable reputation by June 27, 1941, the day his *U-556* encountered HMS *Nasturtium*, HMS *Celandine*, and HMS *Gladiolus*, three of those Flower-class corvettes for which Prime Minister Churchill had so much hope. They did themselves proud that day in the open sea south of Iceland and Greenland, trailing the *U-556* like bulldogs. *U-556* had been out a long time and needed yard work. One of the electric motors was running badly. During the chase it began heating up, and the engineer closed it down. Then, under the depth-charging, the boat took several tons of water aft, and the second electric motor began making a loud, rattling noise. They could not get at it to fix it because of the water. Still, they had to use it because the depth-charging was very close, and as they used it, the corvettes above zeroed in on the noise. Then the depth-charging grew worse. It was the radio mate's job to log the depth charges, and he sat there in his little cubical, writing.

Close, he wrote, after the first salvo.

Closer, he wrote, after the second.

Closer still . . .

Quite close . . .

Then the radioman ran out of words. The depth charges were raining down, each salvo closer than the last.

Under this tremendous pressure of noise and jolting, the crew grew rebellious. They spoke of mutiny and surfacing to surrender.

Amidships, the midshipman drew his pistol.

"I shall shoot on the spot any man who does not get back to his station."

The men returned to battle stations. "They were more afraid of my pistol than of the depth charges," he later said.

But the charges kept raining down. The control room

sprang a leak, and then the second electric motor coughed and died. Without underwater power they were helpless. The only thing left to do was surface and try to escape by using the diesels. Wohlfahrt gave the orders, and the boat moved up to the surface. When the conning tower broke water the gun crew was already opening the hatch, and the diesels started. But the boat no sooner came up than the first shell exploded on the conning tower. As the men came out they saw the first British warship, moving up to ram, only 400 yards off.

One officer had the special detail of setting the explosive charges in the boat in just such an emergency, when capture seemed imminent. But this officer was the first to leap off the bridge and into the sea, swimming toward the British ship, carrying with him the keys to the box of explosive charges. Those aboard could not get into the box. Fortunately for the Germans the boat was so badly damaged that she sank by herself, as the crew got off. The German who had abandoned his duty to blow up the submarine was the first aboard the British vessel, shouting "I am an officer." His fellows determined that they would deal with him later.

Two days afterward another promising captain, Lieutenant Lohmeyer, encountered five British escorts a bit farther to the east, and they sent the *U-651* to the bottom. In Paris once again there was gloom. Four U-boats lost in June. It was too many.

Altogether, however, in the summer of 1941 the U-boat campaign reached a peak. In June Doenitz had thirty-five boats out, with twenty-five of them in western Atlantic waters. The Italians had more boats out than ever, too, and their successes rose as they gained experience.

Admiral Doenitz had some good luck. His boats in the South Atlantic had been able to make double cruises because the German navy had been able to send supply ships south to serve them with oil, provisions, and ammunition. Lieutenant Commander Guenter Hessler's *U-107* earned a new record down there: sinking 90,000 tons on one cruise. Of course the "cruise" lasted from the first of April until the middle of June, courtesy of the supply ships.

* * *

The British could take heart from the fact that shipping losses actually dropped lower than those of May (down from 323,000 tons to 260,000 tons), even with the increased number of assaults on the convoys. Also, they sank those four U-boats in June. One of these, *U-651*, "had the unusual distinction of carrying one of the most unpleasant crews which have ever been interrogated," according to the British monthly U-boat war report. It was an indication of what had happened to the U-boat service in the months of expansion:

Otto Kretschmer, captured in that spring of 1941, had proved to be an officer and gentleman of the sort the British could understand. On the way back to England aboard the *Walker*, he played bridge with Commander McIntyre, leader of the escort group that had captured him. When interrogated, he had refused to give military information, but he was obviously not enamored of the Nazi cause. Rather, he was a professional naval officer doing his job.

The captain of the *U-651* was an entirely different sort: Kapitaenleutnant Peter Lohmeyer, born in Zanzibar, educated in Germany, a former flier who had served in the Luftwaffe during the Spanish civil war. Whereas Kretschmer had the complete loyalty of his crew, Lohmeyer did not. His first lieutenant, Karl Joseph Heinrich, was described by the interrogators as "unpleasant . . . uncouth and ill informed." The engineer officer, Benno Brandt, was called "the worst specimen of a prisoner yet encountered." The younger officers, the British found, were totally Nazified. They had been steeped in propaganda and their conversation, said the British, "consisted of propaganda quotations which they did not understand." The interrogators also found the crew completely lacking in naval discipline—a sign that the U-boat service was beginning to show some serious cracks.

What troubled Doenitz most was the inability of the U-boat scouts to find and hold the course of a convoy. The reason for this was a bold decision of the Admiralty to make more use of the Ultra decryptions. German aircraft and German U-boats would find a convoy and report its position, course, and speed to Berlin and to Doenitz. But by the time Doenitz sent U-boats out to intercept, the British would have deciphered the message and radioed the convoy new routing instructions that would take the ships quite away from the point Doenitz had chosen for interception. It happened so many times that summer that Doenitz's staff began to smell a rat.

Fortunately the belief of the Germans in the absolute inviolability of their code machines was not seriously shaken. Commander Meckel, Doenitz's communications officer, was forced to the conclusion that the British radar must be even more effective than it really was.

July and August were not very satisfactory months for the U-boat high command, even though no boats were lost in July. August saw the sinking with all hands of Zimmermann's *U-401* by British escorts on the third day of the month. Then on August 9 the Soviet submarine *SC-307* caught von Mittelstaedt's *U-144* on the surface in the Gulf of Bothnia. Two more U-boats went down to British aircraft, March's *U-452* on August 25 and Lieutenant Commander Hans Rahmlow's *U-570* two days later. It was months before Admiral Doenitz learned the truth of the loss of the *U-570*, one of the most dismal stories ever told about the German U-boat force.

On the morning of August 24, Rahmlow took *U-570* out of Norway's Lo Fjord on her first patrol. He had a month's food supply aboard and fourteen torpedoes. When the cruise ended he was to take the boat into La Pallice, on the Bay of Biscay, one of the new U-boat havens. He would continue operations thereafter with La Pallice as home port. But from the beginning it seemed unlikely that Rahmlow would ever make La Pallice. The valves of one of the diesel engines were not properly seated and the engines overheated. After this was fixed, something went wrong with the injector pumps, and then the boat was discovered to be taking water through one of the torpedo tubes. That fault, caused by a bump on the bottom during trials, was supposed to have been corrected in the yard. After the crew stopped the leakage, water was then found in the exhaust system. That, too, was fixed. Meanwhile the weather worsened, and many of the new crewmen fresh from submarine school became so hopelessly seasick that they could not stand watch.

The *U-570* passed north of the Faroe Islands and moved into her operations area south of Iceland. The area was empty. On August 26 Doenitz ordered the boat to another square on his grid to join in a wolf pack attack on a convoy, but by the time the boat got there the convoy had changed course. *U-570* was ordered to take a northerly course and try to intercept.

She never found the convoy, nor did any of Doenitz's other captains. But running all night on the surface at high speed in a heavy sea was exhausting the green crew, and at 8:30 A.M. on August 27 the *U-570* submerged so the crew could get a little rest. The boat was then about eighty miles south of Portland, Iceland. Two hours later Rahmlow brought her up, at the precise moment that a Hudson bomber of 269 Squadron was overhead on an antisubmarine sweep. As the conning tower popped out of the water the Hudson dived from 500 to 100 feet and plopped four depth charges all around the U-boat. Set shallow, they made an enormous noise, although most of their explosive power was dissipated. But the explosions did smash some instruments inside the submarine, water came into the boat, and the men began shouting that they would all die from chlorine poisoning. An experienced U-boat captain would have dived and set about the repairs immediately. But this new skipper joined in the panic of his crew. He ordered the men to don their life vests and go into the conning tower. He brought the boat up all the way, and the men poured out onto the deck. The bomber opened fire with machine guns, and the men jammed back into the conning tower. But down below the others were pushing up, and their upward pressure was so great that they forced those on top back out; then the others came out with a white flag and a white board to signify their surrender.

All day long the men huddled around the conning tower in heavy seas. Late in the day the Hudson was replaced by a Catalina flying boat, which circled and threatened the submarine with its guns. At some point the radio operator went below and sent a message to Admiral Doenitz, telling him that *U-570* could not submerge and had been captured. The confidential papers and the cipher machine were destroyed, and someone took a hammer to the attack computer.

At 10:50 P.M. the armed trawler *Northern Chief* approached and warned the Germans that if they tried to scuttle they would not be saved. Rahmlow assured the British he would not. Some of the crew went below and got some sleep. Others worried on deck. At 3:30 A.M. the trawlers *Kingston Agate* and *Northern Prince* joined up and then the destroyers *Burwell*, *Wastwater*, and *Windermere*. The Canadian destroyer *Niagara* arrived at 8 A.M. An airplane came over and dropped bombs, creating more confusion. The Germans began to complain that they had surrendered. Why didn't somebody save them? The British told them to be quiet, that if they saved their ship they, too, would be saved. A half hour later a line was passed from the *Burwell* to the submarine. The *Windermere* stood to windward and pumped oil to calm the sea. The Germans had a terrible time with the line since their decks were awash. The *Burwell* handled badly in the heavy sea and the line parted. Then the U-boat began to settle by the bow. The British told Captain Rahmlow to blow ballast and lighten the boat. He did nothing. The British fired on the boat with machine guns and wounded five men. Rahmlow blew ballast, and he hung out his shirt to call the attention of his captors to the fact that he had surrendered.

Early in the afternoon a Carley float was launched by the *Kingston Agate*, and the wounded were taken off the submarine. They were then put ashore at Reykjavik. The submarine was pulled and hauled, the tow breaking several times, until finally it was beached at Thorlakshafn. When it was examined it was found to be almost totally undamaged. One ballast tank had been holed. No chlorine had been generated. The engines were in fine working order, and although the batteries were depleted, the lights still ran.

So why had the *U-570* surrendered?

Naval intelligence asked the chief petty officers, who were old hands in the navy, although mostly new to submarines. Incompetence and no training was the answer, and it applied to officers and men. Captain Rahmlow was thirty-two years old and had served in the navy for thirteen years, but he had only recently transferred to U-boats. He had served on a training boat in the Baltic, and this was his first seagoing fighting command. He had simply panicked from inexperience.

There was no help to be found from the junior officers. The first lieutenant, Bernhard Berndt, had six years in the navy but was brand-new to U-boats. The junior officer, Walter Christiansen, had just been commissioned in the spring. He knew virtually nothing about anything. Erick Mensel, the engineer officer, was an old hand from the lower deck who had just been promoted. He was the only one aboard who had ever been on a war cruise in a U-boat.

So the British had a nice new U-boat to play with. They would clean her up and christen her HMS *Graph* and use her to learn all they could about the enemy. The Germans had lost another U-boat crew, and the British could now see the strain beginning to show in Doenitz's celebrated attack force.

11

U-Boat Men Never Quit

In August 1941, Winston Churchill crossed the Atlantic in the battleship *Prince of Wales* to meet President Roosevelt off Argentia, Newfoundland. One result of their talks was a decision that the United States would take an active role in the Battle of the Atlantic. U.S. warships would begin escorting British convoys. It was, of course, a decision that the United States would enter the sea war, but Americans were not told of it in that way.

American participation in the Battle of the Atlantic, no matter how concealed in August 1941, helped make August a lean month for Admiral Doenitz. Had it not been for the finding of two convoys, it would have been a disastrous month for the U-boats. On August 4, Lieutenant Heinz

Joachim Neumann's *U-372* trailed Convoy SL 81, bound home to Britain from Sierra Leone, and Neumann called up Doenitz. The admiral diverted all boats anywhere near the area to the spot, and in twenty-four hours, *U-372*, *U-74*, and *U-75* sank five ships. Even more satisfactory for the Germans was finding convoy OG 71, bound from the United Kindom to Gibraltar. Lieutenant Walter Kell in *U-204* opened the proceedings at 2 A.M. on August 19 by sinking the Norwegian destroyer *Bath*. Thereafter a wolf pack of five U-boats sank ten more ships out of that convoy, including the corvette *Zinnia*.

But to counter all that the British had their enormous prize of the month, a German U-boat in virtually perfect condition, the *U-570*. They brought her back to Britain and began studying the characteristics of Doenitz's latest ocean-going boats.

When the crew of *U-570* came ashore in Britain they were taken first to London, for interrogation in "the cages." Then they were split up, the enlisted men going to one POW camp, and the officers to POW Camp No. 1, at Grizedale Hall, a converted mansion overlooking Lake Windermere in northern England. All the officers except Lieutenant Rahmlow went there. He was held in London for further questioning.

At Grizedale, the officers of *U-570* found themselves back in a military atmosphere, under the command of Otto Kretschmer, who had been promoted after his capture to Korvettenkapitaen (Lieutenant Commander) and was thus senior officer of POW Camp No. 1. Kretschmer had been made responsible for the behavior of his fellow officers, and he had put in force the system of German naval discipline. When the British newspapers, which were forever clamoring for more war news, were given the story of the *U-570*, Kretschmer read about it and was aghast. When the officers of the boat arrived at the camp, minus the captain, the other U-boat officers refused even to talk to them. A U-boat had been captured intact by the enemy. One of the most stringent demands of Admiral Doenitz was that any U-boat crew facing capture must destroy their boat. Not only had *U-570* not been destroyed, he learned, but no attempt had even been made to destroy it. From the reports in British newspapers, Kretschmer had learned that the *U-570* had surrendered to an aircraft, and that when warships showed up, Skipper Rahmlow had allowed himself to be persuaded to leave his ship and paddle a dinghy to a destroyer, where, of course, he was held. That act had deprived the crew of the *U-570* of their leader. Kretschmer knew that he would not have behaved in a similar fashion. Putting himself in the place of Rahmlow he said he would have fought it out, and certainly would have destroyed the boat before quitting.

He ordered a secret court of inquiry into the matter, a court manned by the senior German POW officers of his camp. The council of honor, as they called it, was directed by Kretschmer. Lieutenant Commander Hesselbarth (one of the officers Kretschmer had been training for command) and two other U-boat officers made up the council.

Before the council were the questions of possible cowardice by captain and officers in the face of the enemy, the conduct of the captain, and the failure of the crew to scuttle the submarine.

The junior watch officer and the engineer officer were first to appear before the council. Under questioning they told their stories. They had been obeying orders. No, they had not refused to surrender the boat. The first lieutenant, who was in charge after the captain left the *U-570*, had followed his orders from the captain.

After the members of the council of honor considered the testimony they agreed that the junior officers had not shown any dash, but that they had not been guilty of cowardice, so the others were informed that these young men were to be "taken out of Coventry" and accepted as honorable fellows. Kretschmer formally shook hands with each of them and welcomed them to Grizedale Hall.

The case of Lieutenant Bernhard Berndt, the executive officer, was another matter. As senior officer aboard the boat after the captain left it, he was in a position to scuttle the boat and had not. He might also have refused earlier and ordered the captain placed under arrest. The council of honor asked its questions:

Had he remembered that Naval Battle Instructions stipulated that no U-boat might fall into enemy hands through any action by the crew?

He had.

Why had he not countermanded the captain's order to surrender?

He was completely concerned with the safety of the crew.

Did he realize that the capture of the U-boat would give the enemy secrets that would endanger the lives of hundreds of crew members to follow them to sea?

Yes.

Did he realize that by giving the enemy a U-boat intact he had helped the enemy win the war?

Yes.

Did he value his own life and those of his fellow crew members above the welfare of the naval service?

Yes.

These were not the right answers. The lieutenant might have been forgiven for acting improperly in excitement. After all, it was no easy task for a first lieutenant to try to put his captain under arrest, and it might not have worked, anyhow. But the lieutenant had not only acted improperly, he now justified his actions against the best interests of the U-boat service. There was only one possible verdict: he was found guilty of cowardice in the face of the enemy, and the council stipulated that as soon as Germany's forces occupied England, Lieutenant Berndt was to be handed over to higher authority for court-martial. Meanwhile he was to be excluded from the life of the camp. Two officers were appointed to intercede between him and the others.

A few days later, Lieutenant Berndt was so overcome with remorse that he asked to be allowed to commit suicide. Kretschmer appeared contemptuous. But a little more time passed, and through the grapevine the camp learned that the *U-570* had been taken to Barrow-on-Furness, awaiting the unraveling of red tape that would make her a part of the Royal Navy, and that she was lying moored to a buoy in the channel there. Kretschmer decided that an attempt should be made to scuttle her before she could be of any more use to the British, and he called a meeting of his senior officers. Lieutenant Berndt was to be given a chance to redeem his honor: he would be helped to escape from the camp, he would go to Barrow-on-Furness, and he would scuttle the boat.

Even now, the details of the escape of Lieutenant Berndt

from Grizedale are held secret by the British authorities and will be until after the year 2000. As will be seen, too many living people would be embarrassed or worse by revelation of the facts, and so Crown authorities are making sure that all concerned are dead before the story is turned loose. Some of the facts have come to light over the years, however, through statements by Kretschmer and others.

So loose was British internal security that by reading available newspapers, magazines, and books, Kretschmer and the others were able to draw a very respectable chart of the harbor at Barrow-on-Furness and make a guess as to where the submarine was moored. They prepared maps and charts for the lieutenant. The escape committee's tailoring department made him a gray suit, and the forgery committee turned out false papers that proclaimed him to be a Dutch seaman. The escape committee also bribed a guard to give them an identity card and emergency ration cards. The escape committee gave the lieutenant his cover story: he had gone on leave, gotten drunk, spent all his money, and was now hitchhiking back to the River Clyde to rejoin his ship.

By now it was October. The day of the escape came, and on that day Kretschmer declared a "singsong" entertainment near the outer fence, between two guard posts. While the guards watched the entertainment, directly beneath one guard station prisoners cut a hole in the barbed wire fence. When the singsong ended, it was after dark, and no one noticed the hole as the prisoners returned to their huts. At 10 P.M. the lieutenant went through the fence. Somebody suspected something, for at midnight the camp was turned out for inspection; the prisoner's escape was discovered when they found an overcoat buttoned up between two pillows on his bed.

The alarm was sounded, and the Home Guard throughout the county was called out. But the prisoner had escaped and managed to hide that night. The next day he was discovered while trying to make his way to Barrow-on-Furness. He told his cover story and the Home Guardsmen believed it, but someone said at least they ought to check with the camp to be sure this Dutchman was not the escaped prisoner. As they neared the camp in a truck he made a break for it and was shot in the back. He was badly wounded and was taken to a nearby farmhouse, where he died before a doctor could arrive.

All was now forgiven by the German officers, and Lieutenant Berndt was buried with full military honors in the cemetery at the village of Ambleside.

From the maps and other documents that Lieutenant Berndt had been carrying, the camp commander Colonel James R. Veitch of the Grenadier Guards soon had a pretty good idea of the extent and nature of the plot, and he informed higher authority in London. Kretschmer was told that he had been responsible for an act of war, committed while a prisoner. Had it been successful it would have been sabotage, punishable under British military law by death. Veitch said that nothing would be done this time, but . . .

A few hours after the death of Lieutenant Berndt, Lieutenant Commander Rahmlow arrived at POW Camp No. 1. Kretschmer refused to shake hands with him and informed him that he, too, would be subject to examination by a council of honor for his part in the surrender of the *U-570*. But before anything could happen, Colonel Veitch whisked Rahmlow off to the punishment block, for protection. Then Rahmlow was sent to another camp at Carlisle, one that housed Luftwaffe officers who would not be likely to know or care much about U-boat affairs.

The *U-570* affair had deep repercussions, however. Not long afterwards, two Luftwaffe pilots escaped from the Carlisle prison camp, stole a Hurricane fighter, and began the flight toward the continent. As they flew above the channel the engine began coughing, and they turned back to make an emergency landing, out of gas. They came that close to making their escape. They were first believed by the RAF to be deserters and were handled very roughly and promised courts-martial. But when the authorities discovered that they were POWs who had very nearly pulled off the perfect escape, their RAF captors were enormously impressed and amused and treated them like kings until they were loaded with presents and sent back to prison camp.

The War Office, which was responsible for all prisoners of war, was not at all amused. Further, it became known at about this time that POWs, and particularly U-boat POWs, were functioning very effectively as German intelligence agents. The fact was that they were the only enemy intelligence agents in all England, the professionals having been picked up at the beginning of the war and either punished or turned to work for the Allies. The U-boat men's intelligence work functioned directly under Doenitz. Following the escape of that POW prisoner from Canada, Doenitz had established a private code with his U-boat officers, a code virtually unbreakable by all the usual methods, since it involved personal substitutions. As Doenitz knew, the POWs would be allowed to receive and send mail. The problem was to get the messages through the censors, to the families, who would turn over the letters to the U-boat command. The U-boat command would prepare the replies, then, and the families would send them back to the POWs. Thus Kretschmer and other officers were able to keep Doenitz informed of many events that affected the U-boat force. By the fall of 1941 the code was known to exist, and parts of it had been broken. All this was too much for the War Office, which decided that certain categories of POWs were too dangerous to be allowed to remain so close to Germany, and they made arrangements to ship those prisoners to Canada. Foremost among those to go would be the U-boat officers.

12

Failure Story

While the wheels were grinding slowly in London to work out a plan with the Canadians for the latter to take over control of some of the prisoners of war, Kretschmer and his companions remained at Grizedale Hall, as obdurate as ever. Shortly after his capture, Kretschmer had been called to a meeting with Captain Creasy, the British director of antisubmarine warfare, but the German commander revealed no military secrets at all. Creasy had not expected him to;

although Kretschmer had very little use for the Nazis, he was a loyal U-boat man, a proud member of a proud force. The U-boat people took care of their own and they punished their own. Very shortly after Rahmlow showed up at Grizedale Hall and was quickly sent off to another camp for his own safety, so did another U-boat captain arrive under strange circumstances. He was Lieutenant Foerster of *U-501*, who had been caught on the surface on the western side of the Atlantic by a pair of Canadian warships. One, the *Moosejaw*, rammed the U-boat. As the two craft closed, Foerster, forgetting his duty to boat and country, jumped off the conning tower to the Canadian ship's forecastle. In doing this, of course, he abandoned his own ship and his shipmates. His first lieutenant took over and scuttled the boat before she could be captured. When Foerster arrived at Grizedale Hall he was greeted by an angry Kretschmer who announced that there would be another court of honor inquiry. But the British were now aware of the goings on, and within a few hours Foerster was whisked off to another camp and kept away from the other U-boat men for the remainder of the war.

Kretschmer was beginning to wonder what was going on within the service to allow for such slackness. Then the loss of Meyer's *U-207* reaffirmed at least one captain's adherence to the old standards. *U-207* was caught in mid-Atlantic by HMS *Leamington* and HMS *Veteran* and sent to the bottom with every man.

The next U-boat to get into trouble was Lieutenant Wilhelm Kleinschmidt's *U-111*. The *U-111* had sailed from Wilhelmshaven in the second week of May 1941 on her maiden cruise, and she headed up through the North Sea, around Britain and then west. She sank several ships from convoys and participated in several wolf pack attacks. On this cruise she was involved peripherally in the actions of the battleship *Bismarck* and the cruiser *Prinz Eugen*, both of which had gone to sea to raid British shipping. The *U-111*'s role was to direct the German raiders to the convoy it was then shadowing. The *Bismarck* caught the old battlecruiser *Hood* and sank her, and, in turn, fell afoul of the British *Prince of Wales* and carrier planes, which sank the German battleship. The *U-111* participated in the German hunt for survivors of the *Bismarck*, and the crew saw hundreds of bodies floating in life jackets and rafts with dead men lashed to them. The *U-111* had then turned north and refueled from a tanker, and just after she was fueled the tanker was sunk, almost in the act of fueling another U-boat. The *U-111* rescued the surviving seamen from the tanker. She also must have secured torpedoes from the tanker, because the *U-111* stayed out until the middle of June, then put in at Lorient.

The crew had two weeks leave in Germany after this long patrol while the upper deck was fitted with four torpedo containers. Also, the repair parties made an unpleasant discovery: a sack filled with sand in one of her diving tanks, an attempt at sabotage. Then, just after orders had been received to go north, came orders inspired by Hitler that changed all Doenitz's plans. The U-boat concentration was to be made in and around the Mediterranean as a part of Field Marshal Rommel's battle for Africa. So, although the crew had just finished painting a polar bear on their conning tower as a good luck symbol (as a pair of horsehoes had been painted on Kretschmer's *U-99*), on August 16 they were told they would sail south. That day the first lieutenant was injured in an accident, and he was replaced by Lieutenant zur See Helmut Fuchs, the junior officer. His place as watch officer was taken by Oberleutnant zur See Friedrich Wilhelm Roesing. Strange days these, for although Roesing was senior to Fuchs, he had no experience in U-boats and could not possibly hold down the first lieutenant's job.

By the petty officers and men of the crew Captain Kleinschmidt was regarded as an old man, too old for U-boat service. He was thirty-four. His reactions, they said, left a great deal to be desired. He was a careful captain, too careful, they indicated. But he obviously had the confidence of Admiral Doenitz, because along came Lieutenant Heinicke, slated to be a new U-boat commander, for a training voyage.

Carrying seventeen torpedoes in all, the *U-111* sailed on the afternoon of August 16 and very nearly was sunk by a British submarine off the coast when she surfaced that night in the rain and pitch darkness. She escaped and sailed down the coast of Africa to Freetown, then across the South Atlantic, and reached the mouth of the Amazon.

On September 10 she sank the Dutch *Marken* with two torpedoes, and thus destroyed a cargo of aircraft on its way to Capetown. Captain Kleinschmidt gave the survivors chocolate, cigarettes, and brandy and sent them off in their boats.

On September 20 the *U-111* sank the *Cingalese Prince* two degrees north of the equator. The *U-111* surfaced, gave the survivors provisions, and then made off again, heading for Lorient. She had been ordered to transfer her torpedoes to *U-67* and *U-68* and then come to Lorient for a new load. She did meet *U-68* and gave her four torpedoes from the deck containers. She did not meet *U-67*, which had been damaged after the original messages were sent and had headed back to Germany.

The crew continued to be displeased and morale was spotty, particularly after someone discovered a long copper bolt in the hydroplane machinery—another attempt at sabotage.

On October 3 the *U-111* heard from Doenitz that a large British merchantman had been damaged in convoy and was lying about 400 miles west of Las Palmas, right on the *U-111*'s route back to Lorient. Captain Kleinschmidt decided to find and sink her. At 8:40 on the morning of October 4 he saw a ship about ten miles away; that vessel turned and came toward him. He was sure this was the freighter *Silverbelle*, about which he had learned. It was not the *Silverbelle*, but the armed merchant cruiser *Lady Shirley.* Kleinschmidt was so obsessed with the idea that this ship was a merchant vessel that he ignored the sound of the hydrophones and the distance. Through the periscope a small ship up close could look like a large ship far away, and when the *Lady Shirley* was only 500 yards off, Kleinschmidt said she was 3,300 yards away. The result was disaster, for the *Lady Shirley* came up and began dropping depth charges when the U-boat was only 50 feet under water. The shallowest of the charges was set at 400 feet. It blew up under the boat and did some damage to the stern. The main problem thereafter, according to the petty officers, was captain's error, for Kleinschmidt was never able to trim the boat properly, which, they said, was because he did not know how. He ordered the U-boat to surface and run on her diesel engines. But apparently there was real damage, for as soon as she surfaced and the engineers started the engines, they blew out in a dense cloud of black smoke that filled the engine room. Kleinschmidt then ordered the boat down, but she was already under fire from the gun crew of the *Lady Shirley*, which was only 500 yards away. Captain Kleinschmidt then opened the conning tower hatch and went up on the bridge to fight with the deck gun. He was followed by Fuchs, by Roesing, by the petty officer and men who manned the 20mm gun on the bridge, and by the deck gun crew. The machine gunner began firing at the *Lady Shirley* and killed that ship's gunlayer; he also killed and wounded several other British sailors. The British continued to shoot, and one shell penetrated the conning tower and ricocheted off the casing of the attack periscope. Apparently it caused some damage to the ammunition being passed up to the U-boat gun crew because the first shell jammed in the gun. Two men of the crew of the U-boat's forward gun were wounded by shells from the *Lady Shirley*, and the other three men ran for shelter. Orders were given to man the after gun, but this was not done.

Down below the U-boat's engineer was trying to get the diesels going. He did get them up to 500 RPM, but once again they stopped and smoke filled the engine room. Lieutenant Heinicke was also in the engine room trying to help out. Captain Kleinschmidt was on the control room ladder handing up ammunition for the forward deck gun when a shell from the *Lady Shirley* burst squarely on the bridge, killing him, Roesing, and Fuchs. The captain's body fell forward down the conning tower and lay sprawled across the lower hatch.

When the crew saw their captain dead, they quit cold. They came up wearing life belts, and Heinicke gave the order to abandon ship. The engineer opened the vents, and the *U-111* sank. The forty-five survivors were taken aboard the *Lady Shirley* (whose crew at that point consisted of nine unwounded seamen and three times that many wounded). One German petty officer tried to organize a party to storm the ship, seize her, and sail for a Spanish port, but the crew of the *U-111* was so disorganized and the men so at odds with one another, that it was impossible. The *Lady Shirley* sailed into Gibraltar and unloaded her prisoners of war.

That month of October 1941, Lieutenant Kell's *U-204* was sunk by the HMS *Mallow* and HMS *Rochester* in the Mediterranean. All were lost.

November began badly for Doenitz with the lost of *U-580* and *U-583*, both from collisions in the Baltic. All the men of the *U-583* went down, although some from the *U-580* were saved.

By this time, early November, the attention of the U-boat corps was forcibly turned to the south with Hitler's repeated demands for more boats to sink more British merchantmen and warships in order to further the action of the German forces in Africa. On November 13 Hitler's demand was met: Lieutenant Friedrich Guggenberger's *U-81* sank the carrier *Ark Royal* on her way back to Gibraltar from search exercises. Less than two weeks later Lieutenant Freiherr von Tiesenhausen's *U-331* sank the battleship *Barham*, and two days later the *U-559* sank the Australian corvette *Paramatta*.

But was it worth it? Hitler said yes. Doenitz said no, it was not worth the effort, for his boys should be out in the Atlantic cutting off Britain's supply lines. Let von Kesselring's Luftwaffe forces sink the British in the Mediterranean. But Hitler was not listening to his naval staff these days, preoccupied as he was with the battle in North Africa and the growing difficulties that had emerged following his summer's attack on the Soviet Union.

On October 3, 1941, Lieutenant Ey's *U-433* pulled into St. Nazaire harbor, thus ending her first war cruise. She had eleven of her fourteen torpedoes still aboard, and she came into port bare—no victory pennants—for she had not sunk a ship. The captain and the crew of this new 750-ton boat represented Doenitz's new problem: too much too fast, with a subsequent deterioration in training and in the efficiency and determination of captain and crew. Also, although the *U-433* had been put into operation for the first time that summer of 1941, she went into dry dock for a refit in October. She had grounded when she set out on her initial war cruise from Trondheim, grounded on a shallow spot in the harbor because the crew was unfamiliar with the territory. She had been attacked by a Catalina flying boat on September 12, and when the captain said to dive, something had clogged up the vents, and she could not, so she had to maneuver on the surface to escape the aircraft's attacks, and she was buffeted about considerably. On September 13 she got involved with Convoy SC 42, but instead of sinking any ships she was attacked by patrol craft and depth-charged severely. So, although *U-433* had accomplished precisely nothing on her first war patrol, she really did need the refit. She was one of the reasons Doenitz's operations officer was distraught; half the U-boat force was down all the time for repairs.

By the luck of the draw, this crew that had done nothing got twelve days leave in Germany after that mission, and Captain Ey, a man of imagination, wrote on the leave passes of all the men: *Kriegsurlaubs Schein—Schwerst Arbeiter—U-boot Fahrer gegen England*. (Warleave certificate—Vital worker—U-boat sailor against England.) This endorsement, somewhat exaggerated because of the lack of accomplishment of this crew, entitled the men to special concessions from travel authorities and extra food rations.

The men had their leave and returned. The boat was still in dry dock, Doenitz's yards were jammed with boats for repair these days. The men hung around the barracks, most of them getting drunk and spending as much time as possible in the brothels. Finally, on November 5, the *U-443* put to sea on her second war cruise. But a leak developed that day in the control room, and she had to turn around and run back to St. Nazaire for repair. More shore leave—more beer, more wine, and more schnapps.

On November 8 the boat was ready to sail, but the captain had not gotten his petty officers organized to control the crew, and three men did not turn up. Shore police found them drunk, sitting outside the railroad station. They were hustled aboard, but somehow managed to bring a keg of beer with them, and they began drinking. A fight developed in the diesel room, where they had settled down to drink, and they had to be ejected forcibly. It was eight hours before they were sober enough to stand watch. Captain Ey had to delay sailing until November 9. When he opened his sealed orders in the Bay of Biscay he learned that he was to operate in the Mediterranean. *U-433* then headed toward Gibraltar, spending most of the daylight hours below the surface to avoid patrolling British aircraft, and passed through the strait at night on the surface without seeing any escorts or patrol boats. On November 16 Captain Ey sighted what he thought was a British cruiser, traveling alone. It was actually the corvette HMS *Marigold*, and Ey was deceived by her camouflage into believing she was much larger. He decided to attack the "cruiser," maneuvered into what he thought was good position, and fired three torpedoes. They missed by so wide a margin that the lookouts of the Marigold never saw one of them. Ey maneuvered again and fired another torpedo, which, he said, hit but did not explode (quite possibly true, given the quality of German torpedoes).

The result of all this activity was the discovery of the U-boat by the corvette crew and the beginning of a hunt. The target was first seen at 10:30 P.M. as a radio bearing. Then it was identified as a U-boat and attacked. Captain Ey dived, and five depth charges came down, but not too close. No damage was done.

The Germans were very relaxed. Half of the crew were asleep, and they were not called to action stations. The *Marigold*'s propellers were heard moving off. The captain called a council of his officers, and after debating for half an hour they decided to surface and move away from the area, without any real worry about the departing British warship.

The "cruiser" was not behaving in the way a crusier should. Her captain had headed away to set up a block search, having lost contact when the first set of depth charges shook up the Asdic set. It was move, and then stop, and move again. About 11:30 P.M. the submarine began to move upward. She came up to 60 feet and stopped. The hydrophone operator listened. Fifteen minutes later came a rush of heavy propeller noise to starboard. The *Marigold* had found her, dead ahead, 1,200 yards off. "The devil had been lying close to us with engines stopped," said the hydrophone operator. The corvette ran in and dropped ten depth charges as Captain Ey tried to go deep, fast. One charge exploded about the U-boat, flattening the machine gun. The others blew up on either side of the boat, delivering simultaneously crushing blows. Every instrument smashed or went dead. The doors of the refrigerator and the lockers burst and poured provisions and personal equipment all over the deck. The spare torpedoes forward broke loose. The welded seams began to break. The tanks ruptured, and compressed air surged throughout the boat. Then the captain blew the ballast tanks to surface, and the U-boat came up, oh, so slowly, the weight of the incoming water trying to drag her down. In the conning tower the captain opened the hatch, and the air pressure blew him upward. The chief quartermaster, standing below him, was blown into the conning tower. The engineer started the starboard engine. But by this time the crew were pouring out of the boat, the port diesel was not started, and the crew began jumping into the water, believing the boat was sinking. She did not sink, the starboard diesel carried her on a zigzag course, empty, for about five minutes. Then the scuttling charges blew up and she sank.

The *Marigold*'s captain sent a boat to pick up survivors, and the British found thirty-eight men, including Captain Ey. Two men had decided they would swim for the Spanish coast thirty miles away, but as far as anyone knew they never made it.

The loss of *U-433* put an end to a U-boat career that was totally undistinguished. Was it the fault of the captain? Or perhaps, was it the fault of the so much foreshortened training program forced upon Doenitz by the war? Or was it merely bad luck?

All these elements certainly played their roles in the U-boat war, as the fate of the *U-95* now indicated. Twelve days after the sinking of the *U-433*, Lieutenant Commander Gert Schreiber passed Gibraltar on his way into the Mediterranean to do Hitler's bidding. His rank was an indication of his experience: he was of the vintage of Prien and Kretschmer, an old hand who had commissioned the *U-95* in the spring of 1940. He was not nearly so well known to the world because his sinkings were still below 100,000 tons, although he had been on six war cruises in the boat. He had sailed in wolf packs and alone, and he was regarded as a perfectly adequate captain, but somehow the genius was just not there, or maybe one could call it luck.

In any event whatever it was that was necessary deserted Schreiber completely on that very night that he brought the *U-95* through the Straits of Gibraltar.

It was a clear night, so bright that the mountains of

Granada could be seen on the Spanish coast. The first lieutenant and three members of the crew were drinking brandy and playing skat in the mess. One boatswain's mate was sitting, watching them; he was scheduled to go on watch soon. From his leather jacket he extracted a notebook and began to read idly, going over an account he had written of the beginning of this voyage, perhaps to be printed in the newspapers back home or broadcast over the radio.

It told in detail of those last hours at Lorient:

> The day we set sail was as such days usually are. The evening before we had the usual farewell celebrations, when the majority of the crew got pretty drunk. But anyone who has had any experience of a U-boat man's life in a French base will understand. Although there is always plenty of time when you're in dock, most of the jobs are always left to the last day—such as handing in chests, cleaning out quarters, taking on fresh provisions, writing personal letters, medical inspection, and so on. Betweentimes everybody brings his personal belongings on board. Everyone knows how cramped things are in a U-boat, but many would certainly be astounded at the amount of things smuggled on board as personal belongings: photos of all kinds and sizes, all sorts of French perfumes, souvenirs, necklaces, rings, and so on—everybody has his own talisman. When everything has been more or less finished, there is a short roll call, and then we are dismissed. Everything has to be on board one hour before we are ready to put to sea, and the short interval is mostly spent in saying goodbye to one's friends. The chronically overthirsty ones take a short "nip" on their way to the boat.
>
> But the last few days a number of things have struck us as curious. Nobody knew what it was exactly, but anyway things were not the same as usual, and there were an awful lot of rumors flying about on board. We were not to remain in the dark for long, for after we had cast off the commander made an announcement.

[Obviously, since the announcement was secret, the boatswain's account deleted it. Obviously, also, the announcement told the men they were not going back to the Atlantic, but into the Mediterranean to help Rommel win a glorious victory.]

It was bad weather, with thick fog and showers, which was not exactly calculated to raise our spirits. The band played cheerful music to see us off. All the men who had been working on board during our long stay in dock were standing on the jetty, and a lot of our friends besides. Of course the fair sex was well represented,, and gave us flowers for the cruise. The Flotillenchef said a few encouraging words, and the commander took his leave. Two boats were going out at the same time. We had to cast off first as we had the outside berth. We waited until the other boat had cast off, too, and then we both moved off in line ahead at full speed past the crowds gathered on the jetty. We could hear the cheering only very faintly because our diesels were making such a noise. We gave three cheers in reply, and the band began to play *"Denn wir fahren gegen England"* and then immediately after that we were swallowed up in the mist. As soon as we had got away the fun started. Of course the escort vessel which was to fetch us wasn't there. It had gone to bring in a U-boat which was returning from a long-distance cruise. After half an hour the U-boat hove in sight, of course, without the escort vessel. Our boat had stopped. Our commander yelled across to them.

"Haven't you seen the escort?"

"Yes, she must be coming soon."

It was gradually getting dark and the commander intended to anchor for the night if the escort did not soon turn up. At that moment the lookout shouted, "Ship on the starboard bow."

The escort came into sight. The noise of our diesels began again, and off we went. After two hours the escort left us. The signaller reported a message from the escort vessel to our commander.

"My escort duty is completed. Wish you and your crew good voyage and much success. Over to you. Thank you."

Whoever was not on watch was standing on the bridge as the weather had improved a bit. It was now pitch dark.

"Escort out of sight," came from the lookout aft.

As soon as we had parted company we went at full speed. In order to get a good distance from the coast and to get clear of the mined area . . .

The boatswain's mate continued to read with pleasure his own prose. The card players slapped down their cards from time to time. Some men snored in their bunks. Several men were on deck smoking. Suddenly, a lookout in the conning tower saw a shadow and gave the alarm, "Lower deck, action stations."

But the alarm was given in such a low voice that no one believed it for a moment. Then down came a seaman who said that the lookout had indeed seen something strange, and the officer of the watch believed it was a submarine. That officer was Lieutenant Hans Spach, who had excellent night vision honed by four years in the Luftwaffe. It could very well be a German U-boat, half a dozen were known to be in these waters just then, and Doenitz was sending more. It could also be one of their Italian allies. But on the other hand, it might be an Allied submarine. Who was to know?

The *U-95* went to action stations then. For an hour all was silent, the boat running on its motors, stalking the unknown's shadow.

Just before 4 A.M. the boatswain's mate who was to go on duty on deck got up from the game and put on his leather jacket.

"Take your life jacket," said one of his companions. "We may be in for something."

But the boatswain's mate had forgotten where he had left his life jacket.

"Plenty of time to get it later if needed," he said, and he went up to the conning tower. Just as he reached the tower the order came to prepare torpedoes, and men began to run forward to open the torpedo tube caps.

Captain Schreiber was now on deck. He was close enough to the other object to see that it was indeed a submarine, but the angle was such that he could not make out the silhouette. He kept maneuvering, still not knowing. Four times he made an approach, and four times the men below opened and closed the torpedo tubes. They began to curse with the exertion and frustration.

Schreiber saw the other submarine turn away, and he ordered the signalman on the bridge to give a challenge in Morse code. Schreiber ordered the gun crew to begin passing ammunition for the deck gun, and he prepared to open fire if the challenge was not properly answered. He called for more speed.

The other submarine was not German, as Schreiber had hoped, but the Dutch boat *O-21*. Her captain recognized the challenge as coming from a German U-boat and fired a torpedo from 2,000 yards.

Lieutenant Spach saw the torpedo first and shouted.

"Torpedo track to port."

The quartermaster, who was standing forward at the port lookout, pushed the lieutenant out of the way, leaped to the bridge rail, looked over the side, and then put the helm hard over to starboard. The torpedo went racing down the port side of the boat, and the boatswain's mate with the leather jacket could hear it hiss as it went by, then he heard a "clang" as the torpedo grazed the U-boat's rudder.

Aboard the Dutch boat, the captain saw the maneuvering and ordered another torpedo fired. This time he aimed two degrees ahead of the U-boat's bow. The lookout in the conning tower saw it come, then heard a loud report that nearly split his eardrums. He saw a red flame and a cloud of smoke, and then he was flying through the air to land on the bridge.

The captain shouted to the men on deck to stick together. Water began to pour down through the hatch into the control room as the boat settled, her bow half blown away. In half a minute *U-95* sank. The Dutch submarine nosed about in the water, picking up survivors, but of the *U-95*'s crew of forty-six men, only a dozen survived, including the officers (all of whom were on deck at the time). It was more bad news for Admiral Doenitz, just what he expected in the restricted waters of the Mediterranean.

13

Enter the U-Boat Killer

In the fall of 1941 Adolf Hitler interfered with Admiral Doenitz's plans again, as the Fuehrer had done at the time of the invasion of Norway. The difference was that this time the interference lasted longer and cost more to the U-boat corps and the German cause. U-boats that were fighting warships in the Mediterranean were not endangering Britain's lifeline to the west, and it showed. But Hitler was fighting a desperate battle for the control of the Mediterranean, and he insisted that the U-boat arm devote most of its attention to that area. Thus in the last months of 1941 British shipping losses in the Atlantic declined enormously. At the end of November, after the sinking of *U-433* and *U-95*, Doenitz reluctantly sent six more U-boats into the Mediterranean and another dozen to patrol off the Spanish and North African coasts. The idea was to deny access to the Straits of Gibraltar to the British convoys sailing south in support of General Auchinleck's Libya offensive. The month of November ended with the sinking of Opitz's *U-206* by a plane of Royal Air Force Squadron 502 in the Bay of Biscay. New days, new problems. The French bases were not so safe now, British air radar was becoming ever more effective.

The German buildup of U-boat forces in the Mediterranean and the eastern approaches to that sea was bound to create powerful opposition by the British. Their whole position in Africa depended on the ability to supply the Eighth Army and Gibraltar and Malta and to keep the sea traffic open. In November and December the Germans made a powerful effort to close off that traffic.

Admiral Doenitz's complaints to Admiral Raeder were becoming louder. The figures he showed, of British shipping losses dropping almost to zero in the Atlantic, had to be impressive, even to the battleship admirals of the German naval staff. Still, OKW remained adamant: at least ten submarines had to be maintained in the Mediterranean at all times and fifteen more outside the Gibraltar approaches.

Doenitz swallowed hard and obeyed. Lieutenant Schlieper's *U-208* headed down south toward the straits and was sunk on December 11 by the corvette *Bluebell*. Three other U-boats passed safely through the straits, however, making a total of eighteen U-boats in the Mediterranean. But what did they do? In the whole of December they sank a total of eleven merchant ships and the cruiser *Galatea*. The results had to be seen as a disaster in terms of the potential out in the Atlantic. And in that same month Doenitz was ordered to send another ten boats into the Mediterranean. He was, he told his associates grimly, being told to send his boys into a trap.

How right he was, for of those eighteen boats in the Mediterranean in December, seven never got out. And as for results, in one night a group of Italian dare-devils riding their little "underwater chariots" did more damage to the British fleet than all the eighteen U-boats. But where the Germans were really making hay was in the Atlantic waters between Gibraltar and England, a narrow gauntlet that every British convoy had to run somehow, past the Bay of Biscay bases of Admiral Doenitz's U-boat force. By December 1 the numerous sinkings in this region caused the British Admiralty to seriously worry about its ability to transport adequate supplies to the forces fighting in North Africa. They were desperate days and desperate actions were demanded. The response of the British was to pour more power into the Mediterranean. Destroyer and corvette construction was proceeding more satisfactorily for the British, although still far from adequate. But emergency measures were also showing results: the British had established a corps of "suicide" fliers who took their fighter bombers aboard merchant ships, and when their convoy was attacked, they were catapulted into the air. Of course there was no place except the sea for them to come down, and their rescue would first of all depend on their being found; it was a very risky life. But the catapult planes did serve their purpose and did harry the German submarines.

More practical for the long run was the British development of the escort carrier. Several of these ships, merchantmen equipped with short flight decks, were being built. The first, ready that fall of 1941, was HMS *Audacity.*

Besides these technical improvements in the war against the U-boats, the British were also beginning to assemble their teams of escorts, trained to work together. At the end of November 1941, Commander Frederic John Walker's 36th Escort Group sailed from Liverpool with an outward bound convoy to Gibraltar. The weather was dreadful, but the same gales that howled above the convoy kept the U-boats down. The 36th Escort Group arrived at Gibraltar with its charges. There Walker learned just how serious the situation was. Captain Creasy flew down from London for conferences about the problem of the U-boats in and around the Mediterranean. The main reason for the flap was the growing cooperation between Goering's Focke-Wulff patrol bombers and Doenitz's submarines. In this cooperation the Admiralty quite properly saw a gravely increased threat, particularly to Gibraltar convoys because of the long French coastline available to the Germans for airfields. Some line officers wanted the escort group to patrol the straits, and they did for two weeks, but they saw no submarines. Patrol, as Creasy knew, was not the answer. He finally authorized action that he believed would help. In mid-December Commander Walker's escort group prepared to take to sea with the important convoy HG 76, bound from Gibraltar for Liverpool. In addition to his own vessels, Walker would have the destroyers *Blankney*, *Stanley*, and *Exmoor*, and that first escort carrier, the *Audacity.* No incident was more telling about the state of the war against the U-boats than the story of Convoy HG 76.

It began with Creasy's words for Walker:

"The enemy has been cutting the Gibraltar convoys to shreds. This is an important convoy and you will be re-enforced with ships of the Gibraltar command. You must arrive as intact as possible."

HG 76 was scheduled to leave Gibraltar at the end of November, but the convoy was postponed because of the appearance of the second and third contingents of U-boats sent down by Admiral Doenitz. The British reply had been to strengthen the air forces by bringing down Hudson Squadron No. 233 and Swordfish scout planets of the Fleet Air Arm. They began something new: attacking the U-boats when they surfaced at night, something they could do with the Leigh light, a strong spotlight that both lit up the sea around a U-boat and blinded the U-boat crew.

During the second week of December many U-boats were reported operating west of Gibraltar. Convoy OG 77 was coming down to the Rock with one escort group. The escorts scheduled to take out HG 76 were released and sent up to help bring OG 77 in, and then did so. Under double escort, the convoy arrived without losing a ship, although it was trailed and reported to Doenitz off Lisbon by *U-434*.

With OG 77 safe in Gibraltar harbor, HG 76 was ordered to sail on the afternoon of December 14. The *Empire Barracuda* and four tankers bound for the Middle East via the Cape of Good Hope sailed four hours later.

HG 76 consisted of thirty-two ships in the nine columns. The escort was the most powerful the British had yet put to sea, a real challenge to Doenitz's U-boats. It consisted of sixteen escort vessels and the *Audacity.* She had been the German motor ship *Hannover*, captured early in the war, and her conversion with a flight deck had been completed this year. The British had brought the escort carrier into use at about the same time that they were fitting out merchant ships to catapult fighters into the air. Already four of those catapult ships were in service on the Gibraltar run. Five other merchant ships were undergoing transformation with flight decks in England, and six escort carriers had been ordered from the United States, but it would be 1942 before any of these would be ready for service. So the *Audacity* was alone, the first escort carrier, the answer of the Battle of the Atlantic committee to the German combination of Focke-Wulff bomber and U-boat.

The *Audacity* carried six American-made fighters, and four Swordfish scout planes. She had already proved her worth on the Gibraltar convoy run, with OG 74, when that convoy was under heavy attack by U-boats and bombers on September 20. One of her planes had shot down a Focke-Wulff that day. Admiral Doenitz had instructed his U-boat skippers to watch out for this carrier and sink her if they could.

Commander Walker was a great deal more than just the commander of the escort group. He was one of that new breed of fighting sailors, the anti-U-boat specialist. From 1926 to 1931 Walker had served as fleet antisubmarine officer in the Atlantic and then the Mediterranean fleets. In 1937 he had been made commander of the antisubmarine school and was thus responsible for development of antisubmarine materials and methods. He held this post at the beginning of the war. Walker had a brief and unfortunate sojourn in China. Then, as noted, he went to the staff of the vice admiral, Dover command. He wangled his way out of this staff job in the fall of 1941 to take over as senior officer of the 36th Escort Group, in his command ship, the little sloop *Stork*.

Everyone connected with HG 76 expected plenty of trouble. The reports of U-boats, the knowledge that the Germans were doing everything possible to beef up their power in the Mediterranean, all pointed to a rough voyage home.

The first indication of trouble came at 11:25 that night of December 14. A Swordfish scout plane from the *Audacity* spotted a U-boat on the surface six and a half miles on the starboard beam of the convoy. The Swordfish circled, came back and dropped two calcium lights and three depth charges, set to explode at 25 and 50 feet. The first two fell 80 feet ahead of the U-boat, which then took violent evasive action, and the third charge dropped 60 feet off the starboard bow. The Swordfish did not have radio, but Commander Walker's *Stork* was alert, and when the watch heard the sound of exploding depth charges the *Stork* raced out to find them. She found two calcium lights and carried out an antisubmarine search but did not find the submarine. Walker then detailed the escorts *Deptford* and *Rhododendron* to continue the search, and he rejoined the convoy.

Thus was the first encounter avoided: the aircraft had given the U-boat a fright as it was closing to attack the convoy, and the *Stork* had put the cap on it.

All was quiet for a time. Shortly after midnight Commander Walker had a signal from the Admiralty noting that a U-boat had reported in to Doenitz on sighting a convoy. But since the *Empire Barracuda*'s tanker convoy had sailed so soon after HG 76, the Admiralty report was a little fuzzy about which convoy the U-boat had been reporting on. That message was not very helpful, but it emphasized what Commander Walker already knew: there was trouble ahead.

At 1:35 on the morning of December 15, that same Swordfish aircraft sighted another U-boat, this one ten miles astern of the convoy. The pilot zoomed down on the U-boat but could not attack because he had dropped all his depth charges on the first one. The U-boat crash-dived.

Commander Walker had the answer to that Admiralty message shortly after 3 A.M. The tanker convoy that had sailed after HG 76 had set a course of 250 degrees and was zigzagging when the *U-77* torpedoed the *Empire Barracuda*. That convoy was escorted by HMS *Wishart* and three corvettes; Lieutenant Heinrich Schonder had shown a considerable amount of daring to come up close and torpedo the steamer through her screen. In the flash of the explosions the conning tower of the *U-77* was visible half a mile away on the starboard bow. One corvette went charging after the U-boat, which went down. HMS *Coltsfoot* began picking up survivors. She obtained what might be a contact, and, taking no chance, dropped depth charges, but nothing happened. She went back to Gibraltar with the survivors, and the other ships of the convoy went on to reach the Cape without further trouble.

Life continued quiet in Convoy HG 76 until 5:37 that morning. Another Swordfish sighted a U-boat off Cape Trafalgar and attacked, dropping two depth charges. One exploded in the swirl made by the U-boat as she dived. There was no evidence of damage, but once more a U-boat had been forced down and away from the convoy.

On the morning of December 15 several missions were flown by Swordfish. No U-boats were sighted. The next day no missions were flown because there was no indication that there were any U-boats in the neighborhood of the convoy. Like the first of anything, the *Audacity* was a rather iffy carrier at best. Her flight deck was short, and her whole bearing was tenuous. As her senior aircraft pilot said:

"Flying had to be kept to minimum, as, under conditions obtaining in *Audacity*, there was always a bigger risk than in other carriers and our normal wastage had so far been about four aircraft per convoy trip."

In this two-day lull from enemy activity, the convoy commodore practiced altering course by various sorts of signals and making emergency turns. The merchant skippers became quite adept at it. But everyone knew the quiet could not last, and on the night of December 16 the Admiralty again reported on U-boat transmissions that indicated at least one U-boat had found the convoy. Commander Walker sped over to the *Audacity* and on this TBS transmitter he asked the carrier to carry out an antisubmarine search at dawn.

It was done. At 9:25 in the morning the plane reported a U-boat on the port beam, twenty-two miles away. Walker then set course at full speed for the position and ordered the *Blankney*, *Exmoor*, *Stanley*, and *Pentstemon* to come with him.

The *Blankney* arrived first and reported no contact. Walker came up and found a doubtful contact. Six charges were dropped, but then there was no contact at all. But Walker was not convinced. He estimated that since the U-boat was moving in the direction of the convoy, it would dive and continue to move up. So he continued to come back on the course the U-boat ought to have followed. At 10:49 the *Pentstemon* gained a positive Asdic contact at 1,100 yards. An attack was made with ten charges set between 150 feet and 385 feet. Contact was then lost, but Walker continued to sweep the area with the *Stork* and the *Stanley* and *Pentstemon*. At 12:47 HMS *Stanley* reported an object on the horizon, bearing 130 degrees. Then the U-boat surfaced, bearing 60 degrees. The U-boat sped along trying to escape but the two destroyers chased and began to close the distance. At 1 P.M. Swordfish from the *Audacity* came up to attack the submarine with machine gun fire. The U-boat's machine gunners shot the plane down. The *Exmoor* and the *Blankney* joined up again, and the three destroyers began firing at seven miles range. The *Exmoor*'s firing was quite accurate, and the U-boat sank at 1:30. The escorts then picked up survivors and learned that they had sunk Lieutenant Commander Arend Baumann's *U-131*. She had been on her maiden cruise, Baumann had first taken her up to the North Atlantic but had then been ordered down south as part of the gang Doenitz brought in to meet Hitler's demands. She had sunk one ship in the North Atlantic and nothing since she had arrived in these southern waters.

Commander Walker remembered that just before the U-boat had surfaced, bearing 60 degrees from the British ships, the *Stanley* had reported an object bearing 130 degrees. There was no way the U-boat could have moved around that much in a few moments. So there was another U-boat out there somewhere. He ordered the *Exmoor* and the *Blankney* to go off and take a look while he led the other ships back to the convoy.

The afternoon was quiet. The Admiralty warned again that the convoy had been sighted by a U-boat and was being shadowed. The commodore changed course to 350 degrees, and the *Stanley* was stationed on the outer screen on the port quarter of the convoy. But the night was very quiet. No attack came.

At 9:06 on the morning of December 18, the *Stanley* reported a U-boat six miles on the port quarter, and the *Blankney*, *Deptford*, and *Exmoor* were ordered to help in the hunt. The convoy altered course again to due north.

The *Stanley* closed on the U-boat at full speed, but the boat dived when she was three miles away. This created a problem because the *Stanley*'s Asdic set had been out of order during the whole trip. But her skipper saw oil and wake off to starboard a mile away from the place where the

U-boat had dived. The *Stanley* then cut back to twelve knots and started dropping single depth charges in a square around this position. Three sides of the square had been completed and nineteen depth charges dropped by the time the *Blankney* came up at 9:23. The *Blankney*'s Asdic was working just fine, and soon she had a firm contact at 800 yards. Her captain increased speed to eighteen knots and charged in to attack. The U-boat turned sharply and passed down the port side of the destroyer about 50 yards away. The destroyer dropped a pattern of six charges.

Contact was regained immediately (the *Blankney* was using improved Asdic), and the ranges and bearings were passed to the *Stanley*, which fired fourteen charges set to explode deep.

Blankney slowed and waited. As soon as the *Stanley* had completed her run, the *Blankney*'s captain started a new one, not giving the U-boat captain time to recover from the last attack. She dropped a six-charge pattern set for medium depths. Six minutes later, as the throwers were being reloaded, *U-434* resurfaced, 2,000 yards away. The *Blankney* increased her speed, and both destroyers opened fire. The U-boat swung stern on, as the *Blankney* prepared to ram, and the destroyer struck her a glancing blow that damaged the destroyer's port side. A whaleboat was lowered so that the destroyermen could board the U-boat, but she sank almost immediately. The destroyers picked up the survivors. She was, they found, a brand-new boat, Lieutenant Heyda's *U-434*, out on her first patrol, and she had sunk nothing.

During the morning two Focke-Wulffs were engaged by planes from the *Audacity*, one enemy plane was damaged and both were driven off. Just before dark, the evening air search was launched by the carrier. Commander Walker complained that they went out too early, but there was nothing to be done about it ex post facto. In proof, however, was the fact that the air search revealed no U-boats, but HMS *Pentstemon* sighted a U-boat about eleven miles off the convoy's port beam. She began to chase, but this Type IX C boat could make more than eighteen knots on the surface and the small escort could not catch up. She began firing her 4-inch gun and firing starshell at 7:20.

The *Stanley* and the *Convolvulus* were then ordered to

assist, and they conducted a sweep but found nothing. *Convolvulus* reported the sound of torpedoes passing from port to starboard, so apparently the U-boat had fired at one of them.

The night became very dark, with no moon and a cloud cover. At 3:45 the *Stanley* was astern of the convoy. She sent a radio signal: U-boat in sight. Commander Walker asked her to send up starshell to indicate her position, but before all this could be settled, he knew her position: she was torpedoed and blew up in a sheet of flame. At the same time torpedoes passed by the *Largo* and the *Stork* but missed. Walker realized then that the U-boat had followed the escorts when they rejoined the convoy and vowed from then on to always use indirect routing.

Just then, Walker was too busy to give any more thought than that to the problem, for the moment he saw the sheet of flame coming up from his escort, he altered course to port and ordered the HMS *Buttercup* to follow. The *Stork* then moved at fifteen knots, dropping single depth charges as she went. At 4:24 she had a contact. As Commander Walker said: "Movement was very slight and the U-boat's position suggested that she was waiting for a ship to stop and pick up *Stanley*'s survivors, thus providing her with another victim."

The *Stork* fired five charges set at 50 feet. The shock knocked out the Asdic. Walker turned and came back, and the Asdic went on again. The U-boat turned, but the *Stork* turned with her and dropped another pattern of depth charges. After a third attack, the U-boat surfaced 200 yards ahead of Walker's sloop. Then came a chase that lasted eleven minutes, the U-boat turning constantly just inside the *Stork*'s turning circle and traveling only two knots less than *Stork*'s maximum speed. Walker kept firing starshell to illuminate the area, and thus he kept track of the U-boat's gyrations. The 4-inch gun could not be depressed far enough to fire at the U-boat so the crew was reduced to "fist shakings and roaring curses at an enemy who several times seemed to be a matter of a few feet away rather than yards."

At 4:48 Walker ended the drama. He managed to ram the U-boat just in front of the conning tower and roll her over. She hung up on the *Stork*'s side, then went by, and he dropped ten charges set at shallow settings. The U-boat began to sink. Walker then went off to look for the survivors of the *Stanley.* He did not have much hope that he would find any survivors, for the explosion had been violent. The *Samphire* was already on the scene, but she came first to the area where the U-boat had been sunk and picked up thirteen survivors. When the *Samphire* reached the *Stanley*'s area she found many dead bodies, but only three survivors.

The *Stork* found twenty-five men in the water and rescued them. She came back and picked up five Germans from the *U-574*. Lieutenant Dietrich Gengelbach had been out on his first cruise, too. At 5:28 Walker signalled the convoy:

"*Stanley* sunk by U-boat. U-boat sunk by *Stork*."

The convoy went on.

At 5:15 on December 19, the *U-108* torpedoed the steamer *Ruckinge*. The torpedo caused her to list, and the captain abandoned ship. Later Walker went back to the wreck and inspected her, and then ordered her sunk by gunfire. A Focke-Wulff came up to watch the proceedings, but stayed off at a respectful distance.

At 11 A.M. on December 19 two Focke-Wulffs appeared near the convoy. The first was shot down by fighter planes from *Audacity.* They damaged the second but it escaped. But through attrition (accidents) the *Audacity*'s operational aircraft were now reduced to three.

At 4 P.M. another Focke-Wulff appeared, flying very low above the water, apparently to confuse the fighters. Two Grumman Martlets shot it down.

A U-boat was sighted by another of the *Audacity*'s planes, but could not be found later by the escorts. They all clustered around the convoy, and the night was spent peacefully, no U-boats in sight.

Activity on the morning of December 20 opened with the usual Focke-Wulff visit at about 9 A.M. The enemy plane was chased into cloud cover and then away by two Martlet fighters. At 5:30 one fighter reported two U-boats ahead of the convoy, but they were too far ahead to chase, so Walker ordered an 80-degree course change to starboard, and he told the aircraft to make the submarine dive, which they did. The *Audacity* moved off by herself with one escort because of the presence of those two U-boats. She began to zigzag. *Audacity* and the convoy both spent a quiet night, having outwitted the U-boats.

At nine o'clock on the morning of December 21 the dawn antisubmarine air patrol discovered two U-boats alongside each other with a plank between them, some twenty-five miles astern of the convoy. The Germans appeared to be working on the port bow of one boat. When the Martlet approached they did not dive but opened fire with their Oerlikon guns. The pilot discovered that the Oerlikons could not fire at above a 70-degree elevation, so he came straight down and shot three men off the plank. The work ceased, the plank was withdrawn, and the two U-boats headed off away from the convoy at slow speed.

Walker sent four escorts out to chase, but they never found the U-boats. Two more U-boats were reported during the day, but the escorts could not find them. At 3:28 the corvette *Marigold* had a contact and dropped depth charges, but without result. Walker decided whatever it was they were firing at, it was probably not a submarine.

By evening it was apparent that the convoy was in the middle of a large number of U-boats and close to the French bases of the Focke-Wulffs. It was evident to Commander Walker that the convoy was going to be continuously shadowed and attacked no matter what, so he decided to take the shortest route back to England.

The commanding officer of the *Audacity* wanted to go to the starboard side of the convoy and work independently for the night. But at this point, Commander Walker could not spare a corvette. He asked the *Audacity* to take position to the port side of the convoy, since he expected the attacks would come from the starboard. But the *Audacity*'s c.o. said no, he wanted to go off, even if alone.

And he did.

Commander Walker decided something special was needed:

> The net of U-boats around us seemed to be growing uncomfortably close in spite of *Audacity*'s

> heroic efforts to keep them at arm's length. I realized that a drastic alteration of course was essential after dark, and decided to stage a mock battle of starshell, depth charges, etc. by *Deptford*'s force away to the southeastward, commencing one hour after dusk.

The mock battle began.

Unfortunately just then one of the merchant ships in the convoy let off a starshell by mistake, which queered the whole game. Then, at 8:30 the starshells went up twelve miles away, and the depth charges could be heard thundering beneath the surface of the sea. It was very impressive, until several of the merchant ships in the convoy also began shooting starshell, which pinpointed the convoy for any submarines around. And Lieutenant Endrass's *U-567* was right there, waiting. With all that lovely light he could scarcely miss, and he torpedoed the steamer *Annavore*, a Norwegian ore freighter, which sank like a rock, leaving only four survivors.

The convoy was in the middle of a turn from 20 degrees to 270 degrees; in spite of the confusion the turn went off nicely. Just then the captain of the ship *Finland* saw a U-boat off to port and tried to ram. But his ship was not quite fast enough and he missed by thirty feet. The surfaced submarine then passed down the line of the convoy and crossed out ahead of the next ship which could not depress its deck gun low enough to fire.

The *Audacity* had left the convoy at 8 P.M. and begun zigzagging, all alone. She was lighted up when those merchant ships started firing starshell in response to Commander Walker's mock battle, and Lieutenant Gerhard Bigalk saw her through the periscope of *U-751*.

Bigalk had been searching for ships all day outside the area of the convoy. His submarine was on its first patrol. It had been driven down by the afternoon air search.

Here is how the whole scene, mock battle and all, appeared to the German U-boat commander.

In the listening instrument I heard screw noises under water and took them to be coming from a convoy. I told myself that I should get to the surface as quickly as possible to see what was actually the matter, so I came to the surface very soon and only a few moments later I saw clouds of smoke, and a few minutes after that I saw the outlines of some destroyers.

Aha, there is a convoy!

We were very glad to have met a convoy only a few days after our departure.

First of all I approached the convoy to see how things were. I discovered a number of destroyers zigzagging wildly and furthest to the left, next to the destroyers, I saw a long, dark shadow, surrounded by several destroyers zigzagging crazily.

Suddenly a wild firing of tracer bullets started up in the east. At this moment my other comrades who were also going for the convoy had probably opened the attack. The destroyers took course for the tracer bullets; the long shadow, which I first took to be a tanker, zigzagged first eastward, then northward, presumably to get away from the convoy. I made for the large shadow immediately, to attack it. Suddenly the shadow turned away sharply and at the same time there was a great firing of rockets from the convoy. The whole area was as light as day. The other U-boats must have been attacking. Ten or fifteen rockets hung over the U-boat as though spellbound. The destroyers nearby also started firing tracer bullets and suddenly I saw in the light of the tracer bullets and the rockets a large aircraft carrier lying in front of us.

Good God! What a chance! An opportunity such as a U-boat commander does not find every day. The whole bridge was wildly enthusiastic.

Now I was in a favorable position for attack. I had to fire. I fired several torpedoes and then came the terrible tension while waiting to see if, or if not, one of them hit its mark.

Then suddenly a fiery detonation aft! A hit aft!

The ship described a semicircle portside, then stopped, unable to maneuver. Apparently my torpedo had smashed her screws. I turned a short distance off to load new torpedoes. Down below in the forward compartment there was a terrific crowding since we had left only a few days before and the forward compartment was full of provisions and all sorts of impossible things necessary for an operational cruise.

My torpedo mate and my torpedo crew worked like mad. We, in the meantime, were standing on the bridge, constantly watching the aircraft carrier, and were terribly excited lest the destroyer should approach and mess up this unique chance.

But apparently the destroyers were furiously busy for way back on the horizon there were bangs and detonations, and tracer bullets were being fired. Our comrades were doing their work.

The torpedo tubes were reported clear for action. Thank God. I made another attack, approaching the ship at a crawling pace so that she should under no account hear me. The water was phosphorescing like mad and I could only proceed very slowly so as not to be discovered by the aircraft carrier, which had stopped. I came nearer and nearer. I don't care any more. I had to get so near that my torpedoes could on no account miss. A gigantic shadow, growing larger all the time!

I had approached so closely that no torpedo could possibly miss, and then I gave permission to fire. The torpedoes left their tubes. Seconds of great tension.

There, hit forward, 20 meters behind the stem. A great detonation with a gigantic sheet of flame. A short time afterwards, another detonation, the middle, again a great column of fire. Hardly had the column of water subsided when a strong detonation was observed forward. Probably ammunition or fuel had been hit. I presumed that petro tanks or something of the kind had been blown up.

> I turned off and in so doing cast another glance at the aircraft carrier. The fore was already flooded and the deck was turning upwards. At that moment destroyers were reported to starboard. They were dashing at top speed towards the aircraft carrier, which was wildly firing distress signals—great stars bursting in the air. I was able to get away from the pursuit. I got a rain of depth charges, but that was of no avail to the English. I escaped.

From the deck of the *Audacity*, the affair had a different look: when the mock battle began at 8:30 the first starshell went up from the convoy, and then the *Annavore* was hit and another went up, so the captain of the *Audacity* knew he was lighted up. He was then about ten miles off the starboard beam of the convoy.

At 8:30 a fitter on the flight deck saw a torpedo approaching from the port side. He started to run toward the bridge to shout a warning, but before he could move the torpedo struck the port side of the engine room. Two white rockets immediately were fired.

The engine room flooded and the lights went out. The confidential books were thrown over the side, and the order was given to abandon ship.

When Commander Walker saw that the *Audacity* had been torpedoed, the *Convolvulus* and *Marigold* were sent to her assistance. These were approaching when they sighted a U-boat on the surface about 500 yards off the carrier. They opened fire.

Aboard the carrier the men on the deck saw more torpedoes coming and lay down on the deck. One hit under the bridge and the other in the ward room, and the deck went up each time. Ten minutes later the carrier sank by the bows. As she went down one of the aircrafts on deck slipped its moorings and plunged down on men in the water causing more casualties.

The escorts chased around, and fired after the fleeing U-boat, but as Lieutenant Bigalk said, it was to no avail. The U-boat escaped.

On December 21 at 10:44 P.M. as the *Deptford* was

moving along the port side of the convoy, she had a contact on her starboard side. She sent up a starshell, and from the bridge the captain saw a U-boat on the surface, closing in on the convoy and preparing to attack. As soon as the U-boat saw the escort, she crash-dived. The *Deptford* then began depth charge attacks on the U-boat. After the third run, which involved just two charges set for 500 feet, the Asdic operator of the *Deptford* heard a double underwater explosion. This must have been the end of Lieutenant Endrass and the crew of *U-567*, taking down another of Germany's most celebrated and most decorated submarine commanders.

Just before midnight on December 21 the escort *Vetch* attacked still another U-boat but without known results. Then at 5:17 on the morning of December 22, the *Deptford* collided with the *Stork*, driving her stem about a third of the way through the sloop's port side. That put the *Stork* out of action as an antisubmarine vessel. She could only make ten knots. The *Deptford* was reduced to eleven knots, nearly all the RDF sets of the escorts had broken down, and the *Audacity* had been sunk. It was hard for Commander Walker not to take a gloomy view of life that day.

But they were coming nearer England, and now friendly aircraft took over what the escorts could no longer handle. A Liberator bomber sighted a U-boat on the surface ten miles off the port bow of the convoy that afternoon, and drove it down. The plane dropped five depth charges. After the last one fell a large upheaval of water was seen and a large patch of oil came up from the deep. It might have been damage to a U-boat. It might also have been a *pillenwerfer*—a device invented by the Germans by which they could fire off an oil canister to make a slick away from their own position and confuse the enemy.

In any event the submarine did not close the convoy.

At 11:15 that morning the usual Focke-Wulff showed up, to remind them that the convoy was still in dangerous waters. The escorts fired on the aircraft, so the pilot stayed off at a respectable distance.

At four o'clock in the afternoon, a Liberator escorting the convoy sighted two U-boats off on the port bow. They both went down and gave no more trouble.

Commander Walker was sure of one thing, he could not continue on a steady course that night and await the attack that was sure to come from those two U-boats. With the resources he had at hand that would be suicidal. There was almost nothing the escorts could do about submarines at night, given their damaged conditions. He decided to stage another little drama. This time he made sure that no starshells would be fired from the convoy's vessels.

At 7:20 the convoy altered course 80 degrees to port. But the escorts *Deptford* and *Jonquil* continued on the course the convoy would have kept had it not turned. Five hours later they staged a mock battle. While they were "fighting" the convoy turned back to its original course.

The ruse worked this time. The convoy was undisturbed during the night, except for one small incident. At 10:20 the escort *Vetch* thought she had a contact and dropped depth charges. The nervous captain of the *Ogmore Castle*, knowing that his escorts were not all they should be and knowing of the ruse, believed he had been torpedoed, and a number of his crew abandoned ship, somehow managing to slip a boat over the side successfully when the ship was moving at seven and a half knots.

When everyone realized that there was no trouble, a search was made for the missing boat. It was found at one o'clock in the morning and then the *Ogmore Castle* rejoined the convoy.

On December 23 the convoy was coming close to England. The escorts *Vanquisher* and *Witch* joined up to give the convoy some real strength again. In the afternoon the *Witch* sighted a submarine conning tower and chased. But the submarine was not found, nor were any others found during the rest of the voyage home. The convoy arrived in England on Christmas day without further incident. It had lost a destroyer and an escort carrier, but only two merchant ships. It had sunk four U-boats, five if you count the *U-127* sunk off Cape Vincent on December 15 by the Australian destroyer *Nestor*, as official British naval historian S.W. Roskill does. That was the sort of exchange Admiral Doenitz could not stand for very long.

The performance of the British escort group in charge of

HG 76 was not generally noted just then on either side of the Atlantic. The attacks on Pearl Harbor and Malaya had brought the Pacific to the center of British and American attention. As Commander Walker prepared to sail, the United States was entering the war. So the success of the protection of Convoy HG 76 went unsung, but Captain Creasy was pleased because Commander Walker had given a show of the enormous expertise the British had now developed in antisubmarine warfare, and had also given a glimpse of the future.

14

The American Station

December's events confirmed Admiral Doenitz's worst fears about the trap of the Mediterranean. Lieutenant Hansmann's *U-127* was lost in the eastern Mediterranean to HMAS *Nestor.* Paulsen's *U-557* was rammed accidentally by an Italian torpedo boat, and all men were killed when the submarine went straight to the bottom. Hoffmann's *U-451* went down under the bombing of a plane from British RAF Squadron 812. Kaufmann's *U-79* and Ringelmann's *U-75* were both sunk in the eastern Mediterranean by British escorts. The Mediterranean, shallow, crowded with ships of too many nations under too many commands, was not a good hunting ground for the U-boats, and the loss of ten boats in December, mostly in this area, proved this fact to Doenitz and to Admiral Raeder. The figures also impressed Hitler, obviously, because some of the pressure on Doenitz was removed. But what made the major change was the official entry of the United States into the war, a development Hitler had hoped could be postponed, but one forced by the Japanese attacks in the Pacific.

From Doenitz's point of view the war status with the

United States was welcome. He was very much aware of the warlike activity of the U.S. naval forces against U-boats, while his own hands had been tied. As of the second week of December 1941, the handcuffs were removed. Doenitz's boys could sink American vessels on sight now. The problem for the admiral was that he had no boats immediately ready for the long-distance run to the American station. The Type IX C 750-ton oceangoing boats were capable of the task, and a patrol life was of about two weeks on station, but some modifications had to be made in matters of fuel tanks, and some rearrangement of the schedule. Hitler still demanded representation in the Mediterranean and the Atlantic around North Africa. Doenitz wanted to remove the boats from the Mediterranean but OKW would not allow it. Since more than half his boats were in dock undergoing repair and maintenance, and the Type IX C boats were new and in short supply, Doenitz could come up with only five suitable boats. The lucky captains were Zapp, Kals, Hardegen, Bleichrodt, and Folkers. They would have first crack at the Americans off their own Atlantic coast. But it would be the third week of December before the first boat could sail, and two weeks more before it could begin operation.

Some of the captains of Type VII 500-ton boats insisted that they also could operate on the far side of the Atlantic although their boats had not been built for such a long voyage. They and their crews were willing to make the sacrifices in comfort and even safety to have the chance. So Admiral Doenitz agreed to give a few of the Type VIIs a chance in the waters of Canada, which was closer to German operating bases than New York by 500 miles.

On January 13, Doenitz unleashed his U-boat attack against America with strikes by five boats operating up and down the Atlantic coast around the 100-fathom curve. They were virtually unopposed; the United States was completely unready for antisubmarine warfare and had no defenses. The largest vessel assigned to the Eastern Sea Frontier, which was the antisubmarine command of the United States, was a 165-foot Coast Guard cutter which had a speed of sixteen knots, a deck gun, and was modified to carry depth charges. There was only one such vessel on the 1,500-mile coast

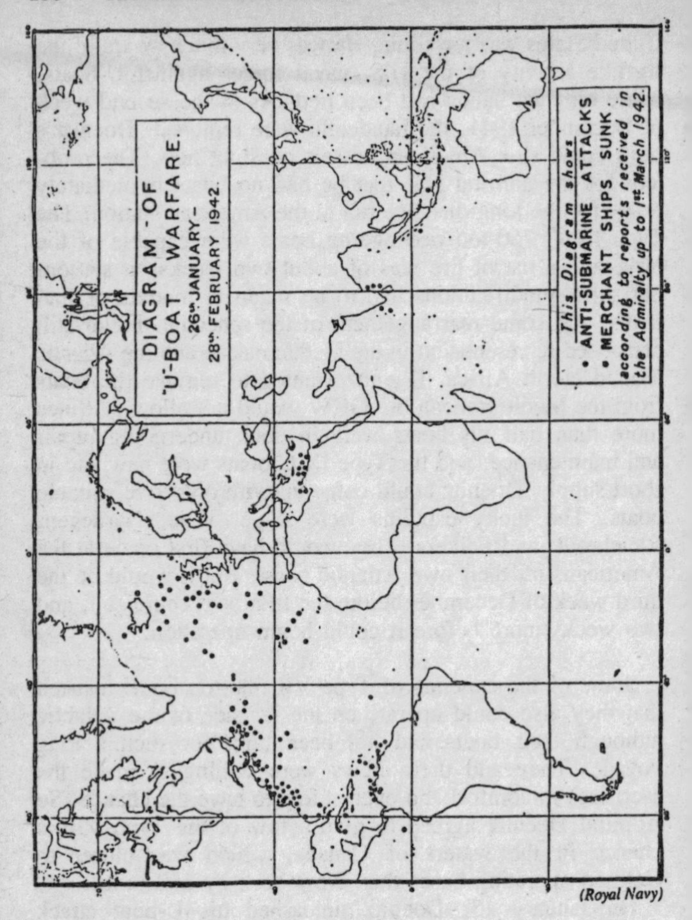

(Royal Navy)

By 1942 the war at sea had moved to the western shore of the Atlantic and the Mediterranean. The greatly increased number of dots indicates the fact: Doenitz's U-boat attack was at its height.

from Florida to Maine. Altogether, the Eastern Sea Frontier had only twenty vessels of any sort, and most of them were too small and too slow to have any effect on U-boats. The U.S. Atlantic Fleet had destroyers (nothing smaller), and the destroyer crews knew the elements of antisubmarine warfare. But the destroyers were part of the fleet, and any use for convoy or antisubmarine patrol was highly restricted because (1) Admiral King did not believe in the convoy system and (2) he intended to keep the Atlantic Fleet destroyers operating with the fleet.

Thus, in January Admiral Doenitz's five lucky U-boat captains all became heroes and returned to Doenitz's command having sunk more than 150,000 tons of shipping in two weeks. Not one boat was even really threatened. The three U-boats lost in January were Schauenberg's *U-577*, sunk by a British plane of Squadron 230 in the eastern Mediterranean, von Fischel's *U-374*, which was surprised by the British submarine *Unbeaten* on January 12 off the east coast of Sicily, and Elfe's *U-93*, sunk on January 15 by HMS *Hesperus* off Malta. Again, the losses were all in the Mediterranean. The *U-93* was a particularly unlucky boat. Lieutenant Opitz, the junior watch officer, had made four cruises aboard her, and, in that time, she had not sunk a thing. On the first cruise he was third officer of the watch. "A damned bad show," he called it. In fact, that cruise had been the subject of a speech by Doenitz to his officers because of the following recollections of Lieutenant Opitz:

> Getting a battleship right in front of your torpedo tubes and then not firing. . . . We sighted a 25,000-ton transport, the battleship *Renown*, and two destroyers in line ahead in broad daylight, coming straight toward us. Everything was ready it was a dead certainty. And a short range too: about 1,000 or 2,000 meters ahead of us. Tubes were ready for action, bow caps off. We could see the enemy's course exactly as they came toward us. They altered course by 10 degrees, otherwise they would have passed right within range of our fire. Our commander didn't see that; he only saw the one destroyer which was on the side, she was still about

800 meters away. Suddenly he saw her coming straight toward us at high speed from the starboard side. He had the periscope out. It was the worst thing that could happen to the boat, to meet destroyers with search gear. The destroyer came at us, we took in the periscope and dived. Everything was ready and then, ,we could hear the search gear and then down came the depth charges . . . then instead of surfacing, the commander remained submerged!

We met a cruiser of the *Leander* class at night. She fired with her guns at us . . . a great shadow looming toward us. Hard over to starboard, utmost speed ahead, stern tube ready . . . dive. We thought perhaps she hadn't seen us yet. Until then, there had been absolutely nothing in sight . . . , a cruiser 2,000 meters away. We were going at utmost speed in front of her. She drew nearer and nearer, and to starboard and to port two shadows bearing down on us. . . . It was the destroyers protecting her flanks. The alarm was sounded. Our knees began to wobble. We submerged and had hardly got down to any depth when the depth charges began to explode. The cruiser passed right over us dropping a pattern of twelve depth charges. Everything in our boat was wrecked. It was terrible! Then after a while she came back again . . . one destroyer remained here . . . and a second one there. The others made off, they'd seen at once that there was a U-boat in such and such position. By next morning we couldn't remain submerged much longer, water had got in. We surfaced, intending if possible, to make a dash for it on the surface in the half-light of dawn. So we surfaced: our main objective was the convoy. We went up into the conning tower. We looked around, and nearly fell down with surprise: exactly 1,000 meters astern of us was a destroyer. The one which had attacked us, lying with her engines stopped.

Our commander again gave the alarm. The first officer of the watch said, "No. We can't do that. If we submerge again we won't have enough air left.'' And so on we chugged slowly through the dawn. Four men watched the destroyer from the conning tower. We hoped she wouldn't spot us. She lay there hardly moving. We looked astern and saw the sun rising. Suddenly the first officer of the watch looked ahead. He just shouted a warning at me and dashed below. We all followed him; we didn't know what was up.

We submerged. About 3,000 or 4,000 meters ahead of us was the convoy and about 2,000 meters ahead was a corvette. We sailed slap into the convoy and it passed right over us. We remained submerged at a great depth and listened: one, two, three depth charges. We did nothing.

The first officer of the watch began grumbling and the commander bawled at him and forbade all criticism. It was his job to decide whether to attack or not. Then we surfaced after the convoy had gone away . . . we tried to find it again.

The first officer, the second officer, a former petty officer, and the chief engineer, the three of them ran the boat together. We ventured to make suggestions, but were shouted down [by the captain].

. . . A Sunderland 500 meters away. We just had time to submerge about 20 meters when a bomb came crashing down right behind our stern. Everything in the boat fell forward, and the whole U-boat shivered. We could just get home. One diesel was still working, but when the engineer finished with that diesel, it failed again. During the night we made one good engine out of the two. One periscope had been wrecked, the mirror smashed. The crankshaft of one of the electric motors had got damaged . . . it kept knocking.

We still had plenty of fuel. We wanted to stay as the convoy was still quite near, but we started for home. Twenty-four hours later we'd already made our report but we got a message from the B.d U [Doenitz] saying ''Go back at full speed after the convoy.'' So we had to go back despite the fact that now we hadn't an earthly chance of catching up with it. Before we got up with them it was time to go home again as we hadn't enough fuel left. We got fired at, too, machine gun fire from aircraft—bullets coming into the conning tower, bombs from aircraft behind and machine gunning at the same time. Salvoes from the cruiser . . .

[Then the *U-93* ran into a new problem.]

It was about midnight and we hadn't seen a thing. We were sailing down much farther south than Gibraltar, clear horizon all the way round, the lookout on the bridge was singing from sheer boredom. We'd been four weeks down south and absolutely nothing had happened. We were sitting on deck having a look around, all of a sudden there was a light, this was at two o'clock in the morning, and the commander shouted from the conning tower:

''Didn't you see something just now?''

''No,'' I said.

''Keep a good lookout for boat signals or something,'' he said.

Has something happened? Have I been asleep? I thought. My lookout point was at the helm. We all scanned the surface again and had just finished when there was a crash.

I jumped automatically over to the port side. I'd scarcely got there when the commander and the chief engineer were on deck.

''We distinctly heard a torpedo,'' they said. ''Someone's trying to torpedo us.''

The whole thing was a mystery. Suddenly there was another crash, again we saw nothing. We made off at utmost speed. The men below insisted they had heard something come swishing past and exploding away in the distance. The floor plates in the control room jumped up.

But there was nothing to be seen, no column of water, nothing at all. They probably saw us in the moonlight, they dived, lay still, let us come on, had a shot and missed.

So the *U-93* got home from that cruise, the captain unnerved. He was more unnerved by Admiral Doenitz's critique of his failures. He did two more cruises after that and sank nothing on either. Then he had to leave. "He was a nervous wreck . . . after sixteen cruises he was absolutely finished."

That skipper was replaced by Elfe, and back to the Mediterranean they went once again, enjoined to be careful and successful. There were always two officers on watch. As Lieutenant Opitz now knew, the Mediterranean was a dreadful place for submarine operations. The phosphorescence in the water was so great that a fired torpedo left an enormous wake. One could even see the propeller wake churning up, leaving a trail after a surfaced U-boat.

On January 15, while the *U-93* was attacking a convoy, she was discovered by HMS *Hesperus*, which launched a persistent attack and sank her. Lieutenant Opitz was a very lucky man, again on the bridge watch at the moment. He went over the side.

> As we got more or less clear, I thought to myself, "Oh boy! You're still alive, you've got away from the whole damned mess."
>
> I struck out with all my strength. Then I looked on the other side and saw a second destroyer coming straight at us. Then the destroyer came through right among us. We were spread over an area of about 50 meters and the destroyer came right through. I take it that some men who couldn't hold out any longer were drowned then. God, how far away she was. Never mind, breathing easily and swimming well, nobody near me now. Suddenly I thought I must be dreaming, for I saw a large shadow, a boat, a cutter, was on the other side. I swam over to her bow and there were two men clinging to it . . .

The war was over for Lieutenant Opitz. Four U-boat patrols, and *U-93* had not sunk a single ship. Those were the perils of the Mediterranean, perils that made Doenitz wish he could withdraw every one of his U-boats from those deadly phosphorescent, shallow waters, and take them out into the deep, green Atlantic where the action was so good on the American side.

Lieutenant Hardegen came home from his first patrol beaming and urging Doenitz to put every boat he had on the American station. He described the ease with which he moved up and down the coast, the city lights that silhouetted the tankers, all those lovely tankers against the shore, the skies that were full of gulls and empty of aircraft. It was a hunter's paradise.

And so it continued in February 1942. The Americans did not have ten coastal defense vessels that could move as fast as a U-boat on the surface. Doenitz was so frustrated by the enthusiastic tales of his captains and his inability to assign Type IX C boats to America that he sent seven Type VII boats off to Canadian waters. One was the *U-85*, under the command of Lieutenant Eberhard Greger. Greger had commissioned the *U-85* on June 7, 1941. On August 6 she had arrived at Trondheim for torpedo practice, during which she was rammed by a destroyer and had to go into dry dock. She finally sailed on her first patrol on August 28. She was one of the U-boats that attacked the convoy SC 42 southeast of Greenland on September 9. Greger fired five torpedoes at the freighter *Jedmoor.* All five were "hot tube runners," which meant they exhausted their power supply without leaving the tube and had to be shoved out to sink to the bottom. Toward evening, the *U-85* came to the surface, and the bridge watch sighted two steamers, one of which was stopped. Doenitz had impressed on Greger the danger of being trapped by a Q-ship, and he was suspicious of this as a trap, so he submerged and moved away.

Greger continued to shadow the convoy, however, and for his trouble was attacked the next day and depth-charged. The boat was damaged, but Greger held on. That evening he exhausted the remainder of his torpedoes against four ships and sank one, the steamer *Thistleglen*. Again the *U-85* was found by the escorts and depth-charged. She made three attempts to surface, but each time she was driven down by aircraft. Early on the morning of September 11 she did manage to surface. The crew worked for ten hours to repair the damage from the depth-charging and then set out for the safety of the base at St. Nazaire. There the *U-85* was laid up for repairs until October 16, which is a good indication of the success in damaging U-boats that convoy escorts sometimes had—a success that was never put into the record books.

The second war cruise of the *U-85* had produced nothing. She found a convoy in heavy weather and lost it again. A Focke-Wulff reconnaissance plane found the convoy again for her, but it was forty miles away, and she had to charge on the surface through a head sea that threatened to drive her under. She had to reduce speed to two-thirds, and then she was attacked by an American long-range bomber. She went down, lost the convoy again, and Greger gave up.

She found another convoy off Newfoundland, but it dispersed in fog, and she got nothing out of it, although another U-boat in the area sank three ships. A valve in the starboard No. 1 cylinder broke and it took twenty-two hours to repair. Greger headed for home, this time Lorient. Obviously Doenitz wanted to see him.

Whatever Lieutenant Greger told the admiral, he managed to clear his skirts, because he did not lose his boat, and it was put in for major overhaul.

In the second week of January, Greger was ordered to the Mediterranean, but then Hitler changed his mind, and freed the boats, so *U-85* was one of those Type VII U-boats sent across the Atlantic as an experiment to operate in Canadian waters.

The *U-85* had a terrible crossing as the diary of Seaman Ungethuem, the ship's baker, shows:

> Jan 11. Aircraft alarm. Seasick. O Neptune!
> Jan 12. Severe vomiting.
> Jan 13. It continues.
> Jan 14. My daughter's birthday. Still sick.
> Jan 15. Weather better. Some of us improving.
> Jan 17. Everyone up and well.
> Jan 18. Sighted steamer but got away in heavy weather.
> Jan 19. Frightful seas.
> Jan 20. Food tastes good again.

On January 21 on the way across, Greger attacked a ship south of Greenland and claimed to have sunk her, but the Allied records did not bear this out. The next day Greger sighted another ship. But the ship she sighted sped away from her and escaped. He came upon another ship lying stopped, again Greger remembered what Doenitz had said about Q-ships, and he broke off his attack and turned away.

Evidently the weather continued to be frightening as they went on station. That seaman's diary again:

> Jan 26. It is getting much colder.
> Jan 28. Below zero.
> Jan 29. Abominably cold.
> Jan 30. The Fuehrer speaks. Off Newfoundland.
> Jan 31. Heavy seas. Barometer rising and falling. We are off New York.

At the beginning of February Doenitz had seen that his U-boats in Canadian waters were not doing anything, so he sent them all down to New York to operate as long as they could. Steering south on February 9, Greger found an escorted Canadian convoy and trailed it. Then along came an unescorted merchant ship, which seemed so much easier, so he left the convoy and trailed the merchantman. She was the 5,000-ton *Empire Fusilier.* Greger attacked, but his torpedo missed, and the *Empire Fusilier* began firing at the submarine with her deck gun. She ran and fought and held the U-boat off for seven hours, but Greger was persistent, and in the end he fired a spread of three torpedoes and one of them sank her.

The *U-85* returned, to St. Nazaire this time, on February 23. She had spent six weeks at sea and had managed more than two weeks on station off North America. Her cruise convinced Admiral Doenitz that the Type VII boats could operate successfully off New York.

The decision was made then that the lucky Greger was to have his chance at a real American cruise, not up in the frozen seas of Canada, but right in the middle of the Happy Hunting Ground, between New York and Hampton Roads.

Greger's *U-85* spent a month undergoing some modifications, to increase her fuel and food capacity, for the 3,000-mile voyage to the United States.

Meanwhile Doenitz's captains were indeed having a field day on the American station. The sinkings for January were 288,000 tons. For February they were 384,000 tons—most of it on the American station. As the end of March neared it was obvious that the sinkings for that month would equal those for the two previous months. For the lucky captains assigned to the American station it was an easy way to make an instant reputation. The number of captains claiming 100,000 tons of shipping shot up week after week, whereas on the British convoy runs through the Atlantic, the U-boats were not having it nearly so easy: Kroening's *U-656* went down on March 1, Mohr's *U-133* seems to have struck one of her own mines on March 14, Gerhick's *U-503* was sunk on March 15, like *U-656*, by aircraft. On March 27 Dumrese's *U-655* fell victim to HMS *Sharpshooter* off Greenland, and Borcherdt's *U-587* was sunk by three British escorts on March 27, and two days later Lohse's *U-585* was sunk in the frozen water off Norway by HMS *Fury* while attacking a convoy on the Murmansk run. Six boats lost in one month, and all men dead in every case. British escort attacks on U-boats had become more ferocious, quicker, and more effective. British use of HF/DF was improving each week. The "hedgehog," a device fixed forward on the deck of an escort, was capable of throwing a half dozen depth charges simultaneously at different angles, fixed to explode at various settings, *ahead* of the ship, which increased the effectiveness of escort attack enormously. Degaussing of Allied vessels worked well against the magnetic exploders; the British had developed Torpex explosive, far more effective than TNT in the depth charges. They were working on a new long-range depth charge thrower called "the squid." Aircraft were getting new depth charges that could be set to explode at 25 feet, thus endangering any U-boat caught on the surface far more than the earlier charges had. No U-boat captain indicated any contempt for enemy aircraft these days. Had it not been for the remarkable successes on the American station Doenitz would have had cause for gloom. But the "happy time" off the U.S. coast gave Doenitz new hopes and brought gloom to the Allies.

* * *

On March 21, Lieutenant Greger's *U-85* sailed from St. Nazaire for the American theater once again. For two days she proceeded submerged, because the British had begun a real campaign to make it hard for the U-boats in the Bay of Biscay. They mined the approaches to the U-boat bases. They sent patrol bombers out to search for submarines heading west. It was not until the *U-85* had been at sea for four days that Lieutenant Greger felt it safe to surface and proceed thus during the daylight hours on the journey west.

In the beginning, the crew enjoyed good weather. For three days the men had virtually a vacation cruise, with sun so warm they could sunbathe on the deck. The sea was as smooth as a mirror and no enemy anywhere around.

But the weather changed. They hit a spring Atlantic storm. They began plowing the heavy seas. The boat pitched and several torpedoes were unseated. One aft damaged one of the electrical motors.

Then, the skies cleared again as Seaman Ungethuem indicated:

> April 4. Cold sea smooth. Baked a big cake. Abominable heat in Gulf Stream.
> April 5. Noon. Magnificent sunshine. Just off America. Thoughts of home.

They repaired the damage to the electric motor as they moved toward America.

> April 7. 300 Nautical miles from land. 660 to Washington.
> April 8. Abominable heat. All stripped bare.
> April 9. Alarm. Only a buoy. Temperature 6 degrees above zero.

(Those last two entries indicate that the U-boat was then on the Great Bank of Newfoundland, near the "cold wall" where the Gulf Stream and the Labrador Current meet, and the temperature can change forty degrees in a few hours.)

On April 10 the *U-85* sank the 5,000-ton Norwegian steamer *Chr. Knudsen*.

At that point, Greger made the decision to leave the 100-fathom curve, where most of the submarines had been operating, and go inshore into shallow water where he was sure the targets had gone. He was quite right, just about the only reasonable defense Admiral Andrews had was to keep his "convoys" close inshore, so they could scud for cover at night. As every U-boat skipper knew, 100 fathoms (600 feet) was barely comfortable depth if an escort got after the boat. But Greger had heard the tales of the other skippers returning triumphantly from the "happy hunting ground," and he was not worried.

> April 11. Off Washington in 164 feet. Cruised submerged.

Lieutenant Greger heard three ships passing, but each time he thought about coming up to attack, he considered the possibilities of Q-ships in shallow water, and he desisted. Finally he decided shallow water was not so good after all, and he headed toward the deeps off New York.

> April 12. Lying on the bottom. All quiet off New York.

On the morning of April 13 the *U-85* was again approaching shallow water off Wimble Shoals near Cape Hatteras. She surfaced south of Bodie Island.

She passed then into the patrol area of the USS *Roper*, one of the handful of destroyers that Admiral Andrews had managed to squeeze out of a reluctant Admiral King. By British standards, the *Roper* was on no business at all; the Royal Navy had given up "patrolling" to try to catch U-boats by 1940, realizing that the effects were minimal as compared to the value of the destroyers in escorting ships. But in this case, the *Roper* had the advantage of being one of so few American defense vessels that the U-boats were careless.

On the morning of April 13, Lieutenant Commander H.W. Howe had his orders for the day: he was to patrol off Wimble Shoals that night. He moved out in the afternoon for the search area.

Just after midnight the *Roper* was cruising in her assigned area at eighteen knots when the radar operator made a contact with an object on the surface at 2,700 yards. Immediately afterward the sonar (American version of British RDF) operator made contact with propeller noises. From the bow of the ship came a hail from the lookout, who reported a wake dead ahead.

Commander Howe increased the speed to twenty knots. The talker called the men to General Quarters. The gun crews of the 3-inch batteries got ready and so did the machine gunners. The torpedomen prepared their tubes. The depth charge crews stood by the Y guns aft.

Whatever was ahead of them was speeding up and taking evasive action. First it swung hard to port, and then immediately afterward, hard to starboard. The destroyer swayed as she followed suit.

Then it was port-starboard-port-starboard . . .

The *Roper* was up to twenty-two knots, and closing. Then from the starboard quarter came a call:

"*Torpedo!*"

Almost immediately the torpedo crossed the wake of the ship, not fifty yards away.

The captain ordered the ship turned hard to starboard, and lit up the searchlight. There in its glare was the surfaced *U-85*.

Then began the chase, the U-boat taking its only advantage, its shorter turning circle, which let the *U-85* circle inside the *Roper*, whose guns could not bear. If Greger could get a little leeway, he could submerge and escape. Meanwhile he brought his gun crews on deck to fight, but the No. 1 machine gun of the *Roper* started firing, and the gun crews crumpled on the deck of the submarine. More men came out of the conning tower. The crew of the *Roper*'s No. 5 3-inch gun found the range and began holing the conning tower. A hit at the waterline brought action. The submarine began to submerge.

Commander Howe could not tell if the U-boat captain was trying to escape by submerging, or if the boat was sinking. The *U-85* disappeared under water, leaving about forty men in the water.

There was a good chance that the *U-85* had escaped, and Commander Howe took no chances. He went through the area dropping depth charges. Unfortunately, some of the charges blew up beneath the German submarine crew in the water, and soon there were only forty bodies and no survivors. The *Roper* moved away then, to safer water, waiting for daylight. At 7:15 the next morning she returned to the scene and found the bodies still floating, and much debris, which indicated that the *U-85* had indeed sunk. Picking up the bodies and examining the materials for naval intelligence, they found Seaman Ungethuem's little diary. The water was very shallow here, and divers were later sent down to investigate the wreck. They found more bodies inside the submarine and not much else of interest. But the Americans had made a start at last. They had sunk their first U-boat.

15

Those Ferocious Escort Groups

In the spring of 1942 the British escort groups were becoming downright ferocious in their assaults on U-boats. On March 18 the British escorts HMS *Keppel*, HMS *Volunteer*, HMS *Badworth*, and HMS *Leamington* were returning from an escort job with an outbound convoy. They were about 125 miles west of Bloody Foreland when, quite unexpectedly, one of them caught a signal from a shore station reporting a U-boat not far to the southeast. They moved that way and soon saw the U-boat on the surface. As they came up, the boat dived. The *Keppel* came up first, found an oil slick, then began an Asdic sweep but found nothing. The *Keppel* then dropped a pattern of ten depth charges on the oil streak, set to explode at various depths from 150 to 300 feet.

Four minutes later the captain of the *Keppel* noted a splash not far from the depth charge disturbances, and he attacked again. This time he got an Asdic contact. The other three escorts came up and soon were attacking. They dropped 139 depth charges, and HMS *Keppel* made one hedgehog attack. That U-boat captain was a good one, he got away. But the ferocity of the attack was something new, and something the U-boats were now having to learn to live with.

April was a very good month for Admiral Doenitz. In exchange for three U-boats (Greger's *U-85*, von Ravenau's *U-702*, which simply disappeared, and Lerchen's *U-252*, which fell to Commander Walker's Escort Group 36) the Germans took half a million tons of Allied shipping.

May cost the U-boat force four more boats: Heinsohn's *U-573*, Friederich's *U-74*, Rathke's *U-352*, and Preuss's *U-568*. But again, the results were enormously satisfactory: the sixty-odd boats that Doenitz had in operation sank over 600,000 tons of ships.

To counter the Allied advances in antisubmarine warfare, Admiral Doenitz had the German advances in submarine warfare, improved direction finding equipment, improved German radar, and above all, the emergence of the "milch cow" submarines, the huge undersea tankers that carried fuel and torpedoes for the boats at sea, thus enabling Doenitz to expand his activities in the Caribbean, the South Atlantic, and the Indian Ocean.

June 1942 was another very productive month for the U-boat force, with 627,000 tons of shipping sunk, in exchange for Fraatz's *U-652*, Henne's *U-157*, and Rostin's *U-158*.

And yet, in this month when U-boat sinkings hit that new high, Doenitz had cause to worry. In the United States shipyards were turning out shipping so quickly that in order to keep up Doenitz had to sink 700,000 tons a month. And Hitler did not seem to understand the seriousness of the problem. Hitler kept diverting the boats, to the Mediterranean and the waters off Norway. Also, the British were improving their antisubmarine weapons quite rapidly. For example, the Leigh aircraft light was now perfected. On the night of June 3, a black Wellington bomber of Squadron 172 went out on an antisubmarine patrol, using one of the Leigh lights. At 1:44 on the morning of June 4 it made contact with a submarine at a range of six miles on the starboard bow. The plane circled and closed, and when the range was one mile the pilot switched on the searchlight. The beam illuminated the U-boat dead ahead, three-quarters of a mile away. The bomber came down to 50 feet and dropped four 250-pound depth charges, set at 25 feet. They fell 35 feet apart. Three of them exploded, straddling the U-boat. The plane circled, and then found another U-boat, turned on the light, and the gunner shot up the conning tower with machine gun fire. Both boats were badly damaged. A new technique had been found to harry the U-boats as they moved in and out of the Bay of Biscay.

During June Doenitz moved more U-boats back into the Central Atlantic. Several convoys were attacked, and ON 100 lost four ships en route from the United Kingdom to North America, but that was not the worst. The story of Convoy HG 84 shows what the British were up against on the Gibraltar run, which went right by Doenitz's Bay of Biscay door, and also something of another new weapon the British had now perfected for convoy protection: Huffduff.

Convoy HG 84 set out from Gibraltar for the United Kingdom in the second week of June. Commander Walker was in charge of the defense of HG 84, twenty-three ships in seven columns with four escorts and a new addition: the rescue ship *Copeland*, which was equipped with Huffduff, the triangulation system for locating the source of high frequency radio transmissions.

The convoy was trailed by Focke-Wulff aircraft almost from the outset. The *Empire Moon* was equipped with a catapult and a Hurricane fighter, and when the bomber came back the second time the Hurricane was flown off and managed to put two bursts into the Focke-Wulff before the enemy escaped into the clouds. The Hurricane then ditched, and the pilot was rescued by Walker's ship HMS *Stork*. It might seem an expensive way to protect a convoy, but those aircraft did deter the enemy.

At 4:10 Walker had a message from the *Copeland*: the Huffduff had picked up a U-boat transmission on the port quarter. With the coordinates in hand, Walker's *Stork* took HMS *Gardenia* to investigate, leaving HMS *Convolvulus* in charge of the convoy. At 5:10 Walker sighted the U-boat, on the surface to the northwest, ten miles off. The *Stork* chased and overhauled the U-boat slowly, but when it was still seven miles away it dived.

Commander Walker:

"*Stork* promptly altered 20 degrees to port with the object of inducing the quarry to go northward and on reaching the probable U-boat area, zigzagged across it in a southeast to northwest direction searching with Asdic. This proved to be a lucky practical shot at a nasty theoretical problem. Contact was gained at 7:51 P.M."

The hunt then began. The U-boat changed course every few minutes and changed its speed and depth. The *Stork* and the *Gardenia* attacked with depth charges and by 9:30 had carried out nine attacks using ninety depth charges. In *Gardenia*'s fourth attack one charge exploded prematurely at twenty feet, carrying away the ship's ensign and damaging the stern of the ship. *Stork*'s depth charge supply ran down to only eighteen depth charges, and Walker decided to get back to the convoy since it was nearly dark, and he left the *Gardenia* there to keep the U-boat down.

Gardenia stayed on, dropping charges until she was down to five. Then she maintained contact with the U-boat, keeping it down, but not attacking. She remained in the area until 1:30 the next afternoon, and then finally lost contact with the U-boat. But, in effect, the escorts had won the round: that particular U-boat was no longer a menace to the convoy.

Meanwhile, as Commander Walker was steaming back to the convoy, *Copeland* passed to the escort *Marigold* a Huffduff bearing of a U-boat on the convoy's starboard bow. The *Marigold* altered course, and half an hour later she came upon the U-boat with its conning tower showing, eight miles off.

HMS *Marigold* chased the U-boat at seventeen knots and overhauled it. She began firing her guns and twenty minutes later the U-boat dived. The corvette made three attacks with depth charges, then lost contact, and turned to rejoin the convoy.

At 8:45 *Copeland* passed to *Convolvulus* a Huffduff bearing of a U-boat directly ahead of the convoy. Twenty-eight minutes later the U-boat was sighted ten miles ahead. HMS *Convolvulus* chased the boat away until it was out of sight.

So, by midnight three U-boats had approached the convoy, and all had been attacked, but none had been sunk. Only one of them managed to get back through the screen, Erich Topp's *U-552*. At 1 A.M. Topp moved up on the starboard side of the convoy and fired a blunderbuss spread of three torpedoes. He was extremely lucky: in rapid order they hit the freighter *Etrib*, the tanker *Slemdal*, and the freighter *Pelayo*, which was the commodore's ship. All three ships sank so rapidly that they did not fire starshell or send radio messages. Commander Walker saw the ships torpedoed, however, and swept around to the starboard side of the convoy to find the submarine, but he was unable to make contact. He sent the *Marigold* astern to fire starshell and snowflake, lighting up the sky, to fool the U-boat into believing the convoy had turned. Then the *Marigold* and the *Copeland* stopped to pick up survivors of the three ships. The convoy went on. At 2:30 the *Stork* was two and a half miles astern of the convoy when the RDF operator reported a contact. A wake soon came into view, and then the submarine dived and turned to starboard. The *Stork* attacked. A loud explosion was heard, but no definite claim could be made. The *Stork* rejoined the convoy.

At 2:35 the *Marigold* was picking up survivors when she had an RDF contact five miles away. She chased and when she was two miles off she saw the U-boat, which then dived. The *Marigold* attacked with depth charges until she lost contact. Then she escorted the *Copeland* back to the convoy.

Lieutenant Commander Topp, meanwhile, had gone ahead and lay in wait for the convoy to come up again. It did, and he fired another spread of torpedoes. This time he hit the steamers *Thurso* and *City of Oxford*. Both sank. The *Stork* carried out a sweep, first astern and then on the starboard quarter, but found no trace of the U-boat.

The *Marigold* and *Copeland* were coming back with their loads of survivors from the first group of ships torpedoed. They stopped and picked up survivors from these two other ships. In all, 176 survivors had been picked up, perhaps two-thirds of the crews of the five ships.

At 7 A.M. a Catalina flying boat joined the convoy and flew over until 3:15. At 11:45 the *Marigold* was transferring survivors to the *Copeland* ten miles astern of the convoy when her lookout sighted a U-boat eight miles off. She chased, but the U-boat dived, and her depth-charging did not sink it.

A Lancaster bomber came out to meet the convoy and found a U-boat dead ahead of the convoy, three miles out. The U-boat dived, and the Lancaster dropped six 250-pound depth charges set to explode at 25 feet. Streaks of oil were seen in the swirl, and a column of water was seen about three-quarters of a mile away. The U-boat conning tower came up, and the Lancaster dropped a 250-pound antisubmarine bomb, which exploded twenty seconds after the conning tower disappeared. It hit twenty yards to the port of the swirl. Another oil patch appeared. It seems likely that the Lancaster's bombing did serious damage to this U-boat.

At 4:50 the *Stork* was given another Huffduff bearing and went out to investigate. A Liberator and a Lancaster came out, and Walker turned the job of searching for the U-boat over to them and went back to the convoy. The Lancaster sighted the U-boat on the surface about five miles off the starboard quarter of the convoy, obviously coming in to attack. When the bomber was still three-quarters of a mile away the U-boat dived. The Lancaster dropped six 250-pound charges to explode at 25 feet, on the track 25 yards ahead of the swirl. When the explosions had subsided a thick patch of oily scum appeared. That was all. The Liberator patrolled around the convoy out twenty miles. At 11:18 P.M. a U-boat was sighted on the surface two miles from the convoy. The Liberator dropped six depth charges set shallow just ahead of the swirl. Another oily patch came up.

The convoy turned to a course 60 degrees to the right of the one it had been following, because so many U-boats had been sighted that day. Walker expected a lot of trouble. At 2:46 on the morning of June 16 the *Convolvulus* sighted a U-boat on the surface four miles on the port bow. *Convolvulus* began firing starshell and then fired on the boat. It dived. The ship chased and got an Asdic contact that guided her to a ten-charge run. The *Convolvulus* then returned to station off the convoy. At 4 in the morning the course was changed again, and no more U-boats were seen.

At 10:30 on the morning of June 16 a Focke-Wulff showed up, and then another joined it. They hung around until 1 P.M. The *Stork* fired a few rounds of antiaircraft shells, and the German bombers went away. Three more escorts joined the convoy that afternoon, and it was covered all day long by Catalina and Sunderland aircraft. In planning for the night, Walker observed that the Focke-Wulffs had known their position as of 1 P.M. The Admiralty that afternoon warned that there were five U-boats in the vicinity of the convoy. The large alterations of course to port on the preceding nights must be known to Doenitz. Adding up all these details, Walker decided to go straight for home, and that was the course set. It was a wise one, for the convoy passed a peaceful night.

On the morning of June 17 the *Stork* developed troubles with her condensers and had to reduce to convoy speed. As a fighting ship she was out of it. Several escorts came and went, including the *Wild Swan*, but the net result was a strengthened escort. All day long the convoy had air cover, but that night it had air visitors. A flight of twelve Ju 88 aircraft came out to bomb the convoy. They found the *Wild Swan*, which was heading back to harbor, as she was moving through a group of Spanish fishing trawlers. The Germans evidently mistook the trawlers for Convoy HG 84 and bombed. Four trawlers sank. They also bombed the *Wild Swan* until she sank, but not before she had brought down four German bombers and caused two others to collide and crash. A hundred and thirty-three survivors were picked up by HMS *Vansittart*.

A Focke-Wulff appeared over the convoy that night at 10:20, but no air attack developed. The next morning the convoy was in the Western Approaches and had air cover all day long. There was no more trouble. Although the convoy had lost five ships, the defense had been quite remarkable. The problem was that the convoy had to come past the Bay of Biscay submarine bases, and that she had been trailed by at least eight submarines on the passage. Lieutenant Commander Topp had been extremely skillful in his attacks on the convoy. Here is Topp's story, as he broadcast it on July 17, 1942, from Radio Luxembourg:

> We had just put to sea from Western France, our course set for the Caribbean, when we met a convoy on our doorstep, you might say. Escort vessels forced us aside and tried to make us submerge; they were very clever. We succeeded in keeping in touch with the convoy throughout the day and directed more submarines to it. Towards evening the convoy made a wide detour, while we stuck close and fired all our tubes, as a result of which two freighters were torpedoed and one tanker blew up. With that the convoy came to life and fired everything it had, Very lights, flares and starshells illuminating everything as though it were daylight. Destroyers and corvettes made a dash for us, but owing to the very unfavourable weather, we were able to shake them off without, however, losing touch with the convoy. In the meantime the torpedo tubes had again been made ready for action. We moved slowly towards the convoy and fired one tube after the other. Three short detonations and three more freighters had been torpedoed [au. note: two]. Utter confusion came upon the convoy [au. note: anything but, Commander Walker maintained perfect convoy discipline all the way]. The enemy had not expected this new attack [au. note: see text]. Destroyers moved about wildly,

partly to pick up survivors, partly to chase the submarines which appeared to be attacking them from all sides . . .

But the fact was that Lieutenant Commander Topp was the only one to get through the cordon. Commander Walker had maintained perfect convoy discipline, and all the other seven boats had been driven off, some with substantial damage. The performance of the escorts, low key, watching their flock and not charging off after submarine contacts, was precisely the sort of performance the Americans had to learn.

For in the spring and early summer of 1942 the great losses again were among ships sailing independently, and the Americans were slow learners about the importance of convoys.

Even so, for the Allies July was the best month of the year so far. One reason: the American defenses were beginning to shape up. Doenitz recognized that the invocation of American convoys meant the system was going to grow, and even as he kept his boats on the American station, he planned for future operations and looked for new weak spots. He would have to transfer his major operations elsewhere.

If he needed proof of what was happening, the story of *U-701* provided it:

On July 7 the *U-701* was cruising off Cape Hatteras. Despite the high number, she was a Type VII boat, built by the small Stuelkenwerft yard. Her captain was Lieutenant Horst Degen, who had been highly recommended to Doenitz and trained on a cruiser by Lieutenant Commander Erich Topp, now one of the top scorers of the German U-boat team. On her first patrol the *U-701* had met with indifferent success in the Western Approaches. On her second patrol she had worked the Iceland area, without much success either. Now she was on her third war patrol. Her change in orders showed that Doenitz had recognized the ending of the "happy time" along the U.S. coast. *U-701* was to lie low, stay on the bottom on her station during the day, and wait for single steamers.

Degen followed Doenitz's orders to the letter, and once again they proved how ingenious the submarine admiral was, and how he used the resources at his command. For *U-701* went on station early in June, she was refueled at sea by a "milch cow," and she was still on station on July 7 off Cape Hatteras. Doenitz might have only a dozen U-boats operating on the American station, but their ability to refuel and rearm at sea made them worth twice as many to the admiral.

On June 6 Degen sank the patrol craft *Kingston Ceylonite* and the freighter *Santore*, and damaged the U.S. destroyer *Bainbridge*, and also damaged tankers. On June 19 he sank the U.S. patrol boat YP 389. On June 26 he damaged the freighter *Tamesis*, and on June 27 he damaged the tanker *British Freedom*. On June 28 he sank the tanker *William Rockefeller.* Then pickings grew slimmer as more and more ships moved in convoy and more and more planes came overhead. Planes were the real problem, they kept the *U-701* on the bottom during most of the daylight hours.

On July 7 the submarine spent almost the whole day on the bottom. By midafternoon the air was so foul that the men were laboring to breathe. Degen decided to chance it and surface. He came to periscope depth and looked around. He saw nothing. He surfaced and as the conning tower came out of the water the men began pouring up, and as the decks cleared, they were out, taking great gulps of fresh air. But then out of the sun came on American Lockheed Hudson bomber, of No. 59 Squadron, on antisubmarine patrol. The lookout saw it very late. Degen hustled the men back down and crash-dived. The bomber was on them, and the first depth charge fell just twenty-five feet short. The second and third were right on target, in the stern, and tore open the pressure hull. In a minute water was pouring into the control room, and she was going down. Degen blew the tanks and she started up again, and he opened the conning tower under water and seventeen of the crew and the captain managed to get out before she sank. The captain remembered swimming upward forever before the dark turned to light and he struggled to the surface.

The pilot of the bomber, Lieutenant Harry J. Kane, dropped four life rafts and then looked around for help for his enemies. He found a Panamanian freighter and gave the position, but the Panamanian freighter went on. Its captain was not going to stop to rescue "goddamned Germans in submarine infested waters."

The survivors clung together in the water, buoyed by their life vests. They never got to the life rafts, which had been dropped too far away. They drifted in the Gulf Stream. It was not so bad at night, but the next day the blazing summer sun was at them all day long. The engineer officer, Lieutenant Bahr, went mad and screamed half the afternoon. He finally choked and sank. Lieutenant Bazies and Ensign Lange decided to swim for shore. They set out and were never seen again. Machinist's Mate Gunter Kunert said they had to stick together. He held the captain's head in his arms. Ironically they were saved from terrible sunburn by the oil coating the surface of the sea—oil from the tankers they and other U-boat men had torpedoed in the past few days.

One by one the survivors died in the heat. The captain lapsed into delirium several times; his men saved him. They drifted sixty miles in the Gulf Stream. On the third day they were sighted by a Coast Guard patrol bomber, which landed and picked them up. Seven men were still alive.

The Americans were learning fast. Lieutenant Kane's approach out of the sun had been everything it ought to be. That month eleven U-boats were sunk, most of them in the Americas, and two of them by American aircraft. The next month the American aircraft sank more. The convoy now was totally accepted, and Captain Creasy had convinced the American navy that dealing with U-boats was not a job for heroes but one for sloggers. The forces had converged: the July sinkings were accomplished by escorts, British, American, and Canadian bombers, and by bombers and escorts working together, a new, deadly combination.*

July also brought a diminution in sinkings, although Doenitz now had 330 U-boats, 140 of them in operation. On the American station, losses went down to 192,000 tons,

---

*Down had gone Hoeckner's *U-215*, von Rosenstiel's *U-502*, Reichmann's *U-153*, Degen's *U-701*, Zimmermann's *U-316*, Heinicke's *U-576*, Bigalk's *U-571*, Oldoerp's *U-90*, von Varendorff's *U-213*, Vogel's *U-588*, and Ostermann's *U-754*.

and overall to 350,000 tons. Doenitz now found that convoys in American waters had made them far less inviting than during the first six months of the year. In July Doenitz's boats going west were mostly heading for the Caribbean and Mexican coastal waters around Tampico and Corpus Christi. Half a dozen boats were sent east of Trinidad and another half dozen to the Freetown area. German U-boat activity in the Mediterranean was sharply reduced; half a dozen U-boats were operating there, but in July they sank only five vessels, and one of them was a 43-ton sailing vessel. The Italians were pressed to increase their activity in the area, but they had their difficulties, too, because British antisubmarine warfare in the Mediterranean was becoming more effective.

On July 9,1942, the Italian submarine *Perla* was on her way to a new base at Leros. The boat was filled with the personal belongings of the crew, stowed in racks like those in a British railway carriage. That day the submarine attacked the British steamer *Manchester City* between Haifa and Beirut. Later in the day she came upon the British corvette *Hyacinth* and fired two torpedoes. The *Hyacinth* evaded by turning hard to port, and they missed by twenty yards astern. The *Hyacinth* then went back to follow the tracks of the torpedoes and made contact at 1,000 yards with a slowly moving object. She dropped six depth charges set between 100 and 150 feet. She then made another attack with depth charges set deep—350 feet—and a third run, wherein they were set deeper—500 feet. After the third run a conning tower came up 80 yards away.

The gun crews of the corvette then began firing. After four minutes an officer was seen peeping around the conning tower of the submarine and waving a white shirt. A boarding party went off to take the surrender, and the boat was towed into Beirut harbor.

Two days later the South African ships *Protea* and *Southern Maid* left Beirut for Cyprus, and at two o'clock in the afternoon they encountered the Italian submarine *Ondina*. She dived and passed under the *Southern Maid* and opened her bow torpedo tubes. The *Southern Maid* launched a depth charge attack, which so damaged the tubes they could not be closed. Water began pouring into the forward torpedo room, and the submarine sank to 250 feet before the diving officer could trim her up. The *Protea* made a second attack. The explosions rolled the submarine completely over, gear broke loose in the galley, and leaks were started. Watertight doors jammed, and the air mechanism went out. The boat stopped. Another depth charge attack loosened the jammed doors, fractured the bedplates of the port engine, and caused water to come in aft. The main trim tanks burst. Chlorine began to spread through the boat, and the crew panicked. The diving officer brought the boat up, the hatch opened, and the men began pouring out. The boat was captured but she was virtually a wreck. In the Atlantic HMS *Lulworth* sank the submarine *Pietro Calvi*, too. July was a bad month for U-boats in general, the Italians as well as the Germans.

In July Doenitz decided to transfer the main attack back to mid-Atlantic where the convoys were still beyond the range of land-based air cover from Britain or from Iceland. Starting in July, he was getting thirty new boats per month, and he was ready to return to the wolf packs.

16

Battle of the Atlantic—New Phase

In the summer of 1942 Admiral Doenitz paid the Americans and their British teachers the honor of moving away from the American shore into mid-Atlantic for his major assault, proof positive that the "happy time" for the U-boat warriors had ended. From this point on, in spite of the increase in size of the U-boat force, sinkings of U-boats would rise constantly. If at war's outbreak, with about fifty boats, Doenitz felt he could only lose two per month without undue concern, he had been forced to change his thinking.

In July 1942, with three hundred boats in service, he lost eleven. In August, he lost nine. This was not 1 percent loss but over 3 percent. The losses were easier to accept because the U-boat force had changed. At the outset of war the U-boat force had been a tight-knit organization. This was no longer true; Doenitz could not feel the same personal camaraderie with his captains as in the past. Once the command post on Dead Man's Lane in Wilhelmshaven had been the exact heart of the U-boat service. But now, with headquarters in Paris, and later in Berlin, the key officers as far as the captains and crews were concerned were the flotilla commanders. Only occasionally could Doenitz be at Lorient or St. Nazaire to shake the hand of a departing captain or to welcome a victorious crew. The war at sea was a bigger, grimmer business than it had been three years earlier.*

After Admiral Doenitz resumed his attention to the transatlantic convoys, Convoy ON 115 was the first to be hit by the U-boats. The time was August 1942. ON 115 was en route from the United Kingdom to North America. Courtesy of *B-Dienst*, the radio intelligence agency in Berlin, which had again broken the British naval codes, Admiral Doenitz had the messages about ON 115's sailing, and its routing, and these were sent out at the first of the month to the U-boats operating off the North American continent. The U-boat was the *U-210* under the command of Lieutenant Commander Rudolf Lemcke, who had been serving in the navy since 1940 but in destroyers until very recently. The story of Lemcke's previous naval career tells a great deal about the problems of the U-boat service in the summer of 1942.

Lemcke was a career naval officer. By 1940 he had attained the rank of lieutenant commander in destroyers, and he participated in the Norway invasion. One night at Narvik he was assigned to supervise an antiaircraft battery ashore, and while making his rounds of the guns he found a young machine gunner asleep at his post. The penalty for sleeping

*From this point on, the loss of U-boats increased so greatly almost every month (forty-one boats sunk in May 1943, for example) that it is unwieldy to try to deal with each boat in the text. See Appendix for official U.S. count of individual sinking listed by month.

on duty at the front was death. Lemcke gave the youngster a choice: he could be reported officially, and everyone knew what would happen. Or he could accept a flogging (illegal) and the matter would be forgotten. Gratefully the young man took the physical punishment. But the story got out; Lemcke was court-martialed, reduced to the rank of ordinary seaman, and sent to the navy's penitentiary at Hela for three months. Before the war that would have been the end of Lemcke's career. He would have been given a dishonorable discharge and probably would have ended up as a seaman on a German tramp steamer, barred forever from promotion to officer's rank. But in the war officers were needed by the navy. At the end of his three months Lemcke was assigned to the most dangerous duty: seaman on a minesweeper. After three months' probation he was promoted to sublieutenant, then to lieutenant. Scouring the lists of young officers the personnel men of the U-boat corps came across his name and noted his excellent service record until the Narvik affair. In the spring of 1942 Lemcke was brought in and offered a U-boat command, and he accepted quickly. He was almost immediately assigned to *U-210*, a brand-new boat. He found that not more than a dozen men of his crew had any previous service in U-boats.

There were so many new men! No wonder Doenitz warned the German people to expect heavy losses; most of his commanders and crews were going out on their first patrols. Brand-new boats with brand-new skippers and brand-new crews: Doenitz had instituted a new sort of training, called *Agru Front*, in which several officers and men were inserted into the crew with the specific purpose of serving as a "fifth column," creating difficulties that the captain and his men had to overcome under sea conditions. Sometimes these could be quite frightening, as the occasion on which one of the "fifth columnists" set the diving planes of *U-210* at 50 degrees, so that when the captain ordered dive, the boat started down like a stone. But even after the *Agru Front* course was passed the men managed to make troubles of their own. Once the diving officer let the pressure rise too high inside the boat, so that when she surfaced and the captain opened the conning tower hatch, he was catapulted onto the bridge and banged his nose. Another time, the machinists started the diesels without opening the intake valves, and the men of the engine room crew felt their eyes popping out of their heads before the vacuum was relieved by opening the intake.

But finally, Admiral Doenitz's training officers indicated that the *U-210* was ready by the navy's new standards to go to sea, and on July 17 she was at Kiel prepared to go out and participate in the new campaign against England. As with all the new boats, an officer from Doenitz's high command came aboard to wish the ship good luck.

"My friends," he said, "you can be proud of yourselves. you have the privilege of sailing on patrol but we must stay behind. You are now under the direct command of the admiral's U-boats. You are one of his grey moths that dot the ocean. We wish you the very best of luck." Then they all sang "We're Sailing Against England," and the officer went away. The next day *U-210* left Kiel and passed through the minefields, then up through the North Sea, by the Faroes, and toward Iceland.

On July 25 the boat was kept down most of the day by aircraft. The captain headed toward Central America. But on the morning of July 29, he sighted Convoy ON 115. He reported to Admiral Doenitz and was told not, *repeat not*, to attack, but to await the coming of other U-boats. For a new skipper Lieutenant Commander Lemcke did himself proud; he managed to keep in touch with the convoy for forty-eight hours, while Doenitz rushed his experienced captains to the scene. They included three of the "Star Turn" captains who had sunk at least 100,000 tons of shipping, and two others.

When the other boats had assembled in the area, then Doenitz gave the signal to attack. *U-210* was not even in the action on the morning of July 31. She was sighted almost immediately by an escort and driven down. Another of the U-boats was sunk here, so *U-210* was lucky. Another of the "new boys," Lieutenant Hardo Rodler von Rothberg, in the *U-71*, attacked a freighter on the evening of August 2, but his torpedoes missed. Lieutenant Commander Topp found the convoy the next day, and his *U-522* damaged the tanker *G. S. Walden* and sank the steamer *Belgian Soldier.* The *U-53* also sank the big motor ship *Lochkatrine*. It was tribute to experience. But then the air cover and coming of more escorts saved the rest of the convoy, for it was very close to the North American coast. Doenitz learned from that, and in the future he would attempt to line up his attacks so the westbound convoys were first hit just as they left the Western Approaches and the eastbound were hit south of Newfoundland. That sort of attack would mean the wolf packs could trail the convoys all the way across and would have the advantage of the broad stretch of no-man's-land where the air cover did not exist. This factor was a key to Doenitz's attack pattern of the summer.

The next convoy found by Doenitz's radio intercepts was SC 94, a thirty-ship convoy, which sailed from Sydney, Cape Breton, on July 31. Five escorts took the convoy out to the edge of the coastal zone, and there it was picked up by six sea escorts led by HMS *Primrose*. The convoy was troubled by fog, which delayed the joining up of another element, but finally on August 3 HMCS *Battleford* brought three more merchant ships up from St. Johns, and then the convoy numbered thirty-three. They did not know it, but their departure, course, and speed were all known to Admiral Doenitz, and he was already moving his submarines up to intercept as close to the edge of the great air gap as possible. The *U-210* was informed, and Lieutenant Commander Lemcke headed for the position indicated by his admiral.

At 6 P.M. on August 3 the convoy altered course in the fog. The commodore's ship, *Trehata*, signaled the change by whistle, but the escorts *Nasturtium* and *Orillia* and six merchantmen did not hear the sound and continued on the old course. Next morning when the fog lifted HMS *Dianthus* was sent out to try to find the erring ships but did not. Again in the evening two escorts tried to find the missing eight ships, but to no avail. At noon on August 5 a radiogram from the *Orillia* reported its position as thirty-three miles south of the main convoy. HMCS *Assiniboine* was then sent out to collect the miniconvoy and bring it back. The convoy turned onto a course to converge with the smaller group, and the six ships formed up in two columns with the two escorts on the sides. But if anyone needed a lesson they got it just before 5 P.M. The SS *Spar*, the lead ship in the outside column, was torpedoed by Lieutenant Gerd Kelbling's *U-593* and went down almost immediately. Kelbling also fired a torpedo at another ship in the miniconvoy, but the *Nasturtium* sighted the torpedo track, and the whole group turned to starboard, and the torpedo missed. The *Nasturtium* then made a blind attack with a trail of depth charges and stopped to pick up thirty-six men and one dog from the *Spar.* The *Orillia* watched over the little convoy, altering course, and when the *Nasturtium* joined up, they led the five ships back to the main convoy.

The *Assiniboine* was six miles away when the *Spar* was torpedoed and she hurried up to the area. At 7:20 that night a large splash near the wreck was seen and the *Assiniboine* hurried up. All she found was bubbles. This might have been from the submarine diving to escape the escort. She hung around the site of the wreck for a while and then set course back to join the convoy. She had some bad news: the smoke of the convoy was clearly visible on the evening of August 5 for thirty miles.

On the morning of August 6 the weather was clear but overcast in mid-Atlantic. Visibility was eight miles. The convoy was steering northeast with the six escorts to port and starboard. At 11:25 *Assiniboine* saw something on the horizon on the port bow of the convoy. Her captain informed the *Primrose*, and the *Assiniboine* was sent off at twenty-two knots to investigate. Soon the object was identified as a U-boat conning tower. The U-boat immediately altered course and moved at high speed on the surface to get away. The *Assiniboine* steered slightly to starboard of the U-boat so that if she dived her captain would be inclined to turn to port, and fired three salvoes from the escort's guns. The shooting was too good for the U-boat captain, who dived, and turned to port, as the skipper of the *Assiniboine* had hoped. This narrowed the area of search, and the *Assiniboine* moved in. Meanwhile the *Dianthus* had been ordered to help out and she came up and the two escorts organized a search pattern. At noon they found the submarine and began dropping depth charges. They lost contact with the submarine then, and began to search to the north.

At 5:12 P.M. a U-boat was sighted six miles off, but it disappeared in the fog a few minutes later.

The *Assiniboine* turned toward the point where the U-boat was last seen and informed the *Dianthus*. They searched until 6:36 when a U-boat was sighted on the surface. This was *U-210*, an entirely different boat than the ones—two or three others—that the escorts had encountered earlier. Lemcke had been lying stopped on the surface, believing himself protected by the fog, when the *Assiniboine*'s RDF picked him up. He had immediately gotten under way and disappeared in the fog. But the *Assiniboine* came up to the last position and turned on her RDF. She circled and it was not long before she came in contact with the U-boat again and then sighted it quite close, at less than 1,000 yards. The *Assiniboine* began firing on the U-boat and the captain elected to stay on the surface and fight rather than submerge. Later, his crew said he could have gotten away if he had dived just then. But Lemcke said no. Here is the story, drawn from the report of the captain of the *Assiniboine* on the action and from the survivors of the *U-210*:

U-boat crew:

The destroyer came on us out of the fog. Captain Lemcke was on the bridge. If he had dived just then we would have gotten away. But he said he could beat them on the surface. He began turning the boat to get inside the destroyer's turning circle and beneath her main armament.

Destroyer captain:

It was impossible to depress the 4.7-inch guns sufficiently at this range, but I ordered them to continue firing, more to keep the guns' crews busy while under fire than in any hope of hitting. One hit was gained on the conning tower, however.

During most of the action we were so close that I could make out the commanding officer on the conning tower bending down occasionally to pass wheel orders. A gun's crew appeared on deck and attempted to reach the forward gun, but our multiple .5-inch machine guns successfully prevented this.

U-boat crew:
We could not man the forward gun but we could and did use the machine guns on the bridge and raked the destroyer's bridge with incendiary bullets, setting it on fire. (One man was killed and thirteen were wounded.) Then the destroyer backed on one engine and got her gun into play. Two shells hit the conning tower and killed every man on the bridge, including Captain Lemcke.

The first lieutenant then took command. He was badly shaken and wounded besides. Even though the conning tower was wrecked and the air intake valves damaged, he gave the order to dive.

Destroyer captain:
Three or four times we just missed him. The officers left the conning tower in order to dive and in the few seconds during which he was on a steady course we rammed him just abaft the conning tower. He was actually in the process of diving at the time.

U-boat crew:
We were struck on the starboard quarter and the water began to come in aft. So at 15 meters the first lieutenant recalled the order to dive and brought the boat up again. There we lay stopped. The diesel engines were soaked and would not start.

Destroyer captain:
I turned as quickly as possible to find him surfacing again but slightly down by the stern, still firing and making about ten knots. After a little maneuvering we rammed him again well abaft the conning tower and fired a shallow pattern of depth charges as we passed. Also one 4.7-inch shell from Y gun scored a direct hit on his bows. He sank by the head in about two minutes.

U-boat crew:
By this time the first lieutenant had become incapable of command. The engineer officer ordered "abandon ship" and the crew went up on deck through the forward hatch. It

was the only hatch that was not jammed. There was time for the radiomen to destroy the secret papers and to smash the radio with a hammer while the engineer officer and a chief petty officer opened a seacock and put an explosive charge in the periscope shaft.

Destroyer captain:
Dianthus appeared out of the fog just in time to see him go. The yell that went up from both ships must have frightened U-boats for about ten miles in the vicinity.

U-boat crew:
At 7:14 P.M. the *U-210*, which had never fired a torpedo except in practice, sank.

While the *Assiniboine* had been chasing the *U-210* the *Dianthus* was chasing another submarine, but her RDF was out of action, and she decided to give up on that job and rejoin the *Assiniboine*, particularly because her captain could hear the sounds of the guns firing. She moved in to pick up survivors as did the *Assiniboine*. A number of them shouted "Heil Hitler" as they came aboard. The *Assiniboine* and *Dianthus* then set course to rejoin the convoy. One U-boat down.

On the way back at 11 P.M. the *Dianthus* sighted another U-boat on the surface about twenty-eight miles from the convoy. The U-boat was only 1,000 yards away, and the *Dianthus* set course to ram, increasing to full speed and manning the guns. One round from the 4-inch gun was fired, but the effect was to blind those on the bridge of the corvette. The U-boat dived just in time to avoid ramming, and *Dianthus* turned into the swirl and dropped depth charges. The boat must have been one of the 1,600-tonners, because the captain of the *Dianthus* said that she was much larger than anything he had ever seen before. He reported to the *Primrose*, and then stuck around the area and continued to attack. The last contact was made shortly after midnight, and then the contacts faded out as the U-boat apparently went deep. At least that is what one of the seamen from the

U-210 told the men of the *Dianthus*. After that, nothing. The *Dianthus* waited in the area, listening, until 7:30 that morning and then set out to rejoin the convoy.

While the two escorts were attacking submarines, the convoy was moving ahead, changing course several times. At 6:14 on August 6 a conning tower was sighted by the *Primrose* seven miles from the convoy. Two escorts chased and the U-boat dived. By the time they reached the position where it had dived visibility was reduced to about a half mile. No contacts were made, and the captain of the *Primrose* had to assume that the U-boat had surfaced and escaped in the fog. He brought them back to the convoy.

At 9:15 that night the *Orillia*, which was on the port bow of the convoy, sighted a U-boat through a clearing in the fog, only about two miles away. It was lying beam on with decks awash, stopped. Apparently the captain was waiting for the convoy to come up so he could attack. The *Orillia* turned and increased to full speed, and the submarine dived. The *Orillia* came up but made a bad attack because someone on the bridge gave the wrong course, and the U-boat got away. Twenty minutes later a periscope was sighted as the *Orillia* was moving parallel to the convoy. Or so someone reported. At this point periscopes were being seen "all over the place," said the captain, who was not very pleased. However, an echo was found in that area, and an attack was made. The captain of the *Orillia* was not convinced that very much of it was real. He returned to the convoy.

At 9:05 astern of the convoy the *Nasturtium* obtained an RDF contact. She turned to follow and soon the Asdic operator heard torpedo noises. The ship turned, and the torpedo passed ahead of her while she was turning. *Nasturtium* continued the sweep but found nothing and returned to station on the convoy. The night thereafter was quiet for Convoy SC 94, until after midnight.

In the first hours of August 8 the convoy screen was reinforced on the starboard side as more light was to be expected from the north. At 2:52 the *Orillia* had a contact and attacked with ten charges. Nothing happened. At 4 A.M.

Nasturtium picked up a contact three miles off to starboard. This persisted and turned out to be real. *Nasturtium* followed and found the U-boat going steadily to the left, trying to get around ahead of the escort. At 4:28 a wake was sighted. Ten minutes later the *Nasturtium* fired a starshell and saw the U-boat. Then the submarine dived. The *Nasturtium* picked up an Asdic contact and attacked. In the next four hours the escort dropped fifty-one depth charges on eight runs. Several times the escort lost contact and made it again. Then the contact was finally lost and not found again. The *Nasturtium* rejoined the convoy.

As of the afternoon of August 8 the score was: one merchant ship sunk, one submarine sunk, at least three other submarines attacked. But at 1:25 that ratio altered rapidly for the worse. The *U-176* got next to the convoy and fired three quick torpedoes. So did Lieutenant Commander Rudolf Kettner's *U-379* at almost that same moment. The result was spectacular: the commodore's SS *Trehata* was the first ship hit. Next was the *Kelso*, then came the *Kaimoku*, the *Anneberg*, and the *Mount Kassion*. All but the *Anneberg* went down immediately, the *Kaimoku* with an intense explosion that indicated an ammunition cargo. The noise and the confusion were so great that the crews of the *Empire Moonbeam*, *Empire Antelope*, and *Radchurch* all abandoned ship, thinking that they, too, had been torpedoed. It was easy to think so in the situation that existed: the *Cape Race* suffered propeller damage from the concussions.

When the crews of *Empire Moonbeam* and *Empire Antelope* realized that their ships were safe, shamefacedly they went back aboard. The captain of the *Radchurch* had remained on board and he tried to get his crew to come back. But the ship was carrying a highly inflammable cargo, and the example of the *Kaimoku* was very vivid in the eyes of the men. They refused to board. The *Radchurch* had to be abandoned and when last seen was drifting as sea, just waiting for a submarine. (The next day she was found by *U-176* who sank her under the impression that it was a coup de grace shot at a wounded ship.)

The vice commodore of the British convoy in the *Empire Scout* now took over the management of the merchant ships.

The *Primrose* sighted a puff of smoke from the diesel engines of the submarine and headed for it. By the time it reached the position the submarine had dived, but a contact was made with the Asdic. The *Primrose* attacked, but the depth charge rail mechanism jammed, and there was no positive result.

The convoy had turned and was now bearing down on the U-boat, a situation any U-boat captain would envy. The *Primrose* then devoted her energies to turning the convoy away from the U-boat. The *Nasturtium* went out to look around, then came back and picked up survivors. The *Battleford* also helped in this task. The *Orillia* swept down the port side of the convoy and screened it. The *Chilliwack* remained on station, on guard.

At 7:10 that night, the coxswain of the *Dianthus*, on duty aft, sighted a conning tower not far from the convoy. Before the report could be confirmed by anyone else a rain squall intervened, but the captain altered course anyhow, and thirty minutes later the U-boat came in view, steering northeast. The U-boat was the *U-379*, which had sunk the *Kaimoku* and the *Anneberg* earlier. The *Dianthus* began to chase. At 8:45 two U-boats were in sight, six miles off and quite close to each other. The starboard boat went off east. HMS *Dianthus* tried to indicate the position to HMS *Broke* whose smoke she saw, but the *Broke* was too far away and could not respond. *Dianthus* went after the second U-boat, firing until the boat went down at a point six miles away.

When the *Dianthus* fired, one shot fell within a yard of the conning tower and scared the officer on watch into diving immediately. This happened just before 9 P.M. This was precisely what *Dianthus* wanted; now she had a boat slowed by being under water and could go after it. At 9:26 she reached the diving position and began a sweep. An hour later the *Chilliwack* joined up, but *Dianthus* sent her back to the convoy, because her captain was half sure he had lost contact. But he did continue to search.

Down below, the hydrophone operator of the *U-379* detected the presence of the corvette and reported to the captain. But Lieutenant Commander Rudolf Kettner said he did not hold with such things as hydrophones. There was nobody up there. The hydrophone operator was talking nonsense. The operator then threw down his headphones in disgust.

Dianthus continued to search. At 10:24 there was still no action, but *Dianthus* swept back to the original position. There she found the U-boat, on the surface. As indicated by the hydrophone incident, this captain was a real character. Here is the assessment of his crew, as gleaned by naval intelligence:

> He must have been the only man who ever tried to make life in a U-boat tolerably comfortable. Once he closed a supply U-boat merely because he wanted some fresh water to wash in. He was called each day at 8 with a cup of coffee, but did not get up until it was time for luncheon, spending the morning in his bunk, dozing and listening to the radio. After luncheon, having eaten well and had plenty of sweets, he had another hour with the radio, followed by a couple hours of sleep. When he woke up, at about 4 P.M., he had a cup of coffee, and then really got down to things, spending the next three hours at his paper work. The crew were ordered to pipe down while he was busy.
>
> At 7 P.M. it was time for dinner and he restored himself with a substantial meal, which was followed by some more music; he then went to his bunk for a short rest before going on watch at midnight. During his watch he'd kept up his strength with snacks consisting of tinned asparagus, coffee, cakes, and beer, not leaving the bridge until 1 A.M. He then put on pyjamas and retired for the night leaving strict orders to be called at 8 A.M. . . .

The *Dianthus*'s long search was finally rewarded with a strong contact. The corvette attacked, with five charges set shallow. The first burst so close to the U-boat that the entire crew was deafened. They could not tell where the rest of the pattern exploded. But at least one must have exploded underneath the U-boat, for it was thrown upwards and most of the switches, gauges, and the lights were put out of action. No water entered but the boat popped to the surface.

The captain fumbled. The engineer officer ordered the tanks blown. The captain hurried to the conning tower and bumbled with the hatch. A petty officer opened it. Kettner led the way out. The *Dianthus* turned to ram, switched on her searchlight, and began firing every gun that would bear.

The captain of the *Dianthus* tells what happened next:

> The U-boat sank after ramming four times and firing seven rounds of 4-inch, 100 rounds of pom-pom and several belts of Hotchkiss. Target was well illuminated by searchlight and snowflakes. Pom-pom was highly effective. At the fourth ramming the U-boat's bow lifted and struck *Dianthus* on starboard side of forecastle.
>
> These 19 minutes between the surfacing and sinking of the U-boat can be described as very lively and gave our crew the opportunity for which during the whole commission they had striven so hard.
>
> Immediately the U-boat sank, the First Lieutenant and the Chief Engine Room Artificer made a survey of the damage and commenced shoring up whilst every attempt was made to pick up survivors. In spite of bringing one of our prisoners on to the bridge to urge his countrymen in the water to swim alongside, it proved a slow process; they only appeared capable of shouting.

The last seen of Lieutenant Commander Kettner, he was swimming about around the sinking submarine, asking who had got his life jacket.

Just before 1 A.M. having picked up only five survivors, the *Dianthus* left the scene, dropping a Carley raft. The presence of that other submarine in the area was not very comforting; the survivors, if there were more, would have to shift for themselves. All that ramming had caused some mighty leaks, but they were shored up and by three o'clock the next afternoon the *Dianthus* was back in position with the convoy.

HMS *Broke* had meanwhile arrived to take over from the *Primrose*, since the captain of the *Broke* was the senior officer present. Unfortunately he did not seem to know his business very well. At midnight another submarine attacked the convoy and fired two torpedoes at *Broke*. They missed but in the excitement the *Broke* botched its job, got out of position, and the U-boat got clean away. Seniority sometimes was a problem in the convoy system.

On the morning of August 9 Liberators came over the convoy and escorted it all day long. *Dianthus* was having a terrible time keeping up, taking water forward constantly from the damage caused to her bows in the rammings. At 5 P.M. Catalina flying boats joined the Liberators, and one sighted a U-boat on the surface steering for the convoy. The Catalina approached, the U-boat dived, the Catalina attacked, oil patch was seen, but not the U-boat. It was not seen again. At 6:08 another Liberator found another U-boat and at 11:20 still another, which she attacked with six charges. The U-boat disappeared.

On the morning of August 10 the Polish destroyer *Blyskawica* was found to be missing. No one knew what had happened to her. A U-boat was sighted near the convoy, and two escorts attacked with no conclusive results except that the U-boat did not attack the convoy.

But at 10:23, *U-660* and *U-438* found the convoy, and in quick succession they torpedoed four ships on the starboard side: the *Condylis*, *Empire Reindeer*, *Oregon*, and *Cape Race*. The *Condylis* swung to starboard and was immediately hit by another torpedo on the port side. The *Oregon*, out of control, rammed the *Cape Race*, and half an hour later she exploded. The *Cape Race* sank. So did the others. A hundred and seventeen survivors were picked up by *Dianthus* and seventy-seven by *Nasturtium*. Only eleven lives were lost.

Except for the fiasco of the *Broke* that night, the conduct of the escorts had been unexceptionable. During the rest of the daylight hours of August 10—until nearly 11 P.M.—the convoy was covered by Liberator and Catalina aircraft, which sighted four U-boats and managed one good attack. The U-boat probably got home again, but it also probably was laid up for repairs for a while. Another air attack that evening was not so effective, but again it prevented the U-boat from closing the convoy. At about the time the aircraft left the convoy two more RDF contacts were made ahead, which meant two more U-boats. But by changing course, the convoy managed to stay away from them and passed a peaceful night.

On the morning of August 11 the escorts were very short of fuel, so the senior officer decided to leave the outer screening to the aircraft. The Polish destroyer showed up, having been bothered by condenser trouble and having dropped back to make repairs. The convoy was getting close to England, and four local escorts showed up at 6:30 on the morning of August 12. They took over, the ocean escorts headed for port, and the convoy reached England without further casualties on August 13. England had to be unhappy about the score of SC 94 and Doenitz was pleased. For the score stood at two U-boats sunk and ten merchantmen lost. With Doenitz's U-boat force standing near 350 and rising at the rate of 30 a month barring attrition, that was not the sort of ratio the British could long bear. Perhaps Doenitz would have to live with a loss ratio of 3 percent. By extrapolation Doenitz would be getting more than his 700,000 tons a month, and that way lay tragedy for Britain.

17

The Noose Tightens

By the end of 1942, several developments had changed the course of the U-boat war. The escort carriers were almost ready to begin operations, which meant the wide Atlantic gap where there was no air cover could be closed. To match that Allied development, the Germans now had many Type IX C long-range Atlantic boats and a number of "milch cow" tanker submarines to supply them. Allied air expertise had improved, but so had German radar and sound detection. The Germans had a search receiver that could pick up British RDF transmissions. They had perfected a device known sometimes as "*das zweite U-boot* [the second U-boat], *S-geraet Vertilger*" (Asdic obliterator) but most often as the "*pillenwerfer*," or pill thrower. There were several variations. One consisted of a charge of six pills, which produced an "Asdic target" lasting about six minutes. Another consisted of a charge that moved at high speed for several hundred yards emitting a noise like the electric motors of a U-boat. A third form produced an oil bubble intended to give aircraft the impression that a submarine had sunk here.

B-Dienst continued to break British sea codes and give Doenitz valuable help, but *B-Dienst* could not prevent the invasion of North Africa in the fall of 1942, and that changed the war again, by giving the Allies new bases in the Mediterranean and adding an American presence that meant more planes.

The big change of that late autumn was there in the Mediterranean, as the Allies seized their first real initiative of the European war. Nor did *B-Dienst* have any idea of the one greatest plus the Allies had: the breach of the German master war codes and the ability to read the most important German messages. Long after the war, when the Enigma story began to emerge, one U-boat officer said ruefully that he believed this was the greatest single factor in the defeat of the U-boats.

But intelligence alone could not win wars, as Doenitz knew because *B-Dienst*'s breach of the British naval codes had not wiped out Allied shipping. The weapons and the men were all important. In this Doenitz had advantages and disadvantages. His technicians were perfecting new submarines, particularly the Walther U-boat, powered by a hydrogen peroxide engine. But the crews of each boat were younger and less experienced than before; Doenitz had to live with the problem of too much too soon.

The naval war did not go well for Germany in the last

months of 1942. Hitler had backed the "superbattleship" concept, and it failed. Finally he decided the navy was an enormous waste of money, and in January 1943, Admiral Raeder resigned, and Admiral Doenitz was appointed commander in chief of the German navy.

In January, the Germans were putting the finishing touches on Dr. Todt's enormous U-boat pens. Lorient and La Pallice were long finished. St. Nazaire and Brest, each of which would accommodate two flotillas, were nearly finished, and Bordeaux was half-finished. When the submarine pens were under construction, they were very vulnerable but ignored by the RAF. Now that it would be of no use, the Allies decided to expend thousands of tons of bombs on submarine pens. Dr. Todt had done his work well. For the next three months the Allied bombers would hit the submarine bases in France, and *not one bomb* would disturb a U-boat inside.

As January 1943 began, Doenitz increased the concentration of U-boats in the North Atlantic until there were thirty-seven boats lurking around the edges of "the Greenland air gap," that part of the Atlantic where it was still impossible to provide air cover for the convoys.

Since the middle of 1942 increased emphasis had been placed by the British Admiralty on the formation of groups of antisubmarine vessels trained to operate under an experienced senior officer, and to operate with aircraft support. In the fall of 1942 the first such permanent group was established, but it had to be cut up a few weeks later because of the extreme need for escorts in various parts of the world. In the fall of 1942, Commander Walker, the most experienced and most successful of the escort group leaders, was promoted to captain and made captain of destroyers at the Western Approaches center at Liverpool. He began shaking up the antisubmarine training program, putting each antisubmarine team through a series of tests and training programs to improve the incidence of sinkings rather than simple sightings and depth-chargings. He had at his disposal HMS *Graph* (the old *U-570*), which obligingly pretended to be a U-boat again for purposes of training. The escorts were sent out to "sink" the U-boat. To do so they had to "hit" with at least one depth charge. But *Graph* was not enough for the job; soon Captain Walker had six submarines masking themselves as the enemy, in order to improve the marksmanship of the escort captains and their crews.

The idea of the large, highly trained support group was never far from his mind. In the winter of 1943 Walker had more vital business, but he was still working on the other program.

January opened with dreadful weather, and unluckily for the U-boats it remained that way most of the month. Since the British were primed for a major increase in the violence of the attack on the North Atlantic convoys, they started out the month with evasive convoy routing, and that worked well.

But as always, when frustrated even temporarily in one direction, Doenitz moved his chess pieces swiftly in another, and the story of Convoy YM 1, bound from the Dutch West Indies to Gibraltar with desperately needed petroleum fuels, was an indication of what Doenitz could now do in the U-boat war.

Convoy YM 1 consisted of nine tankers in five columns, protected by Escort Group B.5, under the commanding officer of HMS *Havelock*. The other escorts were the HMS *Pimpernel*, HMS *Godetia*, and HMS *Saxifrage*. All were equipped with RDF and the *Havelock* also had Huffduff. The convoy sailed on December 28 under air cover of Catalina flying boats. The U-boats found the convoy on the morning of December 29. A Catalina reported a U-boat twenty miles astern of the convoy and attacked with depth charges and a mouse-trap bomb thrower (the American equivalent of the hedgehog). The submarine dived. The escort *Godetia* went to the spot and searched, without success.

For the next three days, the convoy had no difficulty; Doenitz was waiting until the ships got outside the air cover zone and into mid-Atlantic. On the afternoon of January 3 the Admiralty let the convoy know it was being shadowed by U-boats.

One of the new techniques of the Allied ocean escort was fueling at sea, and this was practiced on this convoy. It meant the trough method because of the weather, spilling oil between the vessels to keep the sea down. This, in turn, was giveaway to the enemy, but since they were under surveillance anyhow it was an easy trade-off.

So, during the daylight hours, the fueling went on. At night the convoy closed up.

On the night of January 3, HMS *Havelock* obtained an Asdic contact about 5,000 yards ahead of the convoy. Then an RDF contact was made at a different location, and the original was lost. The *Havelock*'s captain decided he must have an old wreck. Ten minutes later he changed his mind: the tanker *British Vigilance* was torpedoed and went up like a match. The U-boat had come in on the surface, 400 yards on the port bow, torpedoed her, and run the gauntlet down the ship's side and around the stern. Every gun in the convoy that could fire opened on her, but she skidded away into the dark. The *Empire Lytton* tried to ram, and missed by only 20 yards. She also claimed two hundred hits with her Oerlik guns at a range of between 100 and 300 yards.. Certainly part of the story must be accurate, because the *U-514* did not again bother this convoy.

The convoy was not troubled again that night. Escorts picked up the captain of the tanker and twenty-six of the crew, without incident. Next morning a U-boat was reported not far away but not found. In the afternoon the Admiralty sent another message indicating that Doenitz was moving boats around to trail, but the convoy commander changed course from the original routing, because he wanted to get into calmer water for fueling, and thus Doenitz's messages from *B-Dienst*, tapping the British codes, did not help. The convoy was out of touch with U-boats until the evening of January 8. At this time it had passed into the zone where air cover could not be supplied.

At 9:35 on the evening of January 8 the *Havelock* attacked a submarine on the surface, quite close to the convoy, and speeded up to ram. The submarine dived. The *Havelock* dropped depth charges. But while she was doing so, another U-boat, the *U-436*, fired three torpedoes, and two of them hit the *Albert L. Ellsworth* and the *Oltenia*. The *Oltenia* broke in two and sank. The *Albert L. Ellsworth* dropped out of the convoy.

Five minutes after the torpedoes were fired the *Havelock* found a submarine on the surface 1,000 yards away, just about to submerge. She attacked, and heard explosions, but that was all. At the same time the *Pimpernel* found a submarine on the other side of the convoy by RDF and steered toward it, and then saw it on the surface and attacked. The U-boat dived, the *Pimpernel* attacked with depth charges and heard a loud underwater explosion. The contact then faded out. The escorts were back with the convoy by 2 A.M. An hour later the *Pimpernel* made contact with a U-boat on the surface, and got a bearing 155 degrees, 1,400 yards. But this soon faded away, and the *Pimpernel* resumed station. Evidently the convoy was being trailed by a number of U-boats that were moving around testing.

This went on all night long. The *Empire Lytton* was torpedoed. At 5:15 the tanker *Minister Wedel* was torpedoed. Both remained afloat. Then the *Norvik* was hit. The *U-522* had not been lucky, her third torpedo had missed another ship entirely. The *Havelock* went after the submarine with depth charges, but gradually lost contact and returned to the convoy. Meanwhile the captain of the *Saxifrage* had dropped back to confer with the captain of the *Empire Lytton*, which could still make six knots in spite of the torpedoing. But the convoy could not spare an escort to care for her alone and she clearly could not keep up. The crew of the *Empire Lytton* was taken off and she was left for the time being. *U-442* came upon the drifting tanker the next day and sank her.

At 2:15 on the afternoon of January 9 the convoy had another U-boat contact. The *Pimpernel* chased, but found nothing. Six minutes later the *Godetia*, chasing a contact, saw a U-boat fire a torpedo, caught sight of the air bubble as it went, saw the periscope turning and watched the torpedo run 1,500 yards toward the convoy. The tanker *Vanja* turned hard aport and the torpedo missed. The *British Dominion* saw a submarine come down her side and fired on it. The periscope passed along *Godetia*'s side, and she dropped seven depth charges, saw oil come up, and then lost contact. So many U-boat reports were coming in at this point that all escorts were chasing, and none were guarding the convoy. The captain of *Godetia* realized this and broke off his attack and took position on the convoy again.

On the afternoon of January 10, the convoy commander estimated that one U-boat just then was right on the convoy, four more were within easy striking distance, and five more were around the area, coming up. Even so, no attack was made until dusk when a submarine fired several torpedoes, all of which misfired. At 7:23 the *Saxifrage* had an Asdic contact and attacked a submarine, but the attack produced nothing, and the escort rejoined the convoy. Half an hour later a flashlight was seen off the convoy, and it was evident that at least two U-boats were in contact out there.

The fifth attack on the convoy came just before midnight on January 10. The *British Dominion* was hit by three torpedoes on her port side by *U-522*. By the light of her fires the *Vanja* sighted a U-boat 300 yards away and she opened fire, claiming many hits on the conning tower. At least three more U-boats were sighted in the next few minutes; the escorts charged them, the U-boats dived. The *Godetia* had a contact, made an attack, and heard an explosion. But she found nothing else. All the escorts then rejoined the convoy, but for the rest of the night, they made sudden darts out to the side, a mile or two off the convoy. Perhaps that was why the convoy was not attacked again that night. Then came day, and the Australian escort *Quiberon* joined up, and so did covering aircraft for the first time in days. The two remaining tankers of the convoy had seven sea escorts all the rest of the way to Gibraltar, and no further contact with submarines. Doenitz was keeping them where it counted.

By the time the convoy arrived, the full extent of the losses were known. The British had sent tugs and escorts back to pick up the torpedoed ships that were still afloat, but Doenitz's scavengers had been very thorough and all the cripples were sunk. The convoy's final loss was seven of the nine tankers that had sailed. The destruction of YM 1 gave the highest percentage loss in convoy suffered from U-boats so far in the war. In analyzing the defeat, the Admiralty's submarine experts made much of the failure of RDF equipment on two of the escorts, and also of the failure of the four escorts to discover the presence of the submarines until late, and then their failure to launch aggressive attacks in time. But the Germans were now enjoying some of the technical fruits of their own experts, and they were able to detect the escorts much earlier than before, and to break off and escape more easily. But the real problem for Convoy YM 1 summed up the whole difficulty of the British in this winter of decision. There in the Atlantic air defense gap, the convoy had been beset by no fewer then eleven submarines, and if the U-boat captains and crews were not trained as had been those early ones whose names had now become legend, so, too, was it true that the British escort service was digging deep into the manpower pools, bringing up reserve skippers (RN) and hostilities-only-officers (RNVR). What the officers and men of the YM 1 escort group needed was a course at Captain Walker's school. But the problem was: could they be spared from convoy duty long enough to get it?

18
Weeks of Decision

When all was said and done, January 1943 had not been a bad month for the British in the North Atlantic. But if Admiral Doenitz could not control the weather, he could put out ever more boats, and that is what happened in February. It was evident to the British that Doenitz's staff was exercising absolute control over the U-boats, the signals came so frequently that no mistake could be made. The admiral had retained his personal control of the U-boat force even after his selection as commander in chief. He took his U-boat staff to Berlin, as part of the headquarters staff. Rear Admiral Godt, his former chief of staff, became in name

Admiral, U-boats, with Commander Hessler as his chief of staff, but Doenitz was in daily contact, and the organization was very much as it had been before.

The U-boats also had a new approach: they did everything possible to get out ahead of the convoys and wait for them, then attack submerged. That way they could avoid the unpleasantness of detection by the constantly improving British RDF. Convoys were the main points of attack in February.

Convoy HX 224 was a fast convoy, which sailed from North America on January 29.

This eastbound convoy was one of the largest yet: fifty-eight ships in fourteen columns covering fifty-two square miles of sea. It had seven escorts, led by HMS *Highlander*, but *Highlander* had been separated from her old escort group, and this new one had been put together in an enormous rush.

The weather was terrible, and on the night of January 30 it blew a gale, causing a dozen ships on the port wing to heave to and finally to leave the convoy. Just before three o'clock on the afternoon of February 1, Lieutenant Commander Teichert's *U-456* found the convoy, but since it was still within the area covered by aircraft no attack was made then. But as night came, so did the U-boats. At 8 P.M. the *Highlander* estimated that two U-boats were in contact with the convoy. Since it was a moonless night with a high sea running, the escort commander did not anticipate an attack, but it came at 1:15 on the morning of February 2 in a blinding sleet storm; Teichert torpedoed the rear ship in the port outside column. Two escorts were sent out, but the U-boat escaped in the storm.

U-456 continued to shadow and wait for opportunity, but stayed off the convoy until 8 P.M. on the night of February 2. Five U-boats were found then, by RDF and Huffduff. One on the starboard bow closed in to attack, but the escort *Restigouche* attacked her and forced her down and away from the convoy. At 1 A.M. on February 3, in another rainstorm, Teichert again attacked, this time torpedoing the rear ship in the center column. Then, as in the first attack, the U-boat sped off at high speed away from the convoy.

The Huffduff bearings now indicated that three U-boats were around, all on the port side of the convoy. At 3 A.M. the escorts illuminated the whole area with starshells and snowflake, and the expected attack did not materialize.

All this while Teichert had played the role of shadow to the convoy, working on the windward quarter, but closing frequently to check the convoy's course and speed, and sending a high-speed transmission to Doenitz's headquarters, and then dropping back again. The U-boat was still there on February 3. The convoy commander decided to try to trap this boat. The commodore was asked to alter the course of the convoy 20 degrees at 5 P.M., the time the air escort quit for the day, and then to alter back five hours later. Two escorts were ordered to make a sweep astern starting at 9:45, to keep the U-boat down and prevent it from observing the course change. Just before 10 P.M. the *Highlander* heard Teichert make his first report—announcing that he was going to approach the convoy and give course and speed. Simultaneously *Highlander* had a report from one escort that it had gained an RDF contact near the position where *Highlander* had anticipated the U-boat would surface. The two escorts attacked and believed they had done damage. One, the *Londonderry*, was damaged by a torpedo, but not sunk. The shadowing U-boat disappeared, and the convoy arrived in England on February 5 without further incident. Thus one innovative convoy commander had made a big difference in the war against the U-boats.

It did not always work this way, not by far. The U-boats took SG 19 for one ship on February 3; and then met SC 118 on February 5. Doenitz and his staff knew all about SC 118, from messages intercepted and translated by *B-Dienst*. This convoy had sailed from New York with airplanes and other vital war materials bound eventually for Murmansk and the Russians. Because of the deteriorating situation on the Eastern Front, Hitler had very strong feelings about sinking ships bound for the USSR, and Doenitz turned to with special effort. A dozen U-boats were directed to the area where Convoy SC 118 was supposed to be found. The question that worried the command at Lorient was whether or not the British would follow the route laid out in the messages, since HX 224 had been attacked on that same route a few days earlier. They knew the convoy was supposed to do that, because a U-boat had picked up a survivor from one of the HX 224 victims, and he had said as much. They had to hope that the British would assume the route was now clear of U-boats. And that is what occurred. The convoy ran smack into the center of the U-boat patrol line on February 4. More than twenty U-boats made contact with SC 118 in the next six days. They sank nine ships, and the British claimed three U-boats sunk and at least seven damaged. The Germans knew that *U-187*, *U-609*, and *U-624* were sunk, but claimed that only four were damaged. Whatever the case, Doenitz later referred to this encounter as "perhaps the hardest convoy battle of the whole war." The British felt much the same, and they took this occasion to make a few points about it.

Admiral Sir Max Horton had assumed command of the Western Approaches in the fall of 1942. That was one reason Captain Walker was up in Liverpool; Horton was an old submariner who agreed with Churchill that the U-boat had to be conquered and very soon. The new intensity of the anti-U-boat campaign is indicated by what happened *after* SC 118 arrived at Liverpool. In the old days the escort commander would submit his report and it would be examined and filed. If someone at the Admiralty thought it necessary or useful to comment, a letter would be written. No more. The escort captains of SC 118 went to Captain Walker's office for a meeting, and the whole conduct of the convoy was gone over in detail. The purpose was not to rake anyone over the coals but to discover what could have gone better than it did, and why. In this case, the escort commander learned that he should have been at the back of the convoy instead of leading it so he could keep track of all ships falling out and all activity; his captains learned that they would have done better to keep the commander informed of all important incidents and any deviation from his last instructions; the captains also had to learn to be more aggressive any time the convoy was attacked. The U-boats had to be scared. And finally, the commander had to learn to exert a total control on the number of escorts sweeping, chasing, rescuing, or screening, particularly since it was in the blood of a naval man to get into action when it seemed to be indicated.

That was the sort of postgraduate training the escort groups were getting. It was paying off.

On February 17, 1943, the *U-69* sighted the convoy ONS 165 east of Newfoundland. *U-201* joined up. So did *U-403* and *U-525*. The latter two U-boats sank one ship apiece. The British destroyer *Fame* sank the *U-201*, and the destroyer *Viscount* sank the *U-67*. Two for two was the sort of statistic that made Doenitz shiver.

The outward bound convoys took a beating in February. On February 18, again in a storm, the *U-67* found the convoy ON 166, about a day and a half out of the Western Approaches, heading west. Doenitz ordered two wolf packs to the scene. The first arrived and attacked on February 21 off Cape Clear. In the next four days the convoy lost twelve ships and one destroyer. There was a difference: twelve submarines were involved, and no one U-boat sank more than two ships. Doenitz was using a new form of attack, the hit and run, by which he hoped to control his losses. He could do this now with so many boats at sea, although the effect, of course, was to bring to an end the old days of the superheroes, driving in to take three, four, five ships from a single convoy. The British defenses simply would not allow that approach anymore. Not even a Kretschmer could have used the bold surface attack of 1942 and survived for long. As it was, Doenitz lost two U-boats in the attack on Convoy ON 166 because the convoy escort was aggressive: one of the U-boats sank after ramming by the USS *Campbell*, the senior ship in the escort.

The Germans now had a new radar search instrument, which they did not trust (the crews feared radiation poisoning), but they used it from time to time. One U-boat seemed to be using it when the U-boats found Convoy ON 167. It gave the RDF operators something easy to home onto, and consequently the boat shadowing Convoy ON 167 got such a severe pounding from three escorts that the shadowing ended. That is not to say the attacks did. Convoy UC 1, consisting of thirty-two tankers bound from Britain to the West Indies, was attacked 450 miles west of Lisbon. On the first day (February 23) the convoy lost three tankers. But the next day the escorts, which consisted of four sloops, four American destroyers and two frigates, attacked six U-boats, and after that there were no more attacks on the convoy.

All those success sounded encouraging to the Allies and they were indicative of a new spirit of aggression among the convoy escorts. It was badly needed; the sinking figures on U-boats were not nearly so indicative as they seemed at the moment, for Doenitz had a lot more U-boats to lose these days.

At least in intelligence it was a standoff. At *B-Dienst* headquarters in Berlin the plotters had the British naval code broken again for the second time in six months so they were reading all the Admiralty's messages with gratification and glee. One of the most useful daily transmissions from London was the U-boat Situation Report, which was designed to give the commanders of convoys and ships at sea the location of all U-boats out there. It did, but they did not remain as located for long, for the moment Doenitz's staff had the report, the U-boats were moved. Doenitz had an enormous respect for British radar and gave it most of the credit for locating the U-boats. In fact, at the end of February he decided that radar had to be somehow overcome, and he ordered that whenever a boat became aware of radar transmissions, it was to submerge and stay down for at least thirty minutes. The British just then were actually improving their radar. The German Metox (radar detection device) had made this essential. In February, two Liberator squadrons of the RAF were fitted out with the new 10-centimeter SCR 5117 Radar RCS and the 172 Squadron of Wellington bombers equipped with Leigh lights were also equipped with the new radar. Still, that was not the real answer to the questions Doenitz was posing. In London Commander Rodger Winn in the Submarine Tracking Room had the work of Ultra, reading all the German codes, plus the Huffduff system's ground stations, plus the reports of agents in France and Norway to help him outguess Admiral Doenitz. So every time the admiral's staff moved a U-boat or sent the U-boat packs to a coordinate to find a convoy as ordered out by the British, Commander Winn's people warned them off. The net result was a constant game much like tennis, with the ball bouncing back and forth, and the actual results dependent largely on the skills and the numbers of escorts and submarines involved.

From February Doenitz concentrated his U-boats in the North Atlantic. As an Admiralty spokesman put it, "Never before has the enemy displayed such singleness of purpose in utilizing his strength against one objective—the interruption of supplies from America to Great Britain." As a result, engagements were embittered and successes against U-boats reached a record peak. It was probably the best month ever known to the Allies in respect to U-boats sunk (more than a dozen). But the losses of merchant shipping were not so pleasant to contemplate: 359,000 tons, as opposed to 203,000 tons in January. Doenitz ended the month rueful because of the "U-boat vacuum" caused by what he saw as a shortage of U-boats. Doenitz had stated the case in that broadcast to the German people: the U-boats would continue to attack, and they would suffer heavier losses, but they would fight more fiercely.

It was already so fierce, that on March 1 an "Atlantic Convoy Conference" was held in Washington by the British, Canadians, and Americans. Here it was decided that the Americans (whose naval attitudes still had not recovered from the War of 1812) would withdraw from the northern convoy escort service, but would take over the escort of the tanker convoys from Britain to the West Indies, and would provide an escort carrier and five destroyers to work under the British as a hunter-killer team in the North Atlantic. Thus came a new wrinkle in the U-boat war, with the movement of the USS *Bogue* and her five destroyers into action. Another change of enormous importance at the end of February was the establishment of the first Very Long Range aircraft unit, with twenty of them stationed in Iceland and at Ballykelly. There was no longer an "air gap" in mid-Atlantic.

Doenitz, who had not only the full support of Hitler for his U-boat war, and the overall command of German naval forces, but the expectation of improving weather and an ever greater force of U-boats, now moved more confidently. March 1943 could well be the point at which the Germans finally destroyed the British convoy system. Doenitz was set to do just that, as he despatched more than a hundred U-boats into the Atlantic.

In March 1943, Admiral Doenitz's U-boats enjoyed "happy times" again, because he could surround the convoys with as many as twenty U-boats.

The British increased the sizes of convoys, and this made it easier for the U-boats. So did the continued gap in mid-Atlantic, for the coming of the escort carriers had been delayed by production problems.

The U-boats were taking ships from the convoys by the dozens. SC 121 lost fourteen ships.

Then the first of the promised thirty U.S. escort carriers arrived, with Convoy HX 228. Still, the U-boats took six ships from that convoy. SC 122 had plenty of escort, but that convoy lost eight ships, and Doenitz did not lose a single U-boat. In fact, against those three major convoys he had sunk 140,000 tons of ships with the loss of but a single submarine, Lieutenant Rosenberg-Gruszczynski's *U-384*.

During the four days and nights of the attacks on Convoys SC 122 and HX 299 Admiral Doenitz had spent all his available time in the plot room of U-boat headquarters in Berlin's Hotel Am Steinplatz. His thin, determined face was even crossed from time to time by a smile as he contemplated the destruction he was meting out to his enemies and the proof that if he had been given his U-boat program at the beginning of the war, the British by now would have been defeated.

The euphoria continued until March 18 when Doenitz had the first report of a Very Long Range aircraft having penetrated the air gap on the eastern side of mid-Atlantic. Even that was not enough to dampen the euphoria, there still were no U-boat losses. Only on the morning of March 20, when the last night of the double convoy's agony had passed without more losses, did Admiral Doenitz begin to lose his high hopes. A new sort of report was coming in to U-boat headquarters. The reports continued for the rest of the week, and they were sobering:

U-134, coming home: damaged by depth charge attacks
U-190, coming home: damaged by depth charge attacks

U-305, coming home: damaged by four depth charge attacks
U-338, coming home: damaged by air and sea depth charge attacks
U-439, coming home: damaged by depth charge attack
U-527, coming home: damaged by depth charge attack
U-530, coming home: damaged by depth charge attack
U-598, coming home: damaged by depth charge attack from air
U-631, coming home: damaged by depth charge attack from air
U-666, coming home: damaged by two depth charge attacks from aircraft
U-440, coming home: damaged by depth charge attack
U-441, coming home: damaged by depth charge attack from air
U-86, coming home: damaged by depth charge attack
U-228, coming home: damaged by depth charge attack

And then, two even more ominous "non-reports," from *U-328*, which had been sunk by a Flying Fortress on March 19, and *U-665*, which had been sunk by a Wellington in the Bay of Biscay while heading for base. There were no survivors from either boat.

As the other boats straggled in, the damaged and the undamaged, U-boat headquarters began to get an indication of the cost of the "victory." The crews were exhausted after a week or more of operations in hurricane weather. The damage was such that it would be a while before Doenitz could assemble so many submarines in one relatively small area again. And, as March continued, the drums of victory were muted. To be sure the U-boats sank ten more ships that month, another 65,000 tons, and ran the score for March to 627,000 tons total, but the U-boat war had changed again, and not in favor of Admiral Doenitz. Almost overnight several new developments had been brought together, largely through the persistence and drive of Prime Minister Winston Churchill and his Anti-U-Boat Committee of the War Cabinet.

One new factor was the establishment of Atlantic support

groups of escorts. This idea, tried before and not found wanting, except in ships, could now be made permanent war policy. There were enough escorts to establish five escort groups with enough ships assigned to each group to provide a permanent working force of five or six ships that were used to working together. Captain Walker got himself released from shore duty to take over the 2nd Escort Group. Their method of operation represented a new wrinkle in the war against U-boats. Hitherto the convoy escorts could spend only a limited time attacking a stubborn U-boat, then they had to return to their primary duty, the protection of the convoy from onslaught. But the escort groups, which accompanied convoys, were free to turn off and attack and stay as long as seemed indicated with any submarine target. It would make a difference.

Another factor was the volte-face of the United States regarding escorts and air patrol and air escort, after the disaster of SC 122 and HX 228. The long-range aircraft began to appear on the western side of the Atlantic and more were made available to the British for their eastern operations.

The appearance of the escort carrier *Bogue* with a convoy has already been noted. Admiral Doenitz was stunned to receive the news on March 26 when several of his U-boats reported on their failure to close a westbound convoy because of the air cover provided by the small carrier. The Americans promised five of these carriers in short order.

But the greatest change of all to affect Admiral Doenitz's operations came on the British side of the Atlantic in the air. Finally, Coastal Command had the resources to begin truly effective operations against enemy aircraft in the Bay of Biscay, where the Atlantic submarines were mostly based. Bomber Command and the Americans would continue the fruitless plastering of Dr. Todt's almost perfect submarine pens, but Dr. Todt could not protect the U-boats when they were at sea, and in short order this became Admiral Doenitz's most pressing problem. For with U-boats pouring out of the yards at the rate of 30 a month, where was he going to keep them? The protected pens in the Bay of Biscay could accommodate only 120 boats, and already Doenitz had more than that at hand, ready to go. At the end of March 1943, as

Doenitz put in his memoirs, "...the British government concentrated all its efforts on defeating the U-boats. After three and a half years of war we had brought the British maritime power to the brink of defeat in the Battle of the Atlantic—and that with only half the number of U-boats which we had always demanded."

19

Doenitz Answers the Challenge

Admiral Doenitz could not forget that if Hitler and the German military establishment had only listened to him at the outbreak of war, he could have won the war for them with his U-boats before 1943. Perhaps so, perhaps not; but the fact was that Winston Churchill agreed with Doenitz and blessed the lucky stars of Britain for Hitler's turbid crystal ball.

The U-boat war had suddenly turned all topsy-turvy for the Germans. One could not say they were on the defensive, for the U-boat was strictly an offensive weapon, but their offensive was on the defensive. The Americans had suddenly been aroused to a pitch almost as high as that of the British. Their air patrols in the Caribbean and the Azores and off the North American coast had become fearsome. The tale of *U-506* gives an indication.

Lieutenant Eric Wurdemann was the skipper of *U-506* and had been since she was commissioned in the autumn of 1941. On her first patrol she had gone to America, but had been beset with mechanical difficulties and had sunk nothing at all. On her second patrol she had been the first U-boat to enter Mexican waters and did very well, claiming eight ships, six of them tankers. But, of course, that was during the "happy time." She returned to Lorient where Wurdemann was nicknamed "the tanker cracker." On Wurdemann's third patrol he went into the South Atlantic off the west coast of Africa. It was a long patrol, lasting from July 1942 until the first week of November. The *U-506*, of course, was refueled several times by supply boats. She sank five merchant ships and was involved in one of the saddest affairs of the U-boat war—the sinking of the British steamer *Laconia* on September 12, 1942, by the *U-156*. The *Laconia* carried 1,500 Italian prisoners of war and a large number of women and children. When the Germans learned what they had done they rallied all the U-boats in the area to carry out rescue missions, including the *U-506*. The rescue mission was upset by British bombings, but the *U-506* came through unscathed.

Lieutenant Wurdemann had not quite reached the 100,000-ton mark—the standard for award of the *Ritterkreuz*, the Knight's Cross of the Iron Cross—but his exploits had been so remarkable that Doenitz got it for him anyhow.

On the *U-506*'s fourth war patrol she was out for 145 days, sailing from Lorient on December 14, 1942, and returning on May 8, 1943. Her operational area had been the Cape of Good Hope and it took her seven weeks just to reach it. She spent six weeks around Port Elizabeth and sank only two ships for all this effort. When the *U-506* returned to Lorient, what a change the crew saw! The war had turned around. Before, the town was the German playground. Now the men were billeted at the headquarters of the 2nd U-Boat Flotilla, in deep woods outside Lorient, where they had a lake to swim in. But then more boats came in, almost more than Lorient could handle, and they were transferred to live in the air raid shelters of the town. They had one room for the whole U-boat company. There was plenty of water but it was unpotable. The officers were housed each in a small room with bunk, washbasin, and chair, and the lights did not work most of the time. They were told to prepare for a long voyage, they would be going to Penang or Singapore to operate with the Japanese. They were fitted out with tropical uniforms, and a surgeon and a war correspondent from Dr. Goebbels's propaganda agency joined the crew. And just before they left Lorient, the captain of the flotilla sent a mountain of flowers to the boat, usually an honor reserved for a boat coming in from an enormously successful patrol.

At noon on July 6, 1943, the crew went to the quay near the pens on the Scorff at Lorient. There lay the *U-506* alongside the *U-533*, also bound for the Far East. A crowd mostly of Germans from the flotilla assembled to cheer them on, two more U-boat crews going out for high adventure in the Orient. All those flowers covered the U-boat, and someone commented that it looked remarkably like a coffin. "Keep your chins up when the aircraft come," someone shouted.

When the speeches had been made and the band had played, *U-506* and *U-533* sailed. They were escorted out to the bay entrance by two destroyers, and then the destroyers circled and waved off and were gone. The two submarines submerged and crossed the bay submerged, surfacing only by day to avoid those deadly bombers with their Leigh lights, and then submerging the moment an aircraft was sighted. For three days the two submarines kept together, then on the fourth day they were attacked by a British surface force, and the *U-506* lost track of the *U-533*. The men of the *U-506* were sure the *U-533* had been sunk by the British destroyers. (Not true, she was sunk in October, by a British air patrol aircraft, having made it as far as the Gulf of Oman.) They went on, south. On July 12 at 2 P.M. when they were off Cape Finisterre the boat surfaced to charge batteries. It was a misty day, visibility was only about 500 yards, and the radar detection device was manned. They were still charging batteries at about 4 P.M. when a plane came at them, "almost vertically," said the crew. Before they could man the guns the plane dropped six bombs. The first two missed off the starboard beam, the third hit the deck forward, and the last three bombs hit the deck aft.

The Liberator then moved off, circled back, dropped a life raft when the pilot saw that he had destroyed the U-boat, and then was gone. The explosions were so effective that they opened the outer and pressure hulls like a can opener working on a sardine tin; one man saw the plates of the pressure hull collapse to expose a diesel engine. Automatically the captain ordered a crash dive, but everyone just looked at him. Then he called for a life jacket. (U-boat skippers were notorious for disobeying their own safety orders.) There were none above deck, said the men, and no one was going down into that sinkhole. Lieutenant Wurdemann then started below down the conning tower ladder, but before he got to the deck he was in water waist deep so he scurried back up and over the side, and began swimming away as the U-boat sank. Seven men, the bridge watch that had just come on duty and part of the bridge watch that had just gone off duty, were all that were still alive. The others had gone down with the U-boat. The six enlisted men and Lieutenant Hans Schult, the executive officer, had life jackets. Two of the men held the captain up until he told them all he was doing was dragging them down to drown, and they let him go. Soon he disappeared. So did one seaman whose leg had been blown off by a bomb. The others held themselves up for an hour. Someone finally found the raft dropped by the American Liberator and set course for the Spanish coast. For two nights they rowed, turn and turn about, until they were twenty miles from Cape Finisterre. They were sighted by HMS *Hurricane* on July 14 and rescued. Lieutenant Schult spent most of the voyage back to England bad-mouthing the dead captain he had served all through the command. Wurdemann, he said, was a bundle of nerves, looked forty, although he was twenty-nine, and had false teeth which once fell down the conning tower hatch when he was giving orders from the bridge. Small requiem for a man who had been awarded the *Ritterkreuz* and was numbered among the "aces." Poor Schult was understandably upset because he had been promised that he would have the *U-506* after this cruise while Wurdemann was slated to go on to greater glory. Now neither would.

In the last months of 1943 Admiral Doenitz's problem was to rejuvenate the power of the U-boat force. His ultimate weapon had to be a new sort of submarine, but in the interim he had to fight with what he had, a concept he had always accepted and in the past had made into a virtue.

What he had were hundreds of U-boats ill-equipped to fight the most dangerous enemy weapon, the aircraft. So now they had to be equipped. He began experimenting.

Some U-boats were equipped with twin 8mm machine gun mounts on the bridge, single 20mm cannon on each side of the widened gun platform, and a quadruple 20mm gun on the lower platform. Some "flak boats" were built with even more machine guns and small cannon. The use of armour on the bridges was also tried. And new methods of getting out of the Bay of Biscay came into use.

The bay had at first seemed a blessing, and the whole Atlantic operation had been built around it. Now it seemed almost like a trap, for the long-range and medium-range aircraft of Coastal Command found no difficulty in swooping down in large numbers to harry the U-boat force.

The U-boats with their new antiaircraft armament now came out across the bay on the surface in groups, accompanied by escorts which also were equipped with extra antiaircraft guns. They moved at high speed in formation and when a U-boat was singled out by an aircraft for attack, it presented its beam, and all the boats and ships fired up at the attacking aircraft. It made dangerous work for the British planes, but also gave them plenty of opportunities to sink U-boats. In July, eleven U-boats were sunk in the bay. On July 30, seven aircraft and the 2nd Support Group sank three U-boats, two fighting boats, and one "milch cow." The Germans retaliated by arming Dornier 217 bombers with glider bombs to attack the surface ships from high altitude. The sloop *Landguard* was the first hit, and hurt. On August 28 eighteen Dorniers attacked the 1st Support Group in the bay and sank the *Egret* and damaged the *Athabaskan*. With that the support groups were withdrawn and the Coastal Command had the field all to itself once more.

That fall Doenitz tried to concentrate on the South Atlantic and the Caribbean, but the Americans were now almost as aroused as the British. An indication of the intensity with which the Allies now regarded the struggle is a note in the Admiralty's monthly U-boat report:

> Information recently obtained from prisoners of war shows that U-boat crews have been led to expect that if their boat has been so badly damaged in an attack that she must be abandoned, other

> U-boats will be ordered to the position to rescue them. There is every reason to believe that this is being done, possibly providing opportunities for attacking rescuing U-boats as they close the scene of a "kill" and so increasing the bag.

There was a change: in the "happy time" of 1942 Kretschmer and Schepke and the other "aces" liked to linger around the wreck they had just torpedoed or the boats full of survivors, to torpedo the ship brave enough to stop to give aid. Now the shoe was on the other foot!

Where was the safe water now, the happy hunting water of yestermonth? That was a question asked by the men of the *U-513* in that summer of 1943.

The *U-513* had been everywhere. She had fought in the Gulf of St. Lawrence. She had sailed the water off Trinidad. She had worked the North Atlantic and the Azores, and she had been part of one of the most remarkable U-boat spectaculars of the spring of 1943. On April 14, the smell of the victories of March still in their nostrils, the crew of *U-513* moved into the 50-fathom line outside Lorient and, as was the custom, waited there for the boat's turn to be escorted into the Scorff by the usual minesweeper. As she lay there, *U-526* came up. Her captain was junior to the captain of the *U-513*, and furthermore the *U-526* was out on her first patrol, and was returning empty-handed. But what the young skipper lacked in skill he made up in brass, and as the patrol boat came up the *U-526* maneuvered into the lead, which meant that she would reach the quay first and have the benefit of the band and the welcoming committee. The men of the *U-513* were furious, and they sneered at their easygoing captain, Lieutenant Commander Rolf Ruggeberg. That was his way, let the young punks insult him! Small wonder he was not one of the "aces."

So the *U-513* swung in behind the *U-526*, and as usual, the careful Ruggeberg gave the leading U-boat plenty of wake room. The minesweeper took them to the outer boom, hauled in her paravanes, and headed for her own berth. The crew of the *U-526* started taking off their life belts and got ready to dock. Everyone could see the band and the crowd and the commander of the 10th Flotilla and his guard of honor on the quay. All the welcome folderol was about to begin. Then, a mile from the pier, without a warning, a huge gout of water shot up from the side of the *U-526*. She slowed in the water and stopped, she began to sink in the water. From behind, the *U-513* hurried forward to help rescue the men of her sister submarine. On the pier the commander of the 10th Flotilla elbowed aside the honor guard and jumped into his launch and hurried to the scene. Every manned boat in the harbor came speeding up. But the mine—for that is what it was, a mine laid by a British aircraft—had done its work well. The *U-526* went down fast, and although the water was only thirty feet deep, only a dozen men were saved, including the presumptuous captain, whose back was broken, and who died before Lieutenant Commander Ruggeberg could thank him for usurping precedence.

That landing was Ruggeberg's last. He was old for the job of U-boat skipper; he had been naval attaché at Madrid before the war, and Doenitz brought him ashore that summer. The *U-513* was given to Lieutenant Friedrich Guggenberger, the hero who had sunk the *Ark Royal*. Aha! said the men of the crew. Now they were getting somewhere. They had an "ace" for a skipper, and at the very least this ought to mean more Iron Crosses, and longer leaves in Germany. In May they went out to Brazil and the crew began to wonder. Drill. Drill. Drill. The captain did not like their diving time. He did not like the speed with which they got on deck to man the guns. He did not like anything it seemed. It was worse than those weird training rituals at *Agru Front*, said the crew. And Guggenberger was not even lucky. They missed one big ship with three torpedoes. The captain said the crew had done it all by themselves and it was drill, drill, drill again. One day off Trinidad the quartermaster shouted "Flugzeug!" and he ducked.

"Nonsense!" shouted the captain. "*Seeadler!*"

But he pressed the diving alarm just the same, and they went down to argue whether they had seen an aircraft or an albatross.

They hit another ship, which limped into Rio. They missed a third but that was because it was surrounded by swarming aircraft that made Guggenberger nervous. They sank a little coastal steamer. Off Sao Sebastio on July 3 they found a convoy and sank a Liberty ship and the British steamer *African Star.* They missed two more ships, and when they were down to their last two torpedoes Guggenberger decided to use them against the Brazilian destroyer that regularly patrolled off Rio harbor. Brazil, tired of its ships being sunk by U-boats, had entered the war on the Allied side.

With that in mind Guggenberger moved back toward Rio. On July 19 the *U-513* was on the surface, the skipper was lying on his bunk, the quartermaster was giving a steering lesson to a torpedo rating who wanted to change jobs for more outside work, when suddenly out of a cloud came an American navy flying boat. The air alarm sounded and Guggenberger rushed to the bridge. He had never seen a PBM and it looked like "some old crate" that would never live to limp out of the range of his boat's gunfire. But before the antiaircraft guns could open, the "old crate" dropped a stick of bombs which ripped open the forward compartment of the *U-513* and let the water rush in. The stern went up, the men on the deck were thrown into the water, and the *U-513* went down, propellers still churning the air. The U.S. Navy plane circled and dropped a raft and life jackets. The men got into the jackets and swam to the raft and got on. There was just room for the seven survivors sitting back to back, with their feet in the water, except when the sharks came around to nibble! They led a calisthenic life until a few hours later when the USS *Barnegat* came up and saved them.

So where was the safe water? It was not in the Caribbean or the western approaches to the Atlantic any more. How about the southern reaches of the Bay of Biscay?

The *U-454* and the *U-706* left La Pallice together on July 29, 1943, bound for the Central Atlantic. Doenitz was trying something new: the buddy system, in which two boats worked together, not as a wolf pack, with Doenitz directing every move. (U-boat command had finally gotten onto the fact that Huffduff pinpointed those transmissions.) But even in the bay they found the buddy system hard to manage. *U-454* and *U-706* had arranged to come up for short periods four times a day to charge batteries, but on the second day out this plan broke down because they were both attacked by aircraft and had to dive. At 8:30 A.M. on August 1 they saw each other for the last time. Then they lost contact. That day *U-454* was in a bad way. She had been forced to stay below so much of the time that her batteries were virtually exhausted, the air was foul in the boat, and the men were growing sick. Just before 5 P.M. she surfaced again, and almost immediately had an air contact. Two minutes later a Sunderland flying boat came over and the skipper, Lieutenant Burkhard Hacklander, was so desperate to charge those batteries and air the boat that he elected to stay on the surface and fight. The gun crew manned the 20mm guns and started shooting. Down below the wireless operator let U-boat headquarters know they were under attack from the air. The gun crew hit the aircraft's starboard inner engine and knocked it out, and the starboard main fuel tank was punctured. The Sunderland bored in to attack without a tremor, however, and straddled the U-boat with three depth charges. Twelve men who had been on the bridge or passing ammunition were the only survivors. They were picked up by HMS *Kite*. The Sunderland crashed, and her crew were rescued by HMS *Wren*.

That evening, the *U-706* got a message from Berlin that a U-boat nearby was in trouble, having been attacked by aircraft that day. She sped toward the place, but the weather was so rough that by midmorning she had not reached it. The commander of this U-boat, Lieutenant Alexander von Zitsewitz, did not hold much with the new GSR (radar) and said he preferred to rely on his lookouts. So the radar was turned off when Hampden bombers of the RCAF 415 Squadron appeared, attacking with gunfire and depth charges. The *U-706* managed to evade in the high sea, but a Hampden circled, outside the gun range of the submarine. The bridge watch craned their necks as she went around twice. Then von Zitsewitz saw his fate coming at him:

"Aircraft dead ahead," he shouted. "Turn hard-a-port."

The U-boat's machine guns and 20mm guns opened up on the aircraft, a Liberator of the USAAF 4th Antisubmarine Squadron.

"That pilot," said the boat's second Lieutenant, "can really fly—he made a wonderful approach."

And while he was saying it that pilot and his crew were finishing the job. They dropped twelve depth charges, which bracketed the boat. The second lieutenant was trapped by the first depth charge, which closed him into the bridge railings, and freed by the second, which blew the railing away and threw him and three seamen into the water as the boat sank beneath them. The captain did not have to wait, the gunfire from the machine gunners killed von Zitsewitz right there on his bridge, in the Bay of Biscay, U-boat heaven.

So where was the safe water—off Italy, perhaps?

The *U-458* was off Pantellaria between Sicily and Tunisia trailing Convoy MKF 22 on the night of August 22, when she was spooked by an escort, and the attacks began. One ten-charge pattern, another ten-charge pattern, a third ten-charge pattern, and then the *U-458* came up. The escorts HHMS *Pindos* (His Hellenic Majesty's Ship) and HMS *Easton* turned their searchlights on the surfaced U-boat and began firing with such vim that several shouts to cease fire had no effect on the gunners. Neither ship had automatic fire control of its big guns, and they were not very accurate, but the Oerlikons swept the deck of the submarine, and several men jumped into the water to get away from the hail of bullets.

After five minutes the U-boat seemed to get under way, and headed for the *Pindos* as if to ram. The skipper of the *Easton* could not bear to see the U-boat escape so he decided to ram. And he did, striking her abreast of her forward gun. The U-boat rolled over, and sank immediately. Twenty-six survivors, including her skipper, Lieutenant Kurt Diggins, were picked up. No, they said, they had not tried to ram the *Pindos*. The U-boat had been abandoned with her engines running and must have slipped into gear.

So where was the happy water? The Indian Ocean? Off Iceland, Ascension Island—where?

The answer was: nowhere. Between August 1 and November 1, 1943, the Allied air and sea hunters destroyed thirty

U-boats, off Portugal, off the French coast, off Iceland, off Gibraltar, off Ascension Island, off Cape Race, off the Azores, off Morocco, near the British coast, off Recife, off Rio de Janeiro.

No, the autumn of 1943 meant a real crisis for Admiral Doenitz and his U-boat men. But one thing must be said, Doenitz never quit trying. In October he decided to increase the force at Toulon, the old French naval base in the Mediterranean. One of the five boats selected for the reinforcement was the *U-340*, operating under one of the most detested captains in the U-boat force, Lieutenant Joachim Klaus, who was so unpopular with his men that when he was wounded on one transit of the Bay of Biscay by aircraft fire, the men cheered, and when he went out on this third patrol fifteen men deliberately drank polluted water and contracted jaundice so they would not have to sail with him.

The *U-340* had a difficult transition out of the Bay of Biscay, down below most of the time, equipment breaking, unable to stay on the surface for more than three hours in twenty-four, attacked even so twice at night by aircraft. The condition of the batteries was so bad by October 31 that the chief petty officer suggested they turn away and give the batteries a really good charge before going through the Strait of Gibraltar. The captain refused disdainfully. That night the boat was attacked again off Tangier, even though she had taken the precaution of surfacing in the middle of a fishing fleet for company. The Wellington that attacked sent her diving, with her starboard motor knocked out. She struck bottom at 280 feet, and Klaus decided to stay there. They got the motor going again, started moving, and were attacked again. Finally they made it through the strait, but the batteries were dangerously low and Klaus decided to charge them by moving at full speed on the surface to the south. The U-boat had been going along handsomely for two hours when the British ships *Fleetwood*, *Bluebell*, and *Poppy* found her by radar. Klaus decided to sink the destroyer *Fleetwood* and readied his stern tubes to fire on the surface. But at the last moment he lost his nerve and crash-dived. The *Fleetwood* then began a series of attacks. The U-boat was not damaged, but lying on the bottom did not agree with Lieutenant Klaus's constitution. He became nervous. At 4 A.M. he called the crew together and told them the air was almost all gone and that he intended to surface and scuttle the boat. They would all then swim for Spain.

The petty officers knew that this was all drivel. There was nothing wrong with the boat, they had enough air. The chief petty officer and the coxswain were ready to mutiny, but they got no assistance from the engineer officer and the first lieutenant. They were too dispirited to care one way or the other.

So the captain had his way. The tanks were blown, but the boat did not move. She was caught on the bottom by suction. The diving officer began joggling the boat, the suction gave way with a swoosh, and the crew went flying in all directions as the boat shot to the surface. There was nothing in sight. The *Fleetwood* had gone away. The U-boat was abandoned senselessly but at leisure. The men got into the thirty one-man dinghies, the two four-man dinghies, and the eight-man dinghy. The scuttling charges were set. The boat sank and the men got under way in their small craft. After three hours they were taken aboard by a fleet of Spanish fishing boats. Lieutenant Klaus wanted to be put ashore but the fishing captains said no, they would have to stay out until the boats had made their catch.

As it turned out, the *Fleetwood* had gone, but not for long. She came back to investigate the submarine contact, and there instead she saw a handful of Spanish fishing boats manned by men in bright yellow Mae West jackets and with a string of bright yellow dinghies trailing behind. The *Fleetwood* came alongside and her captain saw that "the men were in terrible shape: the second lieutenant who was an art student, had already collapsed from lack of sleep!"

"To the captain of the *Fleetwood*," said the monthly submarine report, "the dictates of humanity were clear and strong—the Medical Officer, who was called into conference, felt exactly the same: it was his duty to take off the exhausted men and give them all the care and attention which his ship could provide."

Lieutenant Klaus protested vigorously. They had achieved neutral territory aboard these Spanish vessels, he said. But the captain of the *Fleetwood* could not agree, and so the men of the *U-340*, having nearly reached safe water, were persuaded by Oerlikon and Browning, rescued, and made prisoners of war. The action of the captain of the *Fleetwood* was certainly a violation of the rules of war, but Whitehall did not bat an eye. One more U-boat and one more U-boat crew would never again sink one of His Majesty's vessels. That was all that counted in London.

20
Twilight

The U-boat war surged back and forth. Late in 1943 and early in 1944 the Allies had the advantage, with the arrival of ever more escort carriers on the Atlantic convoy run. The offensive against Doenitz's boats in the Bay of Biscay was powerful, following the British War Cabinet's demand that three of every ten boats in the bay must be sunk. Must be! More long-range bombers were available when the Americans began heavy production of the four-engined Liberator (B-24) which was ideal for ocean work. U-boat tactics had to change then, and they did. Doenitz ordered the boats to stay down during daylight hours to avoid air attack. This long submergence made the U-boats far less effective, and the results showed in the fall of tonnage sunk. Doenitz kept up the morale of his U-boat men by telling them of the new developments: the Type XXI long-range 1,600-ton boat was in production and by 1945 he would have 350 of them. These boats could go as fast under the sea (sixteen knots) as their corvette enemies went on top. They could stay out for ninety days without replenishment. They would have the schnorkel and would never have to surface on a patrol. They, and the small Type XXIII boats, admirable for work in the shallow waters of British estuaries, and the Type

XXVII boats would change the balance once again, and Germany would win the war at sea. Doenitz said so at a conference of admirals that December 1943, as he prepared. Meanwhile, the new homing torpedo (GNAT) would change the odds.

The GNAT, the German Naval Acoustic Torpedo, was one of Admiral Doenitz's new weapons. It had been perfected in the summer of 1943 and had been used to good effect by the Germans, particularly against escorts in the great convoy battles of September that year. The homing feature made it particularly good against small targets. Another weapon, although it belonged properly to Marshal Goering's Luftwaffe, was the glider bomb, another homing-type weapon, which had been used successfully by the Luftwaffe to drive the hunter-killer groups of British escorts out of the Bay of Biscay in 1943.

Doenitz lost his greatest advantage at the end of 1943 when the British changed their naval codes, and he no longer had instant information about the movement of convoys. Also, he no longer had the freedom of movement of the old days. There were just too many escorts, and too many aircraft buzzing around the waters of the Atlantic, which was still the primary battleground of the naval war as Doenitz had long ago said it would be. It was a tip-off on the state of the U-boat war that most of Doenitz's successes after 1943 were scored in those "soft spots" he was always able to find somewhere, but not on the North Atlantic run. And the sinkings now had dropped down to be counted not in the hundreds of thousands of tons, but in the thousands. Admiral Doenitz gave some voice to his worries and his yearnings in a speech to the German merchant navy conference at Stettin on January 20, 1944:

> The enemy has succeeded in gaining the advantage in submarine defence. We shall catch up with the enemy. The day will come when I shall offer Churchill a first-rate submarine war. The submarine weapon has not been broken by the setbacks of 1943. On the contrary, it has become stronger. In 1944, which will be a successful but hard year, we

shall smash Britain's supply line with a new submarine weapon.

But the tonnage sunk fell below a hundred thousand tons a month and remained stubbornly down. The fact was that the German U-boats were now spending more time trying to secure their survival than attacking the enemy, a real change from the days of 1942 and earlier.

At the end of 1944, the honor roll of German U-boat captains listed ninety-eight names, and of them, the most famous of all was Wolfgang Lueth, winner of the *Ritterkreuz*, the Oak Leaves, the Oak Leaves with Swords, and the Oak Leaves with Swords and Diamonds. Lieutenant Commander Lueth was still alive—for a very simple reason: he had been brought ashore. Of all the skippers Lueth had lasted longest. He had been out in the "canoe" *U-9* at the outset of the war, had graduated upward to the *U-138*, then taken over the *U-43*, and finally the *U-181*. He had served in the beginning in the North Atlantic but was fortunate enough to be moved in the bad days of 1943 into the Indian Ocean where convoys were few and patrol planes and destroyers were far between. Most of the other big winners of the U-boat service were long gone. The mighty Achilles, the wily Endrass, Bad Boy Lemp, the great Prien, the tidy Rollmann, the fiery Schepke—all had gone to feed the fishes at the bottom of the sea. And those were only the supermen who had gone.

Two hundred and forty-four U-boats had been sunk, and in the vast number of cases the sea yielded up either none or few survivors for the prison camps. The Freiherr Siegfried von Foerster, the near-sighted Guggenberger, Jenisch, Kretschmer, Oehrn, Freiherr Hans-Diedrich von Tiesenhausen, and Wohlfahrt were all lucky enough to be prisoners of war. But the luckiest of all were the men who had done their job and had been brought back to teach the younger men and administer the U-boat corps, Doenitz's son-in-law, Hessler, Otto von Buelow, Bleichrodt, Frauenheim, Gysae, Hardegen, Heydemann, and others. There was plenty of raw material still for the grinding of the U-boat war machine; the quality of it was another matter. The U-boat arm suffered from the same shortages and difficulties that had begun to beset all of Germany's armed forces after fifty-two months of war.

The U-boat war had entered its final phase in the middle of May 1944, when British Coastal Command was in a position to start an air offensive against U-boats in Norwegian waters. Three weeks later the Allies landed in Normandy, and two months later they began capturing the U-boat ports in the Bay of Biscay and the U-boats moved to Norway, the North Sea, and back to Germany.

Admiral Doenitz and his brave U-boat men never gave up; even as the odds against them worsened month after month they remained optimistic, counting on new weapons and the enormous power of the Type XXI boat to pull them through. There was no question about the Allied concern over the threats offered by the new weapons, and particularly the Type XXI boat. This boat was the nearest thing to the complete submarine (as opposed to submersible) yet developed, and it was a fearsome weapon, indeed. But as the war moved along, the Allied air attacks on the factories, railroads, yards, assembly points, and ports grew ever more fierce. On March 30, 1945, alone, U.S. Army bombers plastering the ports of Bremen and Hamburg destroyed thirteen U-boats. Similar attacks on Kiel and Hamburg a few days later cost Doenitz another nine boats.

The major tactic of the U-boats in the early days of 1945 was switched: they were to conduct a campaign against British shipping almost in the harbors. Using the new devices, the schnorkel, the homing torpedo that could be fired from any angle, and improved detection gear, the U-boats were to travel to a crossroads or other important shipping point, submerge, and wait. A cruise might consist of moving across the North Sea and waiting for weeks in one spot.

The new tactic and the knowledge that Doenitz's constructors were far along in the production of the Type XXI boats brought a renewed sense of fearful anticipation to the War Cabinet and Royal Navy officers encharged with antisubmarine warfare. But the sinkings did not bear out this concern; they did not reach the 100,000-ton mark again. They might have, had Doenitz been fighting his war in a vacuum, but all the time he was perfecting and preparing to man the Type XXI boats and working on other improvements, the Allied troops on the continent of Europe were moving steadily toward the heart of Germany, and the Allied bombers were dealing destruction to the German naval construction facilities.

Doenitz's boys fought on, displaying that same stubborn fighting quality time and again. Midget U-boats invaded British harbors—and were sunk for the most part by vigilant patrol boats, as on the night of March 24, 1945, when the HMS *Puffin* and motor torpedo boats *764* and *758* were patrolling along the coast, and had a radar contact 1,800 yards out. A searchlight proved it to be a midget submarine. It was too close to be reached by the 4-inch gun. The *Puffin* could not drop depth charges without endangering her two motor torpedo boats behind, so the captain turned, and rammed the midget submarine, abaft the conning tower. The U-boat exploded and showered the ship with burning fuel oil, a coxswain's chair, parts of bodies, and tiny bits of wreckage.

As the Allied troops crossed the Rhine and headed north to cut off the U-boat ports from supply, British and American navies were learning to deal with the new U-boat tactics at sea. The Royal Navy's antisubmarine warfare division took a more hopeful view of the future than did some of the British admirals and air marshals:

> It is anticipated that the Germans will manage for a time to continue to expand their U-boat effort until, at any rate, the ports in Northwestern Germany fall or are cut off from necessary supplies. By no means all the boats estimated to be ready or nearly ready to operate have yet been committed. It does seem, however, that the full weight of attack apprehended may never be effectively launched, owing to the general process of attrition and disorganization to which the German forces are being increasingly subjected.

Indeed, the attack of the U-boats was still ferocious. On March 22, 1945, the *U-339* attacked coastal convoy BTC 103 just off the shore of Britain, hitting one merchant ship with a torpedo. The merchant ship was not sunk but had to be beached in order to save ship and cargo. The submarine then went to the bottom near an old wreck and remained there for thirty hours. Meanwhile three escorts of the 3rd Escort Group came up and swept the area for hours. They spotted the wreck in their Asdic sets, but went on by because it was "nonsubmarine." The senior officer of the escort group assumed that the submarine had "bottomed" but could not find it.

The *U-339* waited for another convoy to come along, and on March 26 one did. This was Convoy EG 3. The same escort group was accompanying the convoy, the senior officer was the captain of the *Duckworth*. This time the senior officer had a plan: he assumed that the submarine was still in the area, and that it would attack from the inshore edge of the swept channel at extreme range with homing acoustic torpedoes. So the *Duckworth* went ahead, dropping depth charges along the side of the channel, while the *Rowley* went two miles farther inside and began dropping charges, and the *Essington* went out seaward and did the same. Almost immediately the *Duckworth* had an Asdic contact. An echo sounder run showed that the submarine was not a nonsubmarine object, and was lying just clear of the bottom in 34 fathoms (204 feet). The *Duckworth* attacked with her hedgehog, and shortly afterward up came two men, one of them alive. The whole affair was over in fifteen minutes. Another U-boat was sunk.

This sort of activity went on, showing that while the Admiralty moaned about the future, the men at sea killed U-boats. Admiral Horton stopped moaning and mined the inshore waters with 8,500 deep-laid mines. The patrols began to sink more U-boats. The U-boats, on their side, were having their own troubles. On March 11, the *U-681* reached the Scilly Isles, having come from Kiel by way of Bergen. She did not have enough fuel for a long patrol; because of Bomber Command's insistence on hitting the oil industry hard the U-boat bases in Norway were short of fuel, and she had been given only about 70 percent of her normal fuel load. The captain of the *U-681*, Lieutenant Werner Gebauer, had a shot at an escort with a regular torpedo and missed. He intended to enter St. Mary's Road at 8 A.M. and lie there like a spider waiting for seaborne flies. He took cross bearings on the Bishop Rock light and the old lighthouse that stood on St. Agnes Rock. He went down to 40 fathoms and headed for a point south of land, intending to pass through St. Mary's Sound. But he hit a rock and stuck on it. Trying to get off he damaged the propellers and the hull. Pressure rose in the inner fuel tank, and oil began pouring out into the control room and the electric motor compartment. The watertight doors were shut and dogged down but too late; the control room was awash with two feet of stinking diesel fuel. The captain brought the U-boat up to periscope depth. He wanted to proceed at that level, but about seven tons of water and oil in the boat sloshed back and forth and made it impossible to steady her. He brought the boat to the surface. Then he found that she could not dive, the trim tanks were gone. He decided to try to make the Irish coast and abandon ship there, but he ran afoul on the surface of a Liberator on the U.S. Navy's 103 Squadron, northwest of Bishop Rock, and as the Liberator ran in to attack, the men manned the 37mm gun to fight back. But the Liberator straddled the U-boat with a stick of depth charges and then came in for another run. The men abandoned ship as the Liberator finished her off. Ships of the 2nd Escort Group picked up most of the crew.

On March 14, the crew of the *U-260* swam ashore at Galley Head in County Cork, Eire, and were interned. Their boat had hit a British mine off the Irish coast. On the night of March 20, the bridge lookout of HMCS *New Glasgow* patrolling off Lough Foyle heard strange noises that sounded like low-flying aircraft. But as they looked around, they saw a schnorkel sticking up three feet, coming at the ship on a collision course about 100 yards forward of the port bow. If they had wanted to they could not have stopped the collision, which occurred just below the wing of the bridge. It was the *U-1003* on her maiden voyage; the schnorkel was wrenched off and the periscope wrecked. The water began pouring down through the broken schnorkel tube and filled the conning tower and spilled down into the control room so that the conning tower lower hatch had to be sealed off. The periscope was useless. The schnorkel was gone. The *U-1003* went down to the bottom, and there the captain shut down his engines and lay in the mud. The *New Glasgow* attacked with depth charges. And so did the other ships of the 26th Escort Group, but they were way off. The next day at dawn the captain brought the *U-1003* up to 60 feet and cruised at that depth all day long, and at dusk surfaced. The men turned to air the boat and charge the batteries, but the escorts found her again and she had to dive. The boat was taking water but the pumps were going. All night long the boat lay on the bottom and the pumps kept going. But the pumps took air and power and by midnight both were exhausted. The skipper brought the *U-1003* up and the men abandoned ship. Strike another of Doenitz's new weapons.

On March 27 in the Minches (Hebrides) the 21st Escort Group found a submarine northeast of the Butt of Lewis. It was following this new plan of Doenitz's, down at 47 fathoms in water with a 66-fathom bottom. The six escorts of the group all attacked, and when they left the submarine was no longer moving. *U-722* would not report back to Doenitz again. That same day not far away HMS *Conn* sank the *U-965*, which was down in the mud, so it was several days before another escort, depth-charging a contact, brought up evidence of the sinking. On March 30 in the same general area, the HMS *Rupert* and HMS *Conn* sank the *U-1021*.

Still there was complaint by a Royal Navy defense force that had gotten spoiled. The defenders were now thinking in terms of exchange: if a month started out with the U-boats sinking two or three steamers, the navy men were not satisfied until they had brought the ratio up to one for one at least. If Captain Walker had still been around he would have thought they were daft, but Captain Walker was not; he had died of a heart attack that winter, as much a victim of antisubmarine warfare and of overwork as any man had ever been. Britain's master of the anti-U-boat defense was gone.

The patrol of one U-boat in the month of April 1945 brought together all the elements of the state of the two arts, offense and defense, in this last phase of the U-boat wars.

The U-boat was the *U-1024* and her skipper was Lieutenant Hans Joachim Gutteck. Her patrol area was designated as the Irish Sea, and she left Kiel on March 3 in convoy with several other submarines. The passage was made entirely submerged, with Gutteck bringing the boat up to snorkel depth from 9 P.M. to 2 A.M. each day and again around noon for ventilation of the boat. It was an easy voyage, making about sixty miles a day, and they saw only two British escorts. One attacked on March 17, but the depth charges were so far away Gutteck could not even be sure they were aimed at his boat. Later that day, the sound of Asdic was again detected by the *U-1024*'s sensitive new equipment. A small corvette appeared, but passed by 5,000 yards away. On March 18 the Asdic detector again found noise, this time a motor yacht. But that was all, and on April 2 Gutteck arrived in the St. George's Channel area. At noon on April 3 Gutteck reached the steamer lanes, and four hours later he was depth-charged. The B.2 Escort Group was bringing ON 294 out from the United Kingdom when the HMS *Highlander* had an Asdic contact and attacked. The ship ran on, turned and came back and attacked again, with the charges set to go off at the bottom. The result was phenomenal: an enormous undersea explosion shook the whole area, and oil and bits of solid matter came to the top. Some aboard the *Highlander* figured they had themselves another submarine.

Aboard the *U-1024*, there was no damage at all. Gutteck cautiously brought the boat up to periscope depth and saw the search unit of two ships, and he fired a single T-5 torpedo at the nearest ship, 600 yards away, and a single T III torpedo at the other ship. Then he ducked down to 165 feet. After eight and a half minutes he heard a strong detonation, crackling noises, and all screw noises ceased. Gutteck headed north, confident that he had sunk a corvette. In fact, both torpedoes had missed.

But the skipper of the *Highlander* was an old hand and he knew that an ammunition ship had sunk here in 1943. What had evidently happened was that the depth charges had blown some unexploded ammunition in that ship at the bottom, and the explosion had caused part of the vessel to rise, to be hit by one of *U-1024*'s torpedoes, thus bringing cheap thrills to the men of both sides but no damage to either.

Two hours after that incident, the *U-1024* encountered another escort, towing a unifoxer—one of the devices the British now used to protect themselves from the acoustic GNAT torpedoes. The unifoxer was making so much noise that Gutteck decided a GNAT shot would certainly fail, and he had been instructed to save his more powerful LUT torpedoes for merchantmen. So he did not attack at all but dropped down to 230 feet instead. The escort was on top of him in a few minutes, having a good contact, and dropped ten depth charges, which did the *U-1024* no harm. The escort went away, and Gutteck proceeded with the current northward.

On April 4 Gutteck tried the alternative convoy route to the west and found nothing. So he headed back northeast, to reach the convoy route off Anglesey at dawn on April 5. He did, and at 6:30 he was nearly surprised by an escort that passed very close by his stern. He headed northeast, sighting a hospital ship and hearing an escort group nearby, but the escorts were out of range. Hearing was the key, the German hearing devices had improved marvelously, and during the day Gutteck heard coastal tankers, big cargo ships, a destroyer and corvettes, all of which he could identify by sound. But for two days the fog covered the area and no attacks could be made. On the afternoon of April 6 Gutteck moved west out of the area to schnorkel in peace, and then back. The fog was still thick so he bottomed and nestled in the mud. He would wait.

On the afternoon of April 7, Convoy HX 346 moved along off Anglesey, in four columns, screened by ships of EG C 5, the close escort group, and EG 25, a support group, five ships in all.

The *U-1024* was still bottomed in about 225 feet of water, sitting on the convoy route off Holyhead. At 4 P.M. the powerful hydrophones of the submarine picked up the unifoxers of the escorts and the boat came up to periscope depth. Visibility had improved since the foggy morning, but Gutteck still could not see what was behind those escorts. He moved between the escorts and at 4:45 saw a big convoy (eighteen ships). Only two of Gutteck's torpedoes had been loaded, both of them with LUT torpedoes because Gutteck had never expected to see such a large convoy. He was preparing to fire when the convoy turned and came directly at him. A merchant vessel loomed up, only 100 yards away and he crash-dived to 60 feet. The merchant ship passed over, and he came back up to periscope depth. At 5:23 he fired the two LUT XIIA torpedoes from tubes 1 and 4. Inclination was 180 degrees, speed ten knots, range 1,100 yards. The torpedoes were set to start "curling" at 1,500 yards, with thirty-knot settings. Translate from submarinese: the torpedoes were fired when the submarine was moving at ten knots, to go out 1,500 yards and turn completely around, then begin closing at thirty knots in concentric circles on the target which was 1,100 yards away.

Unfortunately the torpedo in tube 4 could not be cleared electrically or manually, so only tube 1 actually fired.

When Gutteck fired, the merchant aircraft carrier *Empire MacAndrew* had just flown off her aircraft to base, because they were nearing the end of the voyage. Two of the escorts were preparing to detach from the convoy and head for the River Clyde. The convoy was turning, when at 5:25 the American steamer *James W. Nesmith*, the fourth ship in the fourth column, was hit in the port quarter by a torpedo. There was no panic. The convoy completed the turn and continued heading at 50 degrees, escorted into Liverpool by the escort *Huntsville*. The rescue ship *Rathlin* stood by the torpedoed vessel but there were no casualties and the ship was not sinking. The *Rathlin* moved on toward the Clyde and the HMCS *Belleville*, whose Asdic was out of whack, took the *James W. Nesmith* in tow. The three remaining escorts immediately came up, and the leading ship dropped a buoy at the place of the torpedoing; from now on they would use that point as a center for searches.

After Skipper Gutteck heard the torpedo hit he withdrew southeast, which took him completely out of the area that was being searched. He would have liked to have come to periscope depth to look around, but he was too wise for that, the afternoon sea was smooth and the "feather" might have been a giveaway.

The escorts attacked around the area, dropping depth

charges in rear and hedgehog patterns for several hours, but of course there was nothing there but old wrecks. After the sea roughed up, Gutteck watched from outside with interest. But just before 11 P.M. when one escort came close, Gutteck went down to 264 feet. Twenty deep-set charges came, and some were close, but no damage was done. Gutteck kept his stern to the escorts, which made a difficult target, and he ran for the Irish coast so that he could make some minor repairs and recharge batteries. He also had some problems with one clutch of a diesel.

Just before 4 A.M. Gutteck decided he was far enough away from the trailing escorts to schnorkel for ventilation, and he did. Then he proceeded slowly on his low batteries, planning to recharge that night.

At 11 P.M. Gutteck came up to schnorkel again. The trouble was that in the fog that had come in he could not see the lights of Ireland, which he had intended to use as guidon, and he did not know precisely where he was. He extended the periscope fully and still had no luck. He could hear the escorts behind him blasting away with their depth charges. He bottomed in 125 fathoms and waited for daylight. During April 9 he remained bottomed and did not come to periscope depth until 4:45. Visibility was bad, only 500 yards, and there was no wind. He could not see land and he could not find it by radar. He schnorkeled from midnight to dawn on April 10 but still had not found the solution to the clutch problem. Next morning he moved on back to the convoy route and bottomed at 6:30 A.M.

On the morning of April 11, the HCMS *Strathadam* and the *Thetford Mines* left their submarine hunt and move to intercept Convoy BB 79. At ten o'clock they were detected by *U-1024*. Unifoxers and Asdic noises grew loud in the submarine. Gutteck ordered his men to action stations and remained at periscope depth. At 12:48 the unifoxer noises stopped, and an escort suddenly appeared out of the fog only 30 yards away. Gutteck crash dived to 100 feet. The *Strathadam*, with a contact, moved to attack. She picked up her unifoxer gear and made a hedgehog attack. The pattern hit the water (*U-1024*'s sound man heard it) and exploded on the bottom close by, but no damage was done. Two more hedgehog attacks were carried out, but still no real damage to the U-boat. Gutteck got under way and moved around, slowly and quietly. One attack was very close and did some damage. Gutteck began to edge away.

At 6:11 the *Strathadam* fired another hedgehog attack, and this time the escort was victimized by an accident that happened too often with the hedgehogs. A charge exploded 30 feet above the ship's deck, raked the bridge and forecastle with shrapnel and killed six men and wounded a number of others. The *Strathadam* picked up the ship's doctor from the *Thetford Mines* and made for Belfast at high speed, much to the relief of Lieutenant Gutteck. "She looked pretty practiced in the U-boat hunt."

At 10 P.M. three vessels of escort group EG 8 came up and were instructed to continue the hunt for the U-boat. Gutteck hung around the area, schnorkeling and waiting. The escorts were far enough away for comfort. Just before 2 P.M. on April 12, the *U-1024* rose to periscope depth and sighted, only about 4,000 yards away, five ships in two columns, escorted by but a single trawler. Gutteck fired a spread of three LUT torpedoes, and dived. He saw one hit as he went down, and later heard two explosions. That was true. The steamer *Will Rogers* was hit, and the other two torpedoes simply exploded in the water. Before the disturbance subsided, two escort groups were charging in to the area, dropping single depth charges. Soon the crew of the *U-1024* had counted 120 explosions. Then at 8:25 P.M. the *Loch Glendhu* made contact with the *U-1024*, at 1,600 yards. At first the operators thought it was a stationary target, but the *U-1024* was moving, and her engineer officer did not help much by bumping the keel on the bottom twice. The *Loch Glendhu* attacked, four projectiles fell very close, lights were broken, and the starboard motor stopped. Both compasses went out. The boat went to the bottom. Then two more charges went off, and, as one crewman of the *U-1024* said, "It was hell."

All the overhead fittings fell to the deck. One motor jumped its mountings, the switchboard disintegrated, the galley hatch burst open and water began pouring in. Gutteck ordered the lifesaving gear to be prepared, the tanks were blown, and at 8:45 the boat surfaced 1,500 yards from the *Loch Glendhu*.

As she came up, every escort in sight opened fire. Lieutenant Gutteck ran up through the conning tower hatch, and as he emerged his left hand was shot away. He looked at it, picked his Luger pistol out of his belt and shot himself in the head. The body sprawled on the bridge. So shocking was the sight of the dying captain on the deck that the crew had no more fight in them. Boarding parties came from two escorts, and the U-boat men did not resist. The men from the escorts got the crew off into the escorts and took the U-boat in tow. But on the way into harbor she foundered and sank by the stern.

The *U-1195* had been put in service on her first patrol on February 8 from Kiel. Her captain was Lieutenant Ernst Cordes, who was making his fifth war patrol and had brought his crew from the *U-763*, which was bombed while in harbor. The *U-1195* sailed from Kristiansand on February 15 and patrolled north of the Shetland Islands until Doenitz had a new idea. He ordered the U-boat into port, and she arrived at Bergen on February 22. Just because France was now lost to the Germans did not mean they could not attack the British in the English Channel and this was the task given Cordes. Two days later, February 24, the *U-1195* sailed, this time up around the British Isles, down to Land's End, with orders to patrol in the channel around Bristol and Portsmouth and see what she could sink of the ships heading toward the continent with troops and supplies for the Allied forces.

The *U-1195* arrived off Land's End around April 1, and then began patrol. Off Falmouth she torpedoed a patrol boat. What a change! In the old days the captains would not waste a torpedo on a craft that small, but the war was not the same as Kretschmer's and Prien's war. After that small victory luck got better. On April 6, east of St. Catherine's Point in front of the Isle of Wight the *U-1195* sank the 11,000-ton transport *Cuba*. The crew was picked up by HMS *Nene*.

U-1195 then lay silently in the area, waiting, for the *Cuba* had been part of Convoy VWP 16, which meant more ships. It also meant four escorts, the *Nen*, the *Watchman*, the *Hoste*, and the French corvette *L'Escarmouche*.

After some searching, thinking perhaps the *Cuba* had hit

a mine, the captain of the *Watchman* suddenly announced a contact: "I have got a good echo—stationary—maybe a bloody wreck, but I am going to give it the works, as I pass by just for luck."

The escort came barreling toward the *U-1195* and threw a salvo of hedgehog projectiles. The depth charges blasted the *U-1195*. Lights went out, instruments crashed and shattered. The boat began taking water badly, particularly forward. Captain Cordes gave the order to abandon the forward compartments and move aft. The radiomen destroyed the radio sets. The engineer officer ordered all tanks blown and both motors in full reverse. But the boat would not move, she was too heavy with water.

The *U-1195* carried a crew of sixty-seven men. Some had escape vests, and some had only life vests. Some were in the control room and some in the conning tower, and some in the compass compartment, two were in the engine room. Of these, only eighteen men got to the surface, forty-nine, including Captain Cordes, died with the U-boat.

There was the new U-boat war as it existed, not as it was in the minds of the British admirals and Admiral Doenitz. It was as cruel as any aspect of the war had been, and much more wearing on the U-boat men. They went out and lived in constant danger, under the noses of their enemies, and their rewards were slender, one ship or two, and for each sinking they were bound to come under attack, not by one or two escorts, but by half a dozen or more. The results were ever so slender considering the risks and the losses. This was not the sort of U-boat war the Doenitz could ever win.

He and his U-boat men did see, in the Type XXI boat, the wherewithal for a whole new submarine campaign, and by late April the *U-2511*, the first of the Type XXI boats ready for service, was ordered to the Mediterranean. But it was too late. Lieutenant Commander Adelbert Schnee took the boat out with the highest of hopes, only to be called back on May 4, 1945, by Admiral Doenitz. The events of the war had made it impossible for the U-boat arm to continue.

On May 7 Admiral Doenitz, the new chief of the Third Reich, surrendered to the Allies.

Appendix:
German U-Boat Casualties

(From Office of Chief of Naval Operations, Washington, 1963)

Date	U-Boat	Last Comdr.	Cause of sinking	Position
1939				
14 Sep	U-39	Glattes	HMS *Faulknor, Foxhound & Firedrake*	58-32 N, 11-49 W
20 [22?] Sep §	U-27	Franz	HMS *Fortune & Forester*	58-35 N, 09-02 W
8 Oct	U-12	von der Ropp	Mine	†Straits of Dover
13 Oct	U-40	Barten	Mine	Straits of Dover
13 Oct	U-42	Dau	HMS *Imogen & Ilex*	49-12 N, 16-00 W
14 Oct	U-45	Gehlhaar	HMS *Inglefield, Ivanhoe, Intrepid, Icaras*	†50-58 N, 12-67 W
24 Oct	U-16	Wellner	HMS *Puffin & Cayton Wyke* (damaged by) (Mined & stranded on Goodwins)	†51-09 N, 01-28 E
29 Nov	U-35	Lott	HMS *Kingston, Kashmir & Icarus*	60-53 N, 02-47 E
4 Dec	U-36	Fröhlich	HM Sub. *Salmon*	†57-00 N, 05-20 E
1940				
30 Jan	U-55	Heidel	HMS *Fowey, Whitshed &* Br. Sqdn. 228	48-37 N, 07-46 W
1 Feb	U-15	Frahm	Rammed by German *Iltis* (DD)	Baltic
5 Feb	U-41	Mugler	HMS *Antelope*	†49-21 N, 10-04 W
12 Feb	U-23	von Dresky	HMS *Gleaner*	55-25 N, 05-07 W (mining Clyde)
23 Feb	U-53	Grosse	HMS *Gurkha* in North Channel	†60-32 N, 06-10 W
25 Feb	U-63	Lorentz	HMS *Escort, Narwhal, Inglefield & Imogen*	58-40 N, 00-10 W
20 Mar	U-44	Mathes	HMS *Fortune*	†63-27 N, 0-36 E

§A semiofficial British account (1954) says 20 March.
†No survivors

Date	U-Boat	Last Comdr.	Cause of sinking	Position
14 Feb	U-54	Kutschmann	Mined	(†)North Sea (?) (wreckage found)
13 Apr	U-64	Schulz	HMS *Warspite*'s Sqdn. 700	†68-29 N, 17-30 E
15 Apr	U-49	von Gossler	HMS *Fearless* (& *Brazen*)	68-53 N, 16-59 E
16 Apr	U-1	Deecke	HM Sub. *Porpoise*	†58-18 N, 05-47 E
25 Apr	U-22	Jenisch	Mine	†57-00 N, 09-00 E
10 [29?] Apr	U-50	Bauer	HMS *Amazon* & *Witherington* (*Hero*?)	†62-54 N, 01-56 W
31 May	U-13	Schulte	HMS *Weston*	52-27 N, 02-02 E
3 Jul	U-26	Scheringer	HMS *Gladiolus* & RAAF Sqdn. 10	48-03 N, 11-30 W
— Jul	U-122	Loof	Unknown	†North Sea
3 Aug	U-25	Beduhn	Mine	54-00 N, 05-00 E
20 Aug	U-51	Knorr	HM Sub *Cachalot*	47-06 N, 04-51 W
21 Aug ?	U-102	von Kloth	Unknown	†North Sea?
3 Sep	U-57	Kühl	Norw. SS *Rona* (rammed)	Baltic
30 Oct	U-32	Jenisch	HMS *Harvester* & *Highlander*	55-37 N, 12-20 W
2 Nov	U-31	Prellberg	HMS *Antelope* (& RAF §§)	56-26 N, 10-18 W
21 Nov	U-104	Jürst	HMS *Rhododendron*	†56-28 N, 14-13 W
1941				
7 Mar	U-70 §§§	Matz	HMS *Camellia* & *Arbutus*	60-15 N, 14-00 W
8 Mar	U-47	Prien	HMS *Wolverine*	†60-47 N, 19-13 W
17 Mar	U-99	Kretschmer	HMS *Walker* (& *Vanoc*?)	61-00 N, 12-00 W
17 Mar	U-100	Schepke	YHMS *Walker* & *Vanoc*	61-00 N, 12-00 W
23 Mar	U-551	Schrott	HMS *Visenda*	†62-37 N, 16-47 W
5 Apr	U-76	von Hippel	HMS *Wolvering* & *Scarborough*	58-35 N, 20-20 W
28 Apr	U-65	Hoppe	HMS *Gladiolus*	†60-04 N, 15-45 W
9 May	U-110	Lemp	HMS *Aubrietia*, *Bulldog* & *Broadway* (captured)	60-31 N, 33-10 W
2 Jun	U-147	Wetjen	HMS *Wanderer* & *Periwinkle*	†56-38 N, 10-24 W

§§§The most recently published British research suggests *U-47* and *U-70* sinkings should be transposed.

§§Second sinking: sunk 3-11-40, Schillig Rds., by RAF, raised and recommissioned.

['41] Date	U-Boat	Last Comdr.	Cause of sinking	Position
18 Jun	U-138	Gramitzky	HMS *Faulknor, Fearless, Forester, Foresight & Foxhound*	36-04 N, 07-29 W
27 Jun	U-556	Wohlfahrt	HMS *Nasturtium, Celandine & Gladiolus*	60-24 N, 29-00 W
29 Jun	U-651	Lohmeyer	HMS *Malcolm, Violet, Scimitar, Arabis & Speedwell*	59-52 N, 18-36 W
3 Aug	U-401	Zimmermann	HMS *Wanderer, St. Albans & Hydrangea*	†50-27 N, 19-50 W
9 Aug (28 Jul?)	U-144	v. Mittelstaedt	Torpedoed by Russ. Sub. *SC-307*	†Gulf of Bothnia
25 Aug	U-452	March	HMS *Vascama &* Br. Sqdn. 209	†61-30 N, 15-30 W
27 Aug	U-570*	Rahmlow	Br. Sqdn. 269	62-15 N, 18-35 W
10 Sep	U-501	Förster	HMCS *Chambly & Moosejaw*	62-50 N, 37-50 W
11 Sep	U-207	Meyer	HMS *Leamington & Veteran*	†63-59 N, 34-48 W
4 Oct	U-111	Kleinschmidt	HMS *Lady Shirley*	27-15 N, 20-27 W
19 Oct	U-204	Kell	HMS *Mallow & Rochester*	†35-46 N, 06-02 W
11 Nov	U-580	Kuhlmann	Collision	Baltic (off Memel)
15 Nov	U-583	Ratsch	Collision	†Baltic
16 Nov	U-433	Ey	HMS *Marigold*	36-13 N, 04-42 W
28 Nov	U-95	Schreiber	HNM Sub. *0-21*	36-24 N, 03-20 W
30 Nov	U-206	Opitz	RAF Sqdn. 502	†46-55 N, 07-16 W
11 Dec (Nov?)	U-208	Schlieper	HMS *Bluebell*	†Atlantic, W. of Gibraltar
15 Dec	U-127	Hansmann	HMAS *Nestor*	†36-28 N, 09-12 W
16 Dec	U-557	Paulssen	Rammed by Ital. Torp. boat *Orione*	†35-33 N, 23-14 E
17 Dec	U-131	Baumann	HMS *Exmoor, Blankney, Stanley, Stork, Pentstemon & Audacity* [& 802 Sqdn (RN)]	34-12 N, 13-35 W
18 Dec	U-434	Heyda	HMS *Stanley & Blankney*	36-15 N, 15-48 W
19 Dec	U-574	Gengelbach	HMS *Stork*	38-12 N, 17-23 W
21 Dec	U-451	Hoffmann	Br. Sqdn. 812	35-55 N, 06-08 W
21 Dec	U-567	Endrass	HMS *Deptford & Samphire*	†44-02 N, 20-10 W

*(HMS *Graph* from '47)

Date	U-Boat	Last Comdr.	Cause of sinking	Position
23 Dec	U-79	Kaufmann	HMS *Hasty* & *Hotspur*	32-15 N, 25-19 E
28 Dec	U-75	Ringelmann	HMS *Kipling*	31-50 N, 26-40 E
1942				
9 Jan	U-577	Schauenburg	Br. Sqdn. 230	†32-22 N, 26-54 E
12 Jan	U-374	v. Fischel	HM Sub. *Unbeaten*	37-50 N, 16-00 E
15 Jan	U-93	Elfe	HMS *Hesperus*	36-40 N, 15-52 W
2 Feb	U-581	Pfeiffer	HMS *Westcott*	39-00 N, 30-00 W
6 Feb	U-82	Rollmann	HMS *Rochester* & *Tamarisk*	†44-10 N, 23-52 W
1 Mar	U-656	Kröning	VP-82	†46-15 N, 53-15 W
14 Mar	U-133	Mohr	Mine (her own?)	†38-00 N, 24-00 E
15 Mar	U-503	Gerhicke	VP-82	†45-50 N, 48-50 W
24 Mar	U-655	Dumrese	HMS *Sharpshooter*	†73-00 N, 21-00 E
27 Mar	U-587	Borcherdt	HMS *Leamington, Grove, Aldenham* & *Volunteer*	†47-21 N, 21-39 W
29 Mar	U-585	Lohse	HMS *Fury*	†72-15 N, 34-22 E
— Apr	U-702	v. Rabenau	Unknown	†North Sea (?)
14 Apr	U-85	Greger	*Roper (DD-147)*	†35-55 N, 75-13 W
14 Apr	U-252	Lerchen	HMS *Stork* & *Vetch*	†47-00 N, 18-14 W
1 May	U-573	Heinsohn	Br. Sqdn. 233	(†)37-00 N, 01-00 E
2 May	U-74	Friederich	HMS *Wishart, Wrestler* & Br. Sqdn. 202	†37-32 N, 00-10 E
9 May	U-352	Rathke	USCGC *Icarus (WPC-110)*	34-12 N, 76-35 W
28 May	U-568	Preuss	HMS *Eridge, Hero* & *Hurworth*	32-42 N, 24-53 E
2 Jun	U-652	Fraatz	Br. Sqdns. 815 & 203	31-55 N, 25-13 E
13 Jun	U-157	Henne	USCGC *Thetis (WPC-115)*	†24-13 N, 82-03 W
30 Jun	U-158	Rostin	VP-74	†32-50 N, 67-28 W
3 Jul	U-215	Höckner	HMS *Le Tiger*	†41-48 N, 66-38 W
5 Jul	U-502	v. Rosenstiel	Br. Sqdn. 172	†46-10 N, 06-40 W
6 Jul } 13 Jul	U-153	Reichmann	{ US Army Bomb. Sqdn. 59 & *Lansdowne* (DD-486)	12-50 N, 72-20 W; †09-56 N, 81-29 W
7 Jul	U-701	Degen	US Army Bomb. Sqdn. 396	34-50 N, 74-55 W
11 Jul	U-136	Zimmermann	HMS *Spey, Pelican* & RF *Léopard*	†33-30 N, 22-52 W

['42] Date	U-Boat	Last Comdr.	Cause of sinking	Position
15 Jul	U-576	Heinicke	VS-9 & Amer. MS *Unicoi*	†34-51 N, 75-22 W
17 Jul	U-75	Bigalk	Br. Sqdns. 502 & 61	†45-14 N, 12-22 W
24 Jul	U-90	Oldörp	HMCS *St. Croix*	†48-12 N, 40-56 W
31 Jul	U-213	v. Varendorff	HMS *Erne, Rochester & Sandwich*	†36-45 N, 22-50 W
31 Jul	U-588	Vogel	HMCS *Wetaskiwin & Skeena*	†49-59 N, 36-36 W
31 Jul	U-754	Oestermann	RCAF Sqdn. 113	†43-02 N, 64-52 W
1 Aug	U-166	Kuhlmann	USCG Sqdn. 212	†28-37 N, 90-45 W
3 Aug	U-335	Pelkner	HM Sub. *Saracen*	62-48 N, 00-12 W
4 Aug	U-372	Neumann	HMS *Sikh, Zulu, Croome, Tetcott* & Br. Sqdn. 221	32-00 N, 34-00 E
6 Aug	U-210	Lemcke	HMCS *Assiniboine*	54-25 N, 39-37 W
8 Aug	U-379	Kettner	HMS *Dianthus*	57-11 N, 30-57 W
10 Aug	U-578	Rehwinkel	Czech Sqdn. 311	†45-49 N, 07-44 W
20 Aug	U-464	Harms	VP-73	61-25 N, 14-40 W
22 Aug	U-654	Forster	US Army Bomb. Sqdn. 45	†12-00 N, 79-56 W
28 Aug	U-94	Ites	HMCS *Oakville* & VP-92	17-40 N, 74-30 W
2 Sep	U-222	v. Jessen	Collision	54-25 N, 19-50 E
3 Sep	U-756	Harney	Br. A/C	†57-30 N, 29-00 W
3 Sep	U-705	Horn	Br. Sqdn. 77	†47-55 N, 10-04 W
3 Sep	U-162	Wattenberg	HMS *Vimy, Pathfinder & Quentin*	12-21 N, 59-29 W
12 Sep	U-589§	Horrer	HMS *Faulknor*	†75-04 NN, 04-49 E
14 Sep	U-88§	Bohmann	HMS *Onslow*	†74-50 N, 20-32 E
15 Sep	U-261	Lange	Br. Sqdn. 58	†59-49 N, 09-28 W
16 Sep	U-457	Brandenburg	HMS *Impulsive*	†75-05 N, 43-15 E
23 Sep	U-253	Friedrichs	Br. Sqdn. 210	†68-19 N, 13-50 W
27 Sep	U-165	Hoffmann	Mine & Sqdn. 825	†47-50 N, 03-22 W
2 Oct	U-512	Schultze	US Army Bomb. Sqdn. 99	06-50 N, 52-25 W
5 Oct	U-582	Schulte	Br. Sqdn. 269	†58-41 N, 22-58 W
8 Oct	U-179	Sobe	HMS *Active*	†33-28 S, 17-05 E
9 Oct	U-171	Pfeffer	Mine	47-30 N, 03-30 W
12 Oct	U-597	Bopst	Br. Sqdn. 120	†56-50 N, 28-05 W
15 Oct	U-661	v. Lilienfeld	Br. Sqdn. 120	†53-58 N, 33-43 W
15 Oct	U-619	Makowski	HMS *Viscount*	†53-42 N, 35-56 W
16 Oct	U-353	Römer	HMS *Fame*	53-54 N, 29-30 W
20 Oct	U-216	Schultz	Br. Sqdn. 224	†48-21 N, 19-25 W

§Latest British study transposes these two sinkings also.

['42] Date	U-Boat	Last Comdr.	Cause of sinking	Position
22 Oct	U-412	Jahrmärker	Br. Sqdn. 179	†63-55 N, 00-24 W
24 Oct	U-599	Breithaupt	Br. Sqdn. 224	†46-07 N, 17-40 W
27 Oct	U-627	Kindelbacher	Br. Sqdn. 206	†59-14 N, 22-49 W
30 Oct	U-520	Schwartzkopf	RCAF Sqdn. 10	†47-47 N, 49-50 W
30 Oct	U-559	Heidtmann	HMS *Pakenham, Petard, Hero, Dulverton, Hurworth,* & Br. A/C	32-30 N, 33-00 E
30 Oct	U-658	Senkel	RCAF Sqdn. 145	†50-32 N, 46-32 W
[20] Oct	U-116	Grimme	[VP-74]?	†Atlantic
5 Nov	U-132	Vogelsang	Br. Sqdn. 120	†58-08 N, 33-13 W
5 Nov	U-408	v. Hymmen	VP-84	†67-40 N, 18-32 W
12 Nov	U-272	Hepp	Collision	Baltic (off Hela)
12 Nov	U-660	Baur	HMS *Lotus* & *Starwort*	36-07 N, 01-00 W
13 Nov	U-605	Schütze	HMS *Lotus* & *Poppy*	†37-04 N, 02-55 E
14 [15?] Nov	U-595	Quaet-Faslem	Br. Sqdn. 500 [dmgd. bchd, scuttled]	36-38 N, 00-30 E
14 [14?] Nov	U-259	Köpke	Br. Sqdn. 500	†37-20 N, 03-05 E
16 Nov	U-173	Schweichel	*Woolsey (DD-437), Swanson (DD-443) & Quick (DD-490)*	†33-40 N, 07-35 W
17 Nov	U-331	v. Tiesenhausen	HMS *Formidable*'s Sqdn. 820 & Br. Sqdn. 500§§	37-05 N, 02-24 E
19 Nov	U-98	Eichmann	Br. Sqdn. 608	†35-38 N, 11-48 W
20 Nov	U-184	Dangschat	HNMS *Potentilla*	†49-25 N, 45-25 W
21 Nov	U-517	Hartwig	HMS *Victorious*'s Sqdn. 817	46-16 N, 17-09 W
15 Nov	U-411§	Spindlegger	HMS *Wrestler*	†36-09 N, 07-42 E
8 Dec	U-254	Gilardone	Br. Sqdn. 120, after collision with another U-boat (sunk by HMS *Wrestler*?)	57-25 N, 35-19 W
10 Dec	U-611	v. Jacobs	VP-84	†58-09 N, 22-44 W
15 Dec	U-626	Bade	USCGC *Ingham*	†56-46 N, 27-12 W
26 Dec	U-357	Kellner	HMS *Hesperus* & *Vanessa*	57-10 N, 15-40 W

§See *Dessie* under Italians, inf.
§§Damaged by and surrendered to Sqdn. 500, but signals not seen by 820 Sqdn., who then sank her.

['42] Date	U-Boat	Last Comdr.	Cause of sinking	Position
27 Dec	U-356	Ruppelt	HMCS *St. Laurent, Chilliwack, Battleford, Napanee & St. John*	†45-30 N, 25-40 W
1943				
6 Jan	U-164	Fechner	VP-83	01-58 S, 39-23 W
13 Jan	U-224	Kosbadt	HMCS *Ville de Quebec*	36-28 N, 00-49 E
13 Jan	U-507	Schacht	VP-83	†01-38 S, 39-52 W
15 Jan	U-337	Ruwiedel	Br. Sqdn. 206	†57-40 N, 27-10 W
21 Jan	U-301	Körner	HM Sub. *Sahib*	41-27 N, 07-04 E
— Jan	U-553	Thurmann	Unknown	†53-00 N, 33-00 W
3 Feb	U-265	Aufhammer	Br. Sqdn. 220	†56-35 N, 22-49 W
4 Feb	U-187	Münnich	HMS *Vimy & Beverley*	50-12 N, 36-34 W
7 Feb	U-609	Rudloff	RF *Lobelia*	†55-17 N, 26-38 W
7 Feb	U-624	v. Soden-Fraunhofen	Br. Sqdn. 220	†55-42 N, 26-17 W
10 Feb	U-519	Eppen	US Army A/S Sqdn. 2	†47-05 N, 18-34 W
12 Feb	U-442	Hesse	Br. Sqdn. 48	†37-32 N, 11-56 W
14 Feb	U-620	Stein	Br. Sqdn. 202	†39-27 N, 11-34 W
15 Feb	U-529	Fraatz	Br. Sqdn. 120	†55-45 N, 31-09 W
17 Feb	U-201	Rosenberg	HMS *Fame*	†50-36 N, 41-07 W
17 Feb	U-69	Gräf	HMS *Viscount*	50-50 N, 40-50 W
17 Feb	U-205	Bürgel	HMS *Paladin* & RSAAF Sqdn. 15	32-56 N, 22-01 E
19 Feb	U-562	Hamm	HMS *Isis, Hursley* & Br. A/C	†32-57 N, 20-54 E
19 Feb	U-268	Heydemann	Br. Sqdn. 172	†47-03 N, 05-56 W
21 Feb	U-623	Schröder	RAF Sqdn. 120 (A/C torp.)	†48-68 N, 29-15 W
21 Feb	U-225	Leimkühler	USCGC *Spencer (WPG-36)*	†51-25 N, 27-28 W
22 Feb	U-606	Döhler	USCGC *Campbell* & ORP *Burza*	47-44 N, 33-43 W
23 Feb	U-522	Schneider	HMS *Totland*	†31-27 N, 26-22 W
23 Feb	U-443	v. Puttkamer	HMS *Bicester, Lamerton & Wheatland*	†36-55 N, 02-25 E
24 Feb	U-649	Tiesler	Collision with *U-232*	
4 Mar	U-83	Wörishoffer	RAF Sqdn. 500	†37-10 N, 00-05 E
4 Mar	U-87	Berger	HMCS *Shediac & St. Croix*	†41-36 N, 13-31 W
7 Mar	U-633	Müller	Br. Sqdn. 220	†57-14 N, 26-30 W
8 Mar	U-156	Hartenstein	VP-53	†12-38 N, 54-39 W

['43] Date	U-Boat	Last Comdr.	Cause of sinking	Position
11 Mar	U-432	Eckhardt	RF *Aconit*	51-35 N, 28-20 W
11 Mar	U-444	Langfeld	HMS *Harvester* & RF *Aconit*	51-14 N, 29-18 W
12 Mar	U-130	Keller	*Champlin (DD-601)*	37-10 N, 40-21 W
19 Mar	U-5	Rahn	Collision	54-25 N, 19-50 E
20 Mar	U-384	v. Rosenberg-Gruszcynski	Br. Sqdn. 201	†54-18 N, 26-15 W
21 Mar	U-163	Engelmann	*Herring (SS-233)*	†44-13 N, 08-23 W (lv. Lorient, 3-10)
22 Mar	U-665	Haupt	Br. Sqdn. 172	†46-47 N, 09-58 W
22 Mar	U-524	v. Steinaecker	US Army A/S Sqdn. 1	†30-15 N, 18-13 W
25 Mar	U-469	Claussen	Br. Sqdn. 206	†62-12 N, 16-40 W
27 Mar	U-169	Bauer	Br. Sqdn. 206	†60-54 N, 15-25 W
28 Mar	U-77	Hartmann	Br. Sqdns. 223 & 48	37-42 N, 00-10 E
2 Apr	U-124	Mohr	HMS *Stonecrop* & *Black Swan*	†41-02 N, 15-39 W
6 Apr	U-167	Sturm	Br. Sqdn. 233 (5 Apr; scuttled, 6th)	27-47 N, 15-00 W
6 Apr	U-635	Eckelmann	HMS *Tay*	†58-25 N, 29-22 W
6 Apr	U-632	Karpf	Br. Sqdn. 86	†58-02 N, 28-42 W
7 Apr	U-644	Jensen	HM Sub. *Tuna*	†69-38 N, 05-40 W
10 Apr	U-376	Marks	Br. Sqdn. 172	†46-48 N, 09-00 W
14 Apr	U-526	Möglich	Mine	47-30 N, 03-45 W
17 Apr	U-175	Bruns	USCGC *Spencer (WPG-36)*	48-50 N, 21-20 W
23 Apr	U-602	Schüler	Br. Sqdn. 500 (off Oran)	(†)Mediterranean
23 Apr	U-189	Kurrer	Br. Sqdn. 120	†59-50 N, 34-43 W
23 Apr	U-191	Fiehn	HMS *Hesperus*	†56-45 N, 34-25 W
24 Apr	U-710	v. Carlowitz	Br. Sqdn. 206	†61-25 N, 19-48 W
25 Apr	U-203	Kottmann	HMS *Biter*'s Sqdn. 811 A/C & HMS *Pathfinder*	55-05 N, 42-25 W
27 Apr	U-174	Grandefeld	VP-125	43-35 N, 56-18 W
30 Apr	U-227	Kuntze	RAAF Sqdn. 455	†64-05 N, 06-40 W
2 May	U-332	Hüttemann	RAAF, Sqdn. 461	†44-48 N, 08-58 W
3 May	U-659	Stock	Collision with *U-439*	43-32 N, 13-20 W
3 May	U-439	v. Tippelskirch	Collision with *U-659*	43-32 N, 13-20 W
4 May	U-630	Winkler	RCAF Sqdn. 5	†56-38 N, 42-32 W
7 May	U-465	Wolf	RAAF Sqdn. 10	†47-06 N, 10-58 W
5 May	U-192	Happe	HMS *Pink*	†54-56 N, 43-44 W
5 May	U-638	Staudinger	HMS *Loosestrife*	†53-06 N, 45-02 W
6 May	U-125	Folkers	HMS *Vidette*	†52-31 N, 44-50 W
6 May	U-531	Neckel	HMS *Oribi*	†52-31 N, 44-50 W
6 May	U-438	Heinsohn	HMS *Pelican*	52-00 N, 45-10 W

['43] Date	U-Boat	Last Comdr.	Cause of sinking	Position
7 May	U-447	Bothe	Br. Sqdn. 233	†35-30 N, 11-55 W
4 May	U-109	Schramm	Br. Sqdn. 86	†47-22 N, 22-40 W
7 May	U-663	Schmid	Br. Sqdn. 58	†46-33 N, 11-12 W
11 May	U-528	v. Rabenau	HMS *Fleetwood* & Br. Sqdn. 58	46-55 N, 14-44 W
12 [14?] May	U-185	Hesemann	HMS *Hesperus*	†41-54 N, 31-49 W
12 (14) May	U-89	Lohmann	HMS *Biter*'s Sqdn. 811, HMS *Broadway* & *Lagan*	†46-30 N, 25-40 W
13 May	U-456	Teichert	HMS *Lagan* HMCS *Drumheller* & Br. Sqdn. *423*	†48-37 N, 22-39 W
14 May	U-266	v. Jessen	Br. Sqdn. 86	†47-45 N, 26-57 W
14 May	U-640§§	Nagel	VP-84	†60-10 N, 31-52 W
15 May	U-753	v. Mannstein	Unknown	†47-00 N, 22-00 W
15 May	U-176	Dierksen	VS-62 & Cuban *SC-13*	†23-21 N, 80-18 W
15 May	U-463	Wolfbauer	Br. Sqdn. 58	†45-28 N, 10-20 W
16 (15) May	U-182	Clausen	*Mackenzie (DD-614)*	†33-55 N, 20-35 W
17 (28?) May	U-128	Steinert	VP-74, *Moffett (DD-362)* & *Jouett (DD-396)*	10-00 S, 35-35 W
17 May	U-657§§	Göllnitz	HMS *Swale*	†58-54 N, 42-33 W
17 May	U-646	Wulff	Br. Sqdn. 269	†62-10 N, 14-30 W
19 May	U-954	Löwe	Br. Sqdn. 120	†55-09 N, 35-18 W
19 May	U-209	Brodda	HMS *Jed* & *Sennen*	†54-54 N, 34-19 W
19 May	U-273	Rossmann	Br. Sqdn. 269	†59-25 N, 24-33 W
19 May	U-381	v. Pückler u. Limpurg	HMS *Duncan* & *Snowflake*	†54-41 N, 34-45 W
20 May	U-258	v. Mäszen-hausen	Br. Sqdn. 120	†55-18 N, 27-49 W
21 May	U-303	Heine	HM Sub. *Sickle*	42-50 N, 06-00 E
22 May	U-569	Johannsen	VC-9 from *Bogue (CVE-9)*	50-40 N, 35-21 W
23 May	U-752	Schröter	HMS *Archer*'s A/C	51-40 N, 29-49 W
25 May	U-414	Huth	HMS *Vetch*	†36-31 N, 00-40 E
25 May	U-467	Kummer	VP-84	†62-25 N, 14-52 W
26 May	U-436	Seibicke	HMS *Test* & *Hyderabad*	†43-49 N, 15-56 W
28 May	U-304	Koch	Br. Sqdn. 120	†54-50 N, 37-20 W
28 May	U-755	Göing	Br. Sqdn. 608	39-58 N, 01-41 E
31 May	U-563	Borchardt	Br. Sqdns. 58 & 228 & RAAF Sqdn. 10	†46-35 N, 10-40 W

§§Br. Admiralty advises *U-640* and *-657* should be transposed

Date	U-Boat	Last Comdr.	Cause of sinking	Position
31 May	U-440	Schwaff	Br. Sqdn. 201	†45-38 N, 13-04 W
1 Jun	U-202	Poser	HMS *Starling*	56-12 N, 39-52 W
1 Jun	U-418	Lange	Br. Sqdn. 236	†47-05 N, 08-55 W
2 Jun	U-105	Nissen	Fr. Sqdn. 141	†14-15 N, 17-35 W
2 Jun	U-521	Bargsten	*PC-565*	37-43 N, 73-16 W
4 Jun	U-308	Mühlenpfordt	HM Sub. *Truculent*	†64-28 N, 03-09 W
4 Jun	U-594	Mumm	Br. Sqdn. 48	†35-55 N, 09-25 W
5 Jun	U-217	Reichenback-Klinke	VC-9 from *Bogue (CVE-9)*	†30-18 N, 42-50 W
11 Jun	U-417	Schreiner	Br. Sqdn. 206	†63-20 N, 10-30 W
12 Jun	U-118	Cygan	VC-9 from *Bogue (CVE-9)*	30-49 N, 33-49 W
14 Jun	U-334	Ehrich	HMS *Jed* & *Pelican*	†58-16 N, 28-20 W
14 Jun	U-564	Fiedler	Br. Sqdn. 10	44-17 N, 10-25 W
16 Jun	U-97	Trox	RAAF Sqdn. 459	33-00 N, 34-00 E
20 Jun	U-388	Sues	VP-84	†57-36 N, 31-20 W
24 Jun	U-119	v. Kameke	HMS *Starling*	†45-00 N, 11-59 W
24 Jun	U-194	Hesse	Br. Sqdn. 120	†58-15 N, 25-25 W
24 Jun	U-200	Schonder	VP-84	†59-00 N, 26-18 W
24 Jun	U-449	Otto	HMS *Wren, Woodpecker, Kite* & *Wild Goose*	†45-00 N, 11-59 W
3 Jul	U-126	Kietz	Br. Sqdn. 172	†46-02 N, 11-23 W
3 Jul	U-628	Hasenschar	Br. Sqdn. 224	†44-11 N, 08-45 W
5 Jul	U-535	Ellmenreich	Br. Sqdn. 53	†43-38 N, 09-13 W
7 Jul	U-951	Pressel	US Army A/S Sqdn. 1	†37-40 N, 15-30 W
8 July	U-514	Auffermann	Br. Sqdn. 224	†43-37 N, 08-59 W
8 Jul	U-232	Ziehm	US Army A/S Sqdn. 2	†40-37 N, 13-41 W
9 Jul	U-435	Strelow	Br. Sqdn. 179	†39-48 N, 14-22 W
9 Jul	U-590	Kruer	VP-94	†03-22 N, 48-38 W
12 Jul	U-409	Massmann	HMS *Inconstant*	37-12 N, 04-00 E
12 Jul	U-506	Würdemann	US Army A/S Sqdn. 1	42-30 N, 16-30 W
12 Jul	U-561	Henning	HMS *MTB-81*	38-16 N, 15-39 W
13 Jul	U-607	Jeschonnek	Br. Sqdn. 228	45-02 N, 09-14 W
13 Jul	U-487	Metz	VC-13 from *Core (CVE-13)*	27-15 N, 34-18 W
14 Jul	U-160	v. Pommer-Esche	VC-29 from *Santee (CVE-29)*	†33-54 N, 27-13 W
15 Jul	U-159	Beckmann	VP-32	†15-58 N, 73-44 W
15 Jul	U-135	Luther	HMS *Rochester, Mignonette* & *Balsam* & VP-92	28-20 N, 13-17 W
15 Jul	U-509	Witte	VC-29 from *Santee (CVE-29)*	†34-02 N, 26-02 W

Date	U-Boat	Last Comdr.	Cause of sinking	Position
16 Jul	U-67	Müller-Stöckheim	VC-13 from *Core* *(CVE-13)*	30-05 N, 44-17 W
19 Jul	U-513	Guggenberger	VP-74	27-17 S, 47-32 W
20 Jul	U-558	Krech	US Army A/S Sqdn. 19	45-10 N, 09-42 W
21 Jul	U-662	Müller	VP-94	03-56 N, 48-46 W
23 Jul	U-527	Uhlig	VC-9 from *Bogue* *(CVE-9)*	35-25 N, 27-56 W
23 Jul	U-613	Köppe	*Badger (DD-126)*	†35-32 N, 28-36 W
23 Jul	U-598	Holtorf	VB-107	04-05 S, 33-23 W
24 Jul	U-459	v. Wilamowitz-Möllendorf	Br. Sqdn. 172	45-53 N, 10-38 W
24 Jul	U-622	Karpf	US Army air raid	63-27 N, 10-23 E
26 Jul	U-759	Friedrich	VP-32	†18-06 N, 75-00 W
28 Jul	U-359	Förster	VP-32	†15-57 N, 68-30 W
28 Jul	U-404	Schönberg	US Army A/S Sqdn. 4 & Br. Sqdn. 224	†45-53 N, 09-25 W
29 Jul	U-614	Sträter	Br. Sqdn. 172	†46-42 N, 11-03 W
30 Jul	U-591	Ziesmer	VB-127	08-36 S, 34-34 W
30 Jul	U-504	Luis	HMS *Kite, Woodpecker, Wren, Wild Goose*	†45-33 N, 10-47 W
30 Jul	U-43	Schwandtke	VC-29 from *Santee* *(CVE-29)*	34-57 N, 35-11 W
30 Jul	U-461	Stiebler	RAAF Sqdn. 461	45-42 N, 11-00 W
30 Jul	U-462	Voes	Br. Sqdn. 502	45-08 N, 10-57 W
30 Jul	U-375	Koenenkamp	*PC-624*	†36-40 N, 12-38 W
31 Jul	U-199	Kraus	VP-74 & Brazilian A/C	23-54 S, 42-54 W
1 Aug	U-383	Kremser	Br. Sqdn. 228	†47-24 N, 12-10 W
1 Aug	U-454	Hackländer	RAAF Sqdn. 10	45-36 N, 10-23 W
2 Aug	U-706	v. Zitzewitz	US Army A/S Sqdn. 4	46-15 N, 10-25 W
2 Aug	U-106	Damerow	RAAF Sqdn. 461 & Br. Sqdn. 228	46-35 N, 11-55 W
3 Aug	U-572	Kummetat	VP-205	†11-35 N, 54-05 W
3 Aug	U-647	Hertin	Unknown	(†)Iceland-Faroes
4 Aug	U-489	Schmandt	RCAF Sqdn. 423	61-11 N, 14-38 W
5 Aug	U-34	Aust	Collision with Ger. sub-tender *Lech*	Off Memel
7 Aug	U-615	Kapitzky	VP-205, VP-204, VB-130 & US Army Bomb. Sqdn. 10	12-57 N, 64-34 W
7 Aug	U-117	Neumann	VC-1 from *Card* *(CVE-11)*	†39-32 N, 38-21 W

['43] Date	U-Boat	Last Comdr.	Cause of sinking	Position
9 Aug	U-664	Graef	VC-1 from *Card (CVE-11)*	40-12 N, 37-29 W
11 Aug [3?]	U-604	Höltring	Scuttled as result of attacks by VP-129, VB-107 & *Moffett (DD-362)*	05-00 S, 20-00 W [9-10 S, 29-43 W]
11 Aug	U-468	Schamong	Br. Sqdn. 200	12-20 N, 20-07 W
11 Aug	U-525	Drewitz	VC-1 from *Card (CVE-11)*	†41-29 N, 38-55 W
17 Aug	U-403	Heine	Br. Sqdn. 200 & Fr. Sqdn. 697	14-11 N, 17-40 W
20 Aug	U-197	Bartels	Br. Sqdns. 265 & 259	†28-40 S, 42-36 E
21 Aug	U-670	Hyronimus	Collision	Baltic
22 Aug	U-458	Diggins	HMS *Easton* & HMS *Pindos*	36-25 N, 12-39 E
24 Aug	U-134	Brosin	Br. Sqdn. 179	†42-07 N, 09-30 W
24 (30?) Aug	U-185	Maus	VC-13 from *Core (CVE-13)*	27-00 N, 37-06 W
24 (26?) Aug	U-84	Uphoff	VC-13 from *Core (CVE-13)*	†27-09 N, 37-03 W
25 Aug	U-523	Pietzsch	HMS *Wanderer* & *Wallflower*	42-03 N, 18-02 W
27 Aug	U-847	Kuppisch	VC-1 from *Card (CVE-11)*	†28-19 N, 37-58 W
30 Aug	U-634	Dahlhaus	HMS *Stork* & *Stonecrop*	†40-13 N, 19-24 W
30 Aug	U-639	Wichmann	Russian Sub. *S-101*	†*Kara Sea*
7 Sep	U-669	Köhl	RCAF Sqdn. 407	†45-36 N, 10-13 W
8 Sep	U-983	Reimers	Collision	Baltic
8 Sep	U-760	Blum	Damaged by HMS *Wellington*'s Sqdn. 179	Interned in Spain; surrendered in '45
11 (12?) Sep	U-617	Brandi	Br. Sqdn. 179, *HMS Hyacinth, Haarlem* HMAS *Woolongong*	35-38 N, 03-27 W
19 Sep	U-341	Epp	RCAF Sqdn. 10	†58-40 N, 25-30 W
20 Sep	U-338	Kinzel	Br. Sqdn. 120	†57-40 N, 29-48 W
20 Sep	U-346	Leisten	Marine casualty (diving accident)	†54-25 N, 19-50 E
22 Sep	U-229	Schetelig	HMS *Keppel*	†54-36 N, 36-25 W
27 Sep	U-161	Achilles	VP-74	†12-30 N, 35-35 W
27 Sep	U-221	Trojer	Br. Sqdn. 58	†47-00 N, 18-00 W
4 Oct	U-279	Finke	Br. Sqdn. 120	†60-51 N, 28-26 W
4 Oct	U-336	Hunger	VB-128	†60-40 N, 26-30 W
4 Oct	U-422	Poeschel	VC-9 from *Card (CVE-11)*	†43-18 N, 28-58 W

Date	U-Boat	Last Comdr.	Cause of sinking	Position
4 Oct	U-460	Schnorr	VC-9 from *Card (CVE-11)*	43-13 N, 28-58 W
5 Oct	U-389	Heilmann	Br. Sqdn. 269	†62-43 N, 27-17 W
8 Oct	U-643	Speidel	Br. Sqdns. 86 & 120	56-14 N, 26-55 W
8 Oct	U-610	v. Freyberg	RCAF Sqdn. 423	†55-45 N, 24-33 W
8 Oct	U-419	Giersberg	Br. Sqdn. 86	56-31 N, 27-05 W
13 Oct	U-402	v. Forstner	VC-9 from *Card (CVE-11)*	†48-56 N, 29-41 W
16 Oct	U-470	Grave	Br. Sqdns. 59 & 120	58-20 N, 29-20 W
16 Oct	U-533	Hennig	Br. Sqdn. 244	25-28 N, 56-50 E
16 Oct	U-844	Möller	Br. Sqdns. 86 & 59	†58-30 N, 27-16 W
16 Oct	U-964	Hummer	Br. Sqdn. 86	†57-27 N, 28-17 W
17 Oct	U-631	Krüger	HMS *Sunflower*	†58-13 N, 32-29 W
17 Oct	U-841	Bender	HMS *Byard*	59-57 N, 31-06 W
17 Oct	U-540	Kasch	Br. Sqdns. 59 & 120	†58-38 N, 31-56 W
20 Oct	U-378	Mäder	VC-13 from *Core (CVE-13)*	47-40 N, 28-27 W
23 Oct	U-274	Jordan	HMS *Duncan, Vidette* & Br. Sqdn. 224	†57-14 N, 27-50 W
24 Oct	U-566	Hornkohl	Br. Sqdn. 179	41-12 N, 09-31 W
26 Oct	U-420	Reese	RCAF Sqdn. 10	†50-49 N, 41-01 W
28 Oct	U-220	Barber	VC-1 from *Block Island (CVE-106)*	†48-53 N, 33-30 W
29 Oct	U-282	Müller	HMS *Vidette, Duncan & Sunflower*	†55-28 N, 31-57 W
30 Oct	U-431	Schöneboom	HM Sub. *Ultimatum*	†43-04 N, 05-57 E
31 Oct	U-306	v. Trotha	HMS *Whitehall & Geranium*	†46-19 N, 20-44 W
31 Oct	U-584	Deecke	VC-9 from *Card (CVE-11)*	†49-14 N, 31-55 W
31 Oct	U-732	Carlsen	HMS *Imperialist & Douglas*	35-54 N, 05-52 W
1 Nov	U-340	Klaus	HMS *Fleetwood, Active, Witherington* & Br. Sqdn. 179	35-33 N, 06-37 W
1 Nov	U-405	Hopman	*Borie (DD-215)*	†49-00 N, 31-14 W
5 Nov	U-848	Rollmann	VB-107 & US Army 1st Compron	10-09 S, 18-00 W
6 Nov	U-226	Gange	HMS *Starling, Woodcock & Kite*	†44-49 N, 41-13 W
6 Nov	U-842	Heller	HMS *Starling & Wild Goose*	†43-42 N, 42-08 W
9 Nov	U-707	Gretschel	Br. Sqdn. 220	†40-31 N, 20-17 W
10 Nov	U-966	Wolf	VB-103, VB-110 & Czech Sqdn. 311	44-00 N, 08-30 W

['43] Date	U-Boat	Last Comdr.	Cause of sinking	Position
12 Nov	U-508	Staats	VB-103	†46-00 N, 07-30 W
16 Nov	U-280	Hungerhausen	Br. Sqdn. 86	†49-11 N, 27-32 W
18 Nov	U-718	Wieduwilt	Collision	Baltic
19 Nov	U-211	Hause	Br. Sqdn. 179	†40-15 N, 19-18 W
20 Nov	U-536	Schauenburg	HMS *Nene, Snowberry* & HMCS *Calgary*	43-50 N, 19-39 W
20 Nov	U-768	Buttjer	Collision	Baltic
21 Nov	U-538	Gossler	HMS *Foley* & *Crane*	†45-40 N, 19-35 W
23 Nov	U-648	Stahl	HMS *Bazley, Blackwood* & *Drury*	†42-40 N, 20-37 W
25 Nov	U-849	Schultze	VB-107	†06-30 S, 05-40 W
25 Nov	U-600	Zurmühlen	HMS *Bazley* & *Blackwood*	†40-31 N, 22-07 W
28 Nov	U-542	Coester	Br. Sqdn. 179	†39-03 N, 16-25 W
29 Nov	U-86	Schug	VC-19 from *Bogue (CVE-9)*	†38-33 N, 19-01 W
13 [12?] Dec	U-172	Hoffmann	VC-19 from *Bogue (CVE-9), George E. Badger (AVD-3), DuPont (DD-152), Clemson (DD-186)* & *George W. Ingram (DE-62)*	26-19 N, 29-58 W
13 Dec	U-345	Knackfuss	Mine	†54-06 N, 12-09 E
13 Dec	U-391	Dültgen	Br. Sqdn. 53	†45-45 N, 09-38 W
13 Dec	U-593	Kelbling	*Wainwright (DD-419)* HMS *Calpe*	37-38 N, 05-58 E
16 Dec	U-73	Deckert	*Woolsey (DD-437)* & *Trippe (DD-403)*	36-07 N, 00-50 W
20 Dec	U-850	Ewerth	VC-19 from *Bogue (CVE-9)*	†32-54 N, 37-01 W
21 Dec	U-284	Scholz	Scuttled	55-04 N, 30-23 W
24 Dec	U-645	Ferro	*Schenck (DD-159)*	†45-20 N, 21-40 W

1944

Date	U-Boat	Last Comdr.	Cause of sinking	Position
8 Jan	U-426	Reich	RAAF Sqdn. 10	†46-47 N, 10-42 W
8 Jan	U-757	Deetz	HMS *Bayntun* & HMCS *Camrose*	†50-33 N, 18-03 W
9 Jan	U-81	Krieg	US Army A/C	Pola
9 Jan	UIT-19	-(unknown)-	US Army A/C	Pola
13 Jan	U-231	Wenzel	Br. Sqdn. 172	44-15 N, 20-38 W
— Jan	U-377	Kluth	Unknown	(†)Atlantic
16 Jan	U-544	Mattke	VC 13 from *Guadalcanal (CVE-60)*	†40-30 N, 37-20 W

['44] Date	U-Boat	Last Comdr.	Cause of sinking	Position
17 Jan	U-305	Bahr	HMS *Wanderer* & *Glenarm*	†49-39 N, 20-10 W
19 Jan	U-641	Rendtel	HMS *Violet*	†50-25 N, 18-49 W
— Jan	U-972	König	Unknown	†Atlantic
20 Jan	U-263	Nölke	Mine	†46-10 N, 01-14 W
28 Jan	U-571	Lüssow	RAAF Sqdn. 461	†52-41 N, 14-27 W
28 Jan	U-271	Barleben	VB-103	†53-15 N, 15-52 W
30 Jan	U-314	Basse	HMS *Whitehall* & *Meteor*	†73-45 N, 26-15 E
30 Jan	U-364	Sass	Br. Sqdn. 172	†45-25 N, 05-15 W
31 Jan	U-592	Jaschke	HMS *Starling, Wild Goose* & *Magpie*	†50-20 N, 17-29 W
4 Feb	U-854	Weiher	Mine	53-55 N, 14-17 E
6 Feb	U-177	Buchholz	VB-107	10-35 S, 23-15 W
8 Feb	U-762	Pietschmann	HMS *Woodpecker, (Wild Goose* & *Starling)*	†49-02 N, 16-58 W
9 Feb	U-238	Hepp	HMS *Kite, Magpie* & *Starling*	†49-44 N, 16-07 W
9 Feb	U-734	Blauert	HMS *Wild Goose* & *Starling*	†49-43 N, 16-23 W
10 Feb	U-545	Mannesmann	Br. Sqdn. 612	58-17 N, 13-22 W
10 Feb	U-666	Willberg	HMS *Fencer*'s A/C	†53-56 N, 17-16 W
11 Feb	U-424	Lüders	HMS *Wild Goose* & *Woodpecker*	†50-00 N, 18-14 W
11 Feb	U-283	Ney	RCAF Sqdn. 407	†60-45 N, 12-50 W
14 Feb	U-738	Hoffmann	Diving accident	54-31 N, 18-33 E
14 Feb	UIT-23	Striegler	HM Sub. *Tally Ho*	†04-25 N, 100-09 E
18 Feb	U-406	Dietrichs	HMS *Spey*	48-32 N, 23-36 W
18 Feb	U-7	Loeschke	Collision	54-25 N, 19-50 W
19 Feb	U-264	Looks	HMS *Woodpecker* & *Starling*	48-31 N, 22-05 W
19 Feb	U-386	Albrecht	HMS *Spey*	48-51 N, 22-41 W
24 Feb	U-257	Rahe	HMCS *Waskesiu*	47-19 N, 26-00 W
24 Feb	U-713	Gosejacob	HMS *Keppel*	†69-27 N, 04-53 E
24 Feb	U-761	Geider	VP-63, VB-127, Br. Sqdn. 202, HMS *Anthony* & *Wishart*	35-55 N, 05-45 W
25 Feb	U-601	Hansen	Br. Sqdn. 210	†70-26 N, 12-40 E
25 Feb	U-91	Hungerhausen	HMS *Affleck, Gore* & *Gould*	49-45 N, 26-20 W
1 Mar	U-358	Manke	HMS *Affleck, Gould, Garlies* & *Gore*	45-46 N, 23-16 W
1 Mar	U-709	Ites	*Thomas (DE-102), Bostwick (DE-103)* & *Bronstein (DE-189)*	†49-10 N, 26-00 W

['44] Date	U-Boat	Last Comdr.	Cause of sinking	Position
1 Mar	U-603	Bertelsmann	*Bronstein (DE-189)*	†48-55 N, 26-10 W
4 Mar	U-472	v. Forstner	HMS *Chaser*'s Sqdn. 816 & HMS *Onslaught*	73-05 N, 26-40 E
5 Mar	U-366	Langenberg	HMS *Chaser*'s Sqdn. 816	†72-10 N, 14-45 E
6 Mar	U-744	Blischke	HMCS *St. Catherine's, Chilliwack, Gatineau, Fennel, Chaudière*, HMS *Icarus & Kenilworth Castle*	52-01 N, 22-37 W
6 Mar	U-973	Paepenmöller	HMS *Chaser*'s Sqdn. 816	70-04 N, 05-48 E
10 Mar	U-450	Böhme	HMS *Exmoor, Blankney, Blencathra & Brecon*	41-11 N, 12-27 E
10 Mar	U-343	Rahn	HMS *Mull*	†38-07 N, 09-41 E
10 Mar	U-625	Straub	RCAF Sqdn. 422	†52-35 N, 20-19 W
10 Mar	U-845	Weber	HMS *Forester*; HMCS *St. Laurent, Owen Sound & Swansea*	48-20 N, 20-33 W
11 Mar	UIT-22 [ex-*Alpino Attilio Bagnolini*]	Wunderlich	RSAAF Sqdns. 279 & 262	†41-28 S, 17-40 E
11 Mar	U-380	Brandi	US Army A/C	Toulon
11 Mar	U-410	Fenski	US Army A/C	Toulon
13 Mar	U-575	Boehmer	VC-95 from *Bogue (CVE-9)*; Br. Sqdns. 172 & 206, *Haverfield (DE-393), Hobson (DD-464)*, HMCS *Prince Rupert* & Br. Sqdn. 220	46-18 N, 27-34 W
15 Mar	U-653	Kandler	HMS *Vindex*'s A/C, HMS *Starling & Wild Goose*	†53-46 N, 24-35 W
16 Mar	U-392	Schümann	VP-63, HMS *Affleck & Vanoc*	†35-55 N, 05-41 W
16 Mar	U-801	Branz	VC-6 from *Block Island (CVE-106); Corry (DD-463) & Bronstein (DE-189)*	16-42 N, 30-28 W

['44] Date	U-Boat	Last Comdr.	Cause of sinking	Position
17 Mar	U-1013	Linck	Collision	Baltic
19 Mar	U-1059	Leupold	VC-6 from *Block Island (CVE-106)*	13-10 N, 33-44 W
25 Mar	U-976	Tiesler	Br. Sqdn. 248	46-48 N, 02-43 W
— Mar	U-851	Weingaertner	Unknown	(†)Atlantic
29 Mar	U-961	Fischer	HMS *Starling*	†64-31 N, 03-19 W
30 Mar	U-223	Gerlach	HMS *Laforey, Tumult, Hambledon & Blencathra*	38-48 N, 14-10 E
— Mar	U-28	Sachse	Marine casualty	Baltic (Neustadt)
1 Apr	U-355	La Baume	HMS *Tracker*'s Sqdn. 846 & HMS *Beagle*	†73-07 N, 10-21 E
2 Apr	U-360	Becker	HMS *Keppel*	†73-28 N, 13-04 E
3 Apr	U-288	Meyer	HMS *Tracker*'s Sqdn. 846 & HMS *Activity*'s Sqdn. 819	†73-44 N, 27-12 E
6 Apr	U-302	Sickel	HMS *Swale*	†45-05 N, 35-11 W
6 Apr	U-455	Scheibe	Unknown	†44-04 N, 09-51 E
7 Apr	U-856	Wittenberg	*Champlin (DD-601) & Huse (DE-145)*	40-18 N, 62-22 W
8 Apr	U-2	Schwarzkopf	Collision	Baltic (W. of Pillau)
8 Apr	U-962	Lieseberg	HMS *Crane* & *Cygnet*	†45-43 N, 19-57 W
9 Apr	U-515	Henke	VC-58 from *Guadalcanal (CVE-60); Pope (DD-225), Pillsbury (DE-135), Chatelain (DE-149) & Flaherty (DE-135)*	34-35 N, 19-18 W
10 Apr	U-68	Lauzemis	VC-58 from *Guadalcanal (CVE-60)*	33-25 N, 18-59 W
14 Apr	U-448	Dauter	HMCS *Swansea* & HMS *Pelican*	46-22 N, 19-35 W
16 Apr	U-550	Hänert	*Gandy (DE-764), Joyce (DE-317) & Peterson (DE-152)*	40-09 N, 69-44 W
17 Apr	U-342	Hossenfelder	RCAF Sqdn. 162	†60-23 N, 29-20 W
17 Apr	U-986	Kaiser	*Swift (AM-122) & PC-619*	†50-09 N, 12-51 W
19 Apr	U-974	Wolff	HNorMSub. *Ula*	59-08 N, 05-23 E
24 Apr	U-311	Zander	RCAF Sqdn. 423	†50-36 N, 18-36 W

['44] Date	U-Boat	Last Comdr.	Cause of sinking	Position
26 Apr	U-488	Studt	*Frost (DE-144), Huse (DE-145), Barber (DE-161) & Snowden (DE-246)*	†17-54 N, 38-05 W
27 Apr	U-803	Schimpf	Mine	53-55 N, 14-17 E
28 Apr	U-193	Abel	Br. Sqdn. 612	†45-38 N, 09-43 W
29 Apr	U-421	Kolbus	US Army A/C	Toulon
(11?) Apr	U-108	Brünig	US Army & RAF A/C (Decomm., 17th; Scuttled, May '45)	Stettin
1 May	U-277	Lübsen	HMS *Fencer*'s Sqdn. 842	†73-24 N, 15-32 E
2 May	U-674	Muhs	HMS *Fencer*'s Sqdn. 842	†70-32 N, 04-37 E
2 May	U-959	Weitz	HMS *Fencer*'s Sqdn. 842	†69-20 N, 00-20 W
3 May	U-852	Eck	Br. Sqdns. 8 & 621	09-32 N, 50-59 E
3 May	U-371	Fenski	*Pride (DE-323), Joseph E. Campbell (DE-70),* RF *Sénégalais &* HMS *Blankney*	37-49 N, 05-39 E
4 May	U-846	Hashagen	RCAF Sqdn. 407	46-04 N, 09-20 W
5 May	U-473	Sternberg	HMS *Starling, Wren & Wild Goose*	49-29 N, 21-22 W
6 May	U-66	Seehausen	VC-55 from *Block Island (CVE-106) & Buckley (DE-51)*	17-17 N, 32-29 W
6 May	U-765	Wendt	HMS *Vindex*'s Sqdn. 825, *Bickerton, Bligh & Aylmer*	52-30 N, 28-28 W
13 May	U-1224 *[HIJMS RO-501]*	Norita	*Francis M. Robinson (DE-220)*	†18-08 N, 33-13 W
14–17 May	U-616	Koitschka	*Nields (DD-616), Gleaves (DD-423), Ellyson (DD-454), Hilary P. Jones (DD-427), Macomb (DD-458), Hambleton (DD-455), Rodman (DD-456),*	36-52 N, 00-11 E

['44] Date	U-Boat	Last Comdr.	Cause of sinking	Position
			Emmons (DD-457) & Br. Sqdn. 36	
15 May	U-1234	Wrede	Collision (later raised)	Off Göteborg
15 May	U-731	Keller	VP-63, HMS *Kilmarnock* & *Blackfly*	†35-54 N, 05-45 W
16 May	U-240	Link	Nor. Sqdn. 330	†63-05 N, 03-10 E
18 May	U-241	Werr	Br. Sqdn. 210	†63-36 N, 01-42 E
19 May	U-960	Heinrich	*Niblack (DD-424), Ludlow (DD-438),* Br. Sqdns. 36 & 500	37-20 N, 01-35 E
19 May	U-1015	Boos	Collision	†54-25 N, 19-50 E
21 May	U-453	Lührs	HMS *Termagant, Tenacious* & *Liddesdale*	38-13 N, 16-36 E
24 May	U-476	Niethmann	Br. Sqdn. 210	†65-08 N, 04-53 E
24 May	U-675	Sammler	Br. Sqdn. 4	†62-27 N, 03-04 E
25 May	U-990	Nordheimer	Br. Sqdn. 59	†65-05 N, 07-28 E
27 May	U-292	Schmidt	Br. Sqdn. 59	†62-37 N, 00-57 E
29 May	U-549	Krankenhagen	*Eugene E. Elmore (DE-686)* & *Ahrens (DE-575)*	†31-13 N, 23-03 W
31 May	U-289	Hellwig	HMS *Milne*	†73-32 N, 00-28 E
3 Jun	U-477	Jenssen	RCAF Sqdn. 162	†63-59 N, 01-37 E
4 Jun	U-505	Lange	Captured by VC-8 from *Guadalcanal (CVE-60); Chatelain (DE-149), Jenks (DE-665)* & *Pillsbury (DE-133)*	(Now at Chicago Museum of Science & Industry) 21-30 N, 19-20 W
7 Jun	U-955	Baden	Br. Sqdn. 201	†45-13 N, 08-30 W
7 Jun	U-970	Ketels	Br. Sqdn. 228	45-15 N, 04-10 W
8 Jun	U-629	Bugs	Br. Sqdn. 224	†48-27 N, 05-47 W
8 Jun	U-373	v. Lehsten	Br. Sqdn. 224	48-10 N, 05-31 W
9 Jun	U-740	Stark	Br. Sqdn. 120	†49-09 N, 08-37 W
10 Jun	U-821	Knackfuss	Br. Sqdns. 206 & 248	†48-31 N, 05-11 W
11 Jun	U-980	Dahms	RCAF Sqdn. 162	†63-07 N, 00-26 E
12 Jun	U-490	Gerlach	VC-95 from *Croatan (CVE-25); Frost (DE-144), Inch (DE-146)* & *Huse (DE-145)*	42-47 N, 40-08 W
13 Jun	U-715	Röttger	RCAF Sqdn. 162	62-45 N, 02-59 W
15 Jun	U-860	Büchel	VC-9 from *Solomons (CVE-67)*	25-27 N, 05-30 W

['44] Date	U-Boat	Last Comdr.	Cause of sinking	Position
15 Jun	U-987	Schreyer	HM Sub. *Satyr*	†68-01 N, 05-08 E
16 Jun	U-998	Fiedler	Nor. Sqdn. 333: heavily damaged, scuttled 27th.	61-01 N, 03-00 E
17 Jun	U-423	Hackländer	Nor. Sqdn. 333	†63-06 N, 02-05 E
18 Jun	U-767	Dankleff	HMS *Fame, Inconstant* & *Havelock*	49-03 N, 03-13 W
18 Jun	U-441	Hartmann	Polish Sqdn. 304	49-03 N, 04-48 W
24 Jun	U-971	Zeplin	HMCS *Haida*, HMS *Eskimo* & Czech Sqdn. 311	49-01 N, 05-35 W
24 Jun	U-1225	Sauerberg	RCAF Sqdn. 162	†63-00 N, 00-50 W
25 Jun	U-1191	Grau	HMS *Affleck* & *Balfour*	†50-03 N, 02-59 W
25 Jun	U-269	Uhl	HMS *Bickerton*	50-01 N, 02-59 W
26 Jun	U-317	Rahlf	Br. Sqdn. 86	†62-03 N, 01-45 E
26 Jun	U-719	Steffens	HMS *Bulldog*	†55-33 N, 11-02 W
29 Jun	U-988	Dobberstein	HMS *Essington, Duckworth, Domett, Cooke,* & Br. Sqdn. 224	†49-37 N, 03-41 W
30 Jun	U-478	Rademacher	Br. Sqdn. 86 & RCAF Sqdn. 162	†63-27 N, 00-50 W
2 Jul	U-543	Hellriegel	VC-58 from *Wake Island (CVE-65)*	†25-34 N, 21-36 W
3 Jul	U-154	Gemeiner	*Inch (DE-146)* & *Frost (DE-144)*	†34-00 N, 19-30 W
5 Jul	U-390	Geissler	HMS *Wanderer* & *Tavy*	49-52 N, 00-48 W
5 Jul	U-586	Götze	US Army A/C	Toulon
5 Jul (?)	U-642	Brünning	US Army A/C	Toulon
5 Jul	U-233	Steen	*Card (CVE-11)*'s A/C, *Baker (DE-190)* & *Thomas (DE-102)*	42-16 N, 59-49 W
6 Jul	U-678	Hyronimus	HMCS *Ottawa, Kootenay* & HMS *Statice*	†50-32 N, 00-23 W
8 Jul	U-243	Märtens	RAAF Sqdn. 10	47-06 N, 06-40 W
11 Jul	U-1222	Bielfeld	Br. Sqdn. 201	†46-31 N, 05-29 W
14 Jul	U-415	Werner	Mine	48-22 N, 04-29 W
15 Jul	U-319	Clemens	Br. Sqdn. 206	†57-40 N, 05-00 E
17 Jul	U-361	Seidel	Br. Sqdn. 86	†68-36 N, 08-33 E
17 Jul	U-347	de Buhr	Br. Sqdn. 210	68-35 N, 06-00 E
18 Jul	U-672	Lawaetz	HMS *Balfour* (Scuttled)	50-03 N, 02-30 W

['44] Date	U-Boat	Last Comdr.	Cause of sinking	Position
18 Jul	U-742	Schwassmann	Br. Sqdn. 210	†68-24 N, 09-51 E
21 Jul	U-212	Vogler	HMS *Curzon* & *Ekins*	†50-27 N, 09-51 E
(22) Jul	U-1166	Ballert	Torpedo explosion	Eckernförde
23 Jul	U-239	Vöge	RAF A/C (out of svce., 24 July)	Kiel
23 Jul	U-1164	-(unknown)-	RAF A/C (out of svce., 24 July)	Kiel
26 Jul	U-214	Conrad	HMS *Cooke*	†49-55 N, 03-31 W
29 Jul	U-2323	Angermann	US Army A/C	Bremen
29 Jul	U-872	Grau	US Army A/C	Bremen
30 Jul	U-250	Schmidt	Russian *M-103* (sub)	Gulf of Findland
31 Jul	U-333	Fiedler	HMS *Starling* & *Loch Killin*	49-39 N, 07-28 W
4 Aug	U-671	Hegewald	HMS *Stayner* & *Wensleydale*	50-23 N, 00-06 E
6 Aug	U-736	Reff	HMS *Loch Killin* & *Starling*	47-19 N, 04-16 W
6 Aug	U-952	Curio	US Army A/C	Toulon
6 Aug	U-471	Klövekorn	US Army A/C	Toulon
6 Aug	U-969	Dobbert	US Army A/C	Toulon
9 Aug	U-608	Reisener	Br. Sqdn. 53 & HMS *Wren*	46-30 N, 03-08 W
11 Aug	U-385	Valentiner	RAAF Sqdn. 461 & HMS *Starling*	46-16 N, 02-45 W
12 Aug	U-981	Keller	Br. Sqdn. 502	45-41 N, 01-25 W
13 Aug	U-270	Schreiber	RAAF Sqdn. 461	46-19 N, 02-56 W
12 Aug	U-198	Heusinger v. Waldegg	HMS *Findhorn* & HMS *Godavari*	†03-35 S, 52-49 E
14 Aug	U-618	Faust	Br. Sqdn. 53 & HMS *Duckworth* & *Essington*	†47-22 N, 04-39 W
15 Aug	U-741	Palmgren	HMS *Orchis*	50-02 N, 00-36 W
18 Aug	U-107	Fritz	Br. Sqdn. 201	†46-46 N, 03-39 W
18 Aug	U-621	Stuckmann	HMCS *Ottawa*, *Kootenay* & *Chaudière*	†45-52 N, 02-36 W
19 Aug	U-123	v. Schröter	(Out of Service, 8/44) (RF *Blaison*, '54)	Lorient
19 Aug	U-466	Thater	Scuttled (Blown up?)	Toulon
19 Aug	U-967	Eberbach	Scuttled (Blown up?)	Toulon
20 Aug	U-413	Sachse	HMS *Wensleydale*, *Forester* & *Vidette*	50-21 N, 00-01 W
20 Aug	U-984	Sieder	HMCS *Ottawa*, *Chaudière* & *Kootenay*	†48-16 N, 05-33 W

['44] Date	U-Boat	Last Comdr.	Cause of sinking	Position
20 Aug	U-1229	Zinke	VC-42 from *Bogue (CVE-9)*	42-20 N, 51-39 W
20 Aug	U-9	Klapdor	Russian A/C	Constanza
21 Aug	U-230	Eberbach	Scuttled	Toulon
22 Aug	U-180	Riesen	Mine	†45-00 N, 02-00 W
24 Aug	U-354	Sthamer	HMS *Vindex*'s Sqdn. 825, *Mermaid, Loch* §§ *Dunvegan, Keppel & Peacock*	†74-54 N, 15-26 E
22 Aug	U-344	Pietsch	HMS *Vindex*'s §§ Sqdn. 825	†72-49 N, 30-41 E
24 Aug	U-445	v. Treuberg	HMS *Louis*	†47-21 N, 05-50 W
25 (20?) Aug	U-178	Spahr	Scuttled	Bordeaux
20 Aug	U-188	Lüdden	Scuttled	Bordeaux
25 Aug	UIT-21 [ex-*Guiseppe Finzi*]	-(unknown)-	Scuttled	Bordeaux (out of service after 9/8/43 attack)
25 Aug	U-667	Lange	Mine	†46-10 N, 01-14 W
25 [31?]	U-1000	Müller	Mine	Neustadt (Pillau?)
—Aug	U-766	Wilke	(Out of service, 8/44), (RF *Laubie*, '47)	La Pallice
— Aug	U-129	v. Harpe	(Out of service, 7/44), (later scuttled)	Lorient
25 Aug 10 Sep?	U-18	Fleige	Scuttled (later raised by USSR)	Constanza (Kusten-
25 Aug	U-24	Lenzmann	Scuttled (later raised by USSR)	Constanza dje)
1 Sep	U-247	Matschulat	HMCS *St. John & Swansea*	†49-54 N, 05-49 W
2 Sep	U-394	Borger	HMS *Vindex*'s Sqdn. 825, *Keppel, Mermaid, Whitehall & Peacock*	†69-47 N, 04-41 E
4 Sep	UIT-15, -16, -20		(See: Italian sub. chronology, inf.)	
5 Sep	U-362	Franz	Russian Mine-sweeper *T-116*	†Krakowka I. vicinity
9 Sep	U-743	Kandzlor	HMS *Portchester Castle & Helmsdale*	†55-45 N, 11-41 W

§§Br. Admiralty indicates these two positions should be transposed.

['44] Date	U-Boat	Last Comdr.	Cause of sinking	Position
9 Sep	U-484	Schäfer	HMCS *Dunver, Hespeler* (& RCAF Sqdn. 423?)	†56-30 N, 07-40 W
10 Sep	U-19	Ohlenberg	Scuttled	Turkish coast
10 Sep	U-20	Grafen	Scuttled	Turkish coast
10 Sep	U-23	Arendt	Scuttled	Turkish coast
19 Sep	U-407	Kolbus	HMS *Troubridge, Terpsichore* & ORP *Garland*	36-27 N, 24-33 E
19 Sep	U-865	Stellmacher	Unknown	†North Sea
19 Sep	U-867	v. Mühlendahl	Br. Sqdn. 224 (or engine failure?)	†62-15 N, 01-50 E
23 Sep	U-859	Jebsen	HM Sub. *Trenchant*	05-46 N, 100-04 E
24 Sep	U-565	Henning	US Army A/C	Salamis
24 Sep	U-596	Kolbus	US Army A/C	Salamis
24 Sep	U-855	Ohlsen	Br. Sqdn. 224	†61-00 N, 04-07 E
26 Sep	U-871	Ganzer	Br. Sqdn. 220	†43-18 N, 36-28 W
29 Sep	U-863	v. d. Esch	VB-107	†10-45 S, 25-30 W
30 Sep	U-921	Werner	HMS *Campania*'s Sqdn. 813	†72-32 N, 12-55 E
30 Sep	U-1062	Albrecht	*Fessenden (DE-142) & Mission Bay (CVE-59)*	†11-36 N, 34-44 W
30 Sep	U-703	Brünner	Mine	†Iceland (E. coast)
18 Sep	U-925	Knoke	Unknown (Sailed from Bergen 24 Aug)	†Iceland-Faeroes
4 Oct	U-993	Steinmetz	RAF A/C	Bergen
4 Oct	U-228	Engel	RAF A/C (out of service, 12 Oct)	Bergen
4 Oct	U-437	Lamby	RAF A/C (Put out of service, 13 Oct)	Bergen
4 Oct	U-92	Brauel	RAF A/C (Put out of service, 12 Oct)	Bergen
5 Oct	U-168	Pich	HNM Sub. *Zwaardvisch*	06-20 S, 111-28 E
15 Oct	U-777	Ruperti	RAF A/C	Wilhelmshaven
16 Oct	U-1006	Voigt	HMCS *Annan*	60-59 N, 04-49 W
19 Oct	U-957	Schaar	Rammed 19th by Ger. trspt.; out of service, Narvik, 21st.	
23 Oct	U-985	Wolff	Mine (out of service, 15 Nov)	[63-07 N, 07-45 E?] (or Listerfjord?)
24 Oct	U-673	Gerke	Collision w/mine-sweeper; stranded	59-20 N, 05-53 E

['44] Date	U-Boat	Last Comdr.	Cause of sinking	Position
27 Oct	U-1060	Brammer	HMS *Implacable*'s 1771 Sqdn., Br. Sqdn. 502 & Czech Sqdn. 311	†65-24 N, 12-00 E
28 Oct	U-1226	Claussen	Unknown (Schnörkel accident?)	†Atlantic
— Oct	U-2331	Pahl	Marine casualty	Near Hela (Baltic)
9 Nov	U-537	Schrewe	*Flounder (SS-251)*	†07-13 S, 115-17 E
10 Nov	U-966	Wolf	Collision	Off C. Ortegal, Biscay
11 Nov	U-771	Block	HM Sub. *Venturer*	†69-17 N, 16-28 E
11 Nov	U-1200	Mangels	HMS *Pevensey Castle* *Launceston Castle*, *Portchester Castle* & *Kenilworth Castle*	†50-24 N, 09-10 W
25 Nov	U-322	Wysk	HMS *Ascension* & Norw. Sqdn. 330	†60-18 N, 04-52 W
28 Nov	U-80	Keerl	Diving accident	54-25 N, 19-50 E
30 Nov	U-196	Striegler	Unknown	†Sunda Straits
— Nov	U-547	Niemeyer	Mine	Baltic
6 Dec	U-297	Aldegarmann	HMS *Loch Insh* & *Goodall*	†58-44 N, 04-29 W
9 Dec	U-387	Büchler	HMS *Bamborough Castle*	†69-41 N, 33-12 E
12 Dec	U-416	Rieger	Raised after collision of 30 March	Baltic (off Pillau)
12 Dec	U-479	Sons	Mine	†Eastern Baltic
13 Dec	U-365	Todenhagen	HMS *Campania*'s Sqdn. 813	†70-43 N, 08-07 E
17 Dec	U-400	Creutz	HMS *Nyasaland*	†51-16 N, 08-05 W
18 Dec	U-1209	Hülsenbeck	Diving accident [struck rock]	49-57 N, 05-47 W
19 Dec	U-737	Gréus	Collision with minesweeper	(60-00 N, 05-00 E)
26 Dec	U-2342	Schad v. Mittel-biberach	Mine	†53-55 N, 14-17 E
27 Dec	U-877	Findeisen	HMCS *St. Thomas*	46-25 N, 36-38 W
28 Dec	U-735	Börner	RAF A/C	59-24 N, 10-29 E
30 Dec	U-772	Rademacher	RCAF Sqdn. 407	†50-05 N, 02-31 W
31 Dec	U-906	Unknown	Air attack	Hamburg
31 Dec (Apr '45?)	U-2532	Unknown	US Army A/C	Hamburg
31 Dec (Apr '45?)	U-2537	Klapdor	US Army A/C (& RAF)	Hamburg

['45] Date	U-Boat	Last Comdr.	Cause of sinking	Position
1945				
—Jan	U-650	Zorn	Unknown	†NE of Scotland (?)
10 Jan	U-679	Aust	Mine [Russian A/S vsl. *MO-124*?]	†Baltic
16 Jan	U-248	Loos	*Hayter (DE-212), Otter (DE-210), Varian (DE-798), & Harry E. Hubbard (DD-748)*	†47-43 N, 26-37 W
16 Jan	U-482	v. Matuschka	HMS *Peacock, Hart, Starling, Loch Craggie & Amethyst*	†55-30 N, 05-53 W
17 Jan (11 Mar?)	U-2515	Borchers	US Army	Hamburg
17 Jan	U-2530	Bockelberg	US Army	Hamburg
17 Jan	U-2523	Ketels	US Army &RAF A/C	Hamburg
21 Jan	U-1199	Stollmann	HMS *Icarus & Mignonette*	49-57 N, 05-42 W
24 Jan	U-763	Schröter	Russian A/C	Koenigsberg
26 Jan	U-1172	Kuhlmann	HMS *Aylmer, Calder, Bentinck & Manners*	†53-39 N, 05-23 W
27 Jan	U-1051	v. Holleben	HMS *Tyler, Keats & Bligh*	†52-24 N, 05-42 W
31 Jan	U-3520	Ballert	Mine	†54-27 N, 09-26 E
— Jan	U-1020	Eberlein	Unknown	(†)57-20 N, 04-10 W
— Jan	U-382	Wilke	Collision	Baltic
3 Feb	U-1279	Falke	HMS *Bayntun, Braithwaite & Loch Eck*	61-21 N, 02-00 W
4 Feb	U-745	v. Trotha	Unknown	†Eastern Baltic
4 Feb	U-1014	Glaser	HMS *Loch Scavaig, Nyasaland, Papua & Loch Shin*	†55-15 N, 06-44 W
9 Feb	U-864	Wolfram	HM Sub. *Venturer*	†60-46 N, 04-35 E
14 Feb	U-989	v. Roithberg	HMS *Bayntun, Braithwaite, Loch Eck, & Loch Dunvegan*	†61-36 N, 01-35 W
15 Feb	U-1053	Lange	Casualty in rocket tests	†60-22 N, 05-10 E
16 Feb	U-309	Loeder	HMCs *St. John*	†58-09 N, 02-23 W
17 Feb	U-425	Bentzien	HMS *Lark & Alnwick Castle*	69-39 N, 33-50 E
17 Feb	U-1273	Knollmann	Mine	†59-30 N, 10-30 E
17 Feb	U-1278	Müller-Bethke	HMS *Bayntun & Loch Eck*	†61-32 N, 01-36 W

['45] Date	U-Boat	Last Comdr.	Cause of sinking	Position
18 Feb	U-2344	Ellerhage	Collision	54-09 N, 11-51 E
19 Feb	U-676	Sass	Mine	†Baltic
20 Feb	U-1208	Hagene	HMS *Amethyst*	†51-48 N, 07-07 W
22 Feb	U-300	Hein	HMS *Recruit, Evadne & Pincher*	36-29 N, 08-20 W
24 Feb	U-480	Förster	HMS *Duckworth & Rowley*	†49-55 N, 06-08 W
24 Feb	U-927	Ebert	Br. Sqdn. 179	†49-54 N, 04-45 W
24 Feb	U-3007	Marbach	US Army A/C	Bremen
27 Feb	U-1018	Burmeister	HMS *Loch Fada*	49-56 N, 05-20 W
27 Feb	U-327	Lemcke	VPB-12, HMS *Labuan, Loch Fada & Wild Goose*	†49-46 N, 05-47 W
28 Feb	U-869	Neuerburg	*Fowler (DE-222)* & RF *l'Indiscret*	†34-30 N, 08-13 W
— Feb	U-923	Frömmer	Mine	†Baltic
2 Mar	U-3519	v. Harpe	Mine	†54-11 N, 12-05 E
7 Mar	U-1302	Herwartz	HMCS *La Hulloise, Strathadam & Thetford Mines*	†52-19 N, 05-23 W
10 Mar	U-275	Wehrkamp	Mine	†50-36 N, 00-04 E
11 Mar	U-681	Gebauer	VPB-103	49-53 N, 06-31 W
12 Mar	U-683	Keller	HMS *Loch Ruthven & Wild Goose*	†49-52 N, 05-52 W
12 Mar	U-260	Becker	Mine	51-15 N, 09-05 W
14 Mar	U-714	Schebcke	HMSAS *Natal*	†55-57 N, 01-57 W
15 Mar	U-367	Stegemann	Mine	†54-25 N, 19-50 E
18 Mar	U-866	Rogowsky	*Lowe (DE-325), Menges (DE-320), Pride (DE-323) & Mosley (DE-321)*	†43-18 N, 61-08 W
20 Mar	U-905	Schwarting	Br. Sqdn. 86	†59-42 N, 04-55 W
20 Mar	U-1003	Strübing	HMCS *New Glasgow* [rammed]*	55-25 N, 06-53 W
22 Mar	U-296	Rasch	Br. Sqdn. 120	†55-23 N, 06-40 W
26 Mar	U-399	Buhse	HMS *Duckworth*	49-56 N, 05-22 W
27 Mar	U-965	Unverzagt	HMS *Conn, (Rupert & Deane)*	†58-34 N, 05-46 W
27 Mar	U-722	Reimers	HMS *Fitzroy, Redmill & Byron*	†57-09 N, 06-55 W
29 Mar	U-246	Raabe	HMS *Duckworth*	†49-56 N, 05-25 W
29 Mar	U-1106	Bartke	Br. Sqdn. 224	†61-46 N, 02-16 W
30 Mar	U-1021	Holpert	HMS *Rupert, Conn (& Deane)*	†58-19 N, 05-31 W

*Scuttled, 23d.

['45] Date	U-Boat	Last Comdr.	Cause of sinking	Position
4 Mar	U-3508	v. Lehsten	US Army A/C	Wilhelmshaven
30 Mar	U-429 (ex RS *S-2*)	Kuttkat	US Army A/C	Wilhelmshaven
30 Mar	U-96	Rix	US Army A/C	Wilhelmshaven
30 Mar	U-72	Mayer	US Army A/C	Bremen
30 Mar	U-430 (ex RS *S-3*)	Hammer	US Army A/C	Bremen
30 Mar	U-870	Hechler	US Army A/C	Bremen
30 Mar	U-329	-(unknown)-	US Army A/C	Bremen
30 Mar	U-884	Lüders	US Army A/C	Bremen
30 Mar	U-2340	Klusmeier	US Army A/C	Hamburg
30 Mar	U-350	Niester	US Army A/C	Hamburg (D. Werft)
— Mar	U-348	Schunck	US Army A/C	Hamburg
30 Mar	U-1167	Bortfeld	US Army A/C	Hamburg
30 Mar	U-747	Zahnow	US Army A/C	Hamburg
30 Mar	U-886		US Army A/C	Bremen (on stocks)
31 Mar	U-682	Tienemann	RAF A/C	Hamburg
2 Apr	U-321	Berends	Polish Sqdn. 304	†50-00 N, 12-57 W
3 Apr	U-1221	Ackermann	US Army A/C	Kiel
3 Apr	U-2542	Hübschen	US Army A/C	Kiel
3 Apr	U-3505	Willner	US Army A/C	Kiel
3 Apr	U-1276	Wendt	Br. Sqdn. 224	†61-42 N, 00-24 W
4 Apr	U-749	Huisken	US Army A/C	Kiel
4 Apr	U-237	Menard	US Army A/C	Kiel
4 Apr	U-3003	Kregelin	US Army A/C	Kiel
5 Apr	U-1169	Goldbeck	Mine	†52-03 N, 05-53 W
6 Apr	U-1195	Cordes	HMS *Watchman*	50-33 N, 00-55 W
7 Apr	U-857	Premauer	*Gustafson (DE-182)*	†42-22 N, 69-46 W
8 Apr	U-1001	Blaudow	HMS *Fitzroy* & *Byron*	†49-19 N, 10-23 W
8 Apr	U-2509	Schendel	RAF A/C	Hamburg
8 Apr	U-2514	Wahlen	RAF A/C	Hamburg
8 Apr	U-3512	Hornkohl	RAF A/C	Kiel
8 Apr	U-774	Sausmikat	HMS *Calder* & *Bentinck*	†49-58 N, 11-51 W
9 Apr	U-804	Meyer	Br. Sqdns. 143, 235 & 248	†57-58 N, 11-15 E
9 Apr	U-843	Herwartz	Br. Sqdns. 143, 235 & 248	57-58 N, 11-15 E
9 Apr	U-1065	Panitz	Br. Sqdn. 235	†57-48 N, 11-26 E
10 Apr	U-878	Rodig	HMS *Vanquisher* & *Tintagel Castle*	†47-35 N, 10-33 W
12 Apr	U-486	Meyer	HM Sub. *Tapir*	†60-44 N, 04-39 E

['45] Date	U-Boat	Last Comdr.	Cause of sinking	Position
12 Apr	U-1024	Gutteck	Captured by HMS *Loch Glendhu* (towed by *Loch More*, but sank underway)	53-39 N, 05-03 W
14 Apr	U-1206	Schlitt	Diving accident (grounded)	57-21 N, 01-39 W
14 Apr	U-235	Huisken	Ger. escort vessel *T-17*	†57-44 N, 10-39 E
15 Apr	U-285	Bornhaupt	HMS *Grindall* & *Keats*	†50-13 N, 12-48 W
16 Apr	U-1063	Stephan	HMS *Loch Killin*	50-08 N, 05-52 W
15 Apr	U-1235	Barsch	*Stanton (DE-247)* & *Frost (DE-144)*	†47-54 N, 30-25 W
16 Apr	U-78	Hübsch	Russian forces	Pillau, in dock
16 Apr	U-880	Schötzau	*Stanton (DE-247)* & *Frost (DE-144)*	†47-53 N, 30-26 W
16 Apr	U-1274	Fitting	HMS *Viceroy*	†55-36 N, 01-24 W
19 Apr	U-251	Säck	Br. Sqdns. 235, 143, 248 and Norw. Sqdn. 333	56-37 N, 11-51 E
19 Apr	U-879	Machen	*Buckley (DE-51)* & *Reuben James (DE-153)*	†42-19 N, 61-45 W
21 Apr	U-636	Schendel	HMS *Bazely, Drury* & *Bentinck*	†55-50 N, 10-31 W
21 [22?] Apr	U-518	Offermann	*Carter (DE-112)* & *Neal A. Scott (DE-769)*	†43-26 N, 38-23 W
23 Apr	U-183	Schneewind	*Besugo (SS-321)*	†04-57 S, 112-52 E
23 Apr	U-396	Siemon	Br. Sqdn. 86	†59-29 N, 05-22 W
24 Apr	U-546	Just	*Flaherty (DE-135), Neunzer (DE-150), Chatelain (DE-149), Varian (DE-798), Harry E. Hubbard (DD-748), Janssen (DE-396), Pillsbury (DE-133)* & *Keith (DE-241)*	43-53 N, 40-07 W
25 Apr	U-1107	Parduhn	VPB-103	†48-12 N, 05-42 W
28 Apr	U-56	Miede	US Army & RAF A/C	Kiel
29 Apr	U-0117	Riecken	Br. Sqdn. 120	†56-04 N, 11-06 W
29 Apr	U-307	Krüger	HMS *Loch Insh*	69-24 N, 33-44 E
29 Apr	U-286	Dietrich	HMS *Loch Shin, Anguilla* & *Cotton*	†69-29 N, 33-37 E

['45] Date	U-Boat	Last Comdr.	Cause of sinking	Position
30 Apr	U-242	Riedel	Unknown	(†)U. K. Area
30 Apr	U-548	Krempl	*Natchez (PF-2), Coffman (DE-191), Bostwick (DE-103) & Thomas (DE-102)*	†36-34 N, 74-00 W
30 Apr	U-1055	Meyer	VPB-63	†48-00 N, 06-30 W
— Apr	U-1227	Altmeier	US Army & RAF A/C	Kiel
— Apr	U-677	Ady	US Army & RAF A/C	Hamburg
— Apr	U-982	Harmann	US Army & RAF A/C	Hamburg
— Apr	U-3525	Gaude	US Army & RAF A/C	Baltic
— Apr	U-2516	Kallipke	US Army & RAF A/C	Hamburg
— Apr	U-1131	Fiebig	US Army & RAF A/C	Kiel
30? Apr	U-325	Dohrn	Unknown	†Eng. Channel (I. of Man)
— Apr	U-326	Matthes	Unknown	(†)United Kingdom area
2 May	U-1007	v. Witzendorff	RAF A/C (later mined)	58-54 N, 11-28 E
2 May	U-2359	Bischoff	Br. Sqdns. 143, 235, 248, RCAF Sqdn. 404 & Norw. Sqdn. 333	†57-29 N, 11-24 E
3 May	U-3030	Luttmann	RAF A/C	55-30 N, 10-00 E
3 May	U-3032	Slevogt	RAF A/C	55-30 N, 10-00 E
3 May	U-2540	Schultze	RAF A/C	55-30 N, 10-00 E
3 May	U-2524	v. Witzendorff	Br. Sqdns. 254 & 236	55-55 N, 10-45 E
3 May	U-1210	Grabert	RAF A/C	54-27 N, 09-51 E
4 May	U-2503	Wächter	Br. Sqdns. 236 & 254 (damage, beached)	55-37 N, 10-00 E
4 May	U-711	Lange	HMS *Searcher*'s *Trumpeter*'s & *Queen*'s Sqdns. 853, 882 & 846	68-48 N, 16-38 E
4 May	U-2338	Kaiser	Br. Sqdns. 254 & 236	55-37 N, 10-00 E
4 May	U-393	Herrle	Br. Sqdns. 254 & 236	55-37 N, 10-00 E
4 May	U-904	Stührmann	RAF bombs } Scuttled after damage	54-29 N, 09-52 E
4 May	U-746	Lottner	RAF bombs } Scuttled after damage	54-48 N, 09-55 E
4 May	U-876	Bahn	RAF bombs } Scuttled after damage	54-29 N, 09-52 E

['45] Date	U-Boat	Last Comdr.	Cause of sinking	Position
4 May	U-236	Mumm	Br. Sq. 236 & 254 [Scuttled later]	55-37 N, 10-00 E
4 May	U-4708	Schulz	A/C	Kiel (Germaniawerft)
4 May	U-4709		A/C	Kiel (Germaniawerft)
4 May	U-4711	Endler	A/C	Kiel (Germaniawerft)
4 May	U-4712	Fleige	A/C	Kiel (Germaniawerft)
5 May	U-2365	Christiansen	Czech. Sqdn. 311	57-27 N, 10-38 E
5 May	U-2367	Schröder	Collision with U-boat; (raised, '56, for Bundesmarine)	Great Belt
5 May	U-534	Nollau	Br. Sqdn. 206	56-59 N, 11-48 E
5 May	U-3523	Müller	Br. Sqdn. 224	†56-06 N, 11-06 E
5 (4?) May	U-2521	Methner	Br. Sqdn. 547	†56-11 N, 11-08 E
5 May	U-733	Hammer	RAF bombs (Damaged, scuttled)	54-47 N, 09-26 E
5 May	U-3503	Deiring	Br. Sq. 86 (Scuttled off Göteborg, 8th)	56-45 N, 10-49 E
5 May	U-579	Schwarzenberg	RAF bombs	†55-30 N, 10-00 E
6 May	U-1008	Gessner	Br. Sqdn. 86	57-52 N, 10-49 E
6 May	U-2534	Drews	Br. Sqdn. 86	†57-08 N, 11-52 E
6 May	U-853	Frömsdorf	*Atherton (DE-169) & Moberly (PF-63)*	†41-13 N, 71-27 W
6 May	U-881	Frischke	*Farquhar (DE-139)*	†43-18 N, 47-44 W
7 May	U-320	Emmrich	Br. Sqdn. 210	61-32 N, 01-53 E
— May	U-398	Cranz	Unknown	(†)E. Coast Scotland
9 May	U-2538	Klapdor	Mine	Off Marstal, SW Aerö I.
16 May	U-873	Steinhoff	Surrendered	Portsmouth, N.H
3 Jun	U-1277	Stever	Scuttled	W. of Oporto
17 Aug	U-977	Schaeffer	Surrendered	La Plata R., Argentina

N. B.: Over 150 U-boats were scuttled in northern ports the first week in May '45–15 in Wilhelmshaven, 10 at Hamburg, 31 in Travemünde and 26 in Kiel the 2d. and 3d; 56 in Flensburg alone the 5th. From then till the end of June, approximately an equal number of submarine crews surrendered to the Allies from Narvik to Portsmouth, N.H., and a straggler or two at the River Plate as late as mid-August. To pinpoint terminal date and locale for an individual U-boat, consult the general index, as space in the two paragraphs immediately following permits only a skeleton listing of the 300 U-numbers.

Scuttled, May 1945

U-8, -14, -17, -29, -30, -37, -38, -46, -48, -52, -57, -58, -60, -61, -62, -71, -120, -121, -129, -137, -139, -140, -141, -142, -146, -148, -151, -152, -267, -290, -316, -323, -339, -349, -351, -370, -397, -428, -446, -474, -475, -552, -560, -612, -704, -708, -717, -721, -748, -750, -792, -793, -794, -795, -822, -828, -903, -922, -924, -929, -958, -963, -979, -999, -1002, -1016, -1025, -1056, -1057, -1058, -1101, -1132, -1161, -1162, -1168, -1170, -1192, -1193, -1196, -1204, -1205, -1207, -1277, -1303, -1304, -1306, -1308, -1405, -1406, -1407, -2327, -2330, -2332, -2333, -2339, -2343, -2346, -2347, -2349, -2352, -2355, -2357, -2358, -2360, -2362, -2366, -2368, -2369, -2370, -2371, -2501, -2504, -2505, -2507, -2508, -2510, -2512, -2517, -2519, -2520, -2522, -2525, -2526, -2527, -2528, -2531, -2533, -2535, -2536, -2539, -2541, -2543, -2544, -2545, -2456, -2458, -2551, -3001, -3002, -3004, -3005, -3006, -3009, -3016, -3018–3029, -3031, -3033, -3034, -3037–3040, -3044, -3501, -3502, -3504, -3506, -3507, -3510, -3511, -3513, -3516, -3517, -3518, -3521, -3522, -3524, -3526–3530, -4705, -4707, -4710, UIT-2, -3, -6–14.

Surrendered, May - June, 1945

(Over 100 U-boats, here marked ‡, were sunk in deep water in the North Atlantic soon after capitulation; this was the British "Operation Deadlight.")

U-59, -101, -143‡, -145‡, -149‡, -150, -155‡, -170‡, -190, -218‡, -234, -244‡, -245‡, -255‡, -256, -262, -276, -278‡, -281‡, -291‡, -293‡, -294‡, -295‡, -298‡, -299‡, -310, -312‡, -313‡, -315, -318‡, -324, -328‡, -363‡, -368‡, -369‡, -427‡, -481‡, -483‡, -485‡, -510, -516‡, -530, -532‡, -539‡, -541‡, -555, -637‡, -668‡, -712, -716‡, -720‡, -739‡, -758, -764‡, -773‡, -775‡, -776‡, -778‡, -779‡, -802‡, -805, -806, -825‡, -826‡, -827‡, -858, -861‡, -868‡, -873, -874‡, -875‡, -883‡, -889, -901‡, -907‡, -926, -928‡, -930‡, -953, -956‡, -968‡, -975‡, -977, -978‡, -991‡, -992‡, -994‡, -995, -997‡, -1004‡, -1005‡, -1009‡, -1010‡, -1019‡, -1022‡, -1023‡, -1052‡, -1054, -1061‡, -1064, -1102‡, -1103‡, -1104, -1105, -1108, -1109, -1110‡, -1163‡, -1165‡, -1171, -1194‡, -1197‡, -1198‡, -1201, -1202, -1203, -1228, -1230‡, -1231, -1232, -1233‡, -1271, -1272, -1275, -1301‡, -1305, -1307‡, -2321‡, -2322‡, -2324‡, -2325‡, -2326, -2328‡, -2329‡, -2334‡, -2335‡, -2336‡, -2337‡, -2341‡, -2345‡, -2348‡, -2350‡, -2351, -2353, -2354, -2356, -2361‡, -2363‡, -2502, -2506, -2511, -2513, -2518, -2529, -3008, -3017, -3035, -3041, -3514‡, -3515, -4706.

Acknowledgments

In preparing the *Death of the U-Boats* I used a number of sources in the United States, the United Kingdom, and Germany. Primary were the records of the United States Navy Historical Section, particularly the Operational Archives, over which Dr. Dean Allard presides. I used the war diary and other papers of the Eastern Sea Frontier. I also used Vice Admiral Eberhard Weichold's unpublished manuscript, *German Surface Ships, Policy, and Operations in World War II*, prepared for the U.S. Navy. In England I consulted records and works in the Imperial War Museum and the British Museum. But the major source of materials was the Office of Public Records at Kew, in greater London, as with my *The U-Boat Wars*, published in 1984. There the Admiralty records were invaluable, particularly the CAB series and the ADM series, which contain the proceedings of the War Cabinet and its subsidiary bodies and the Admiralty and all the elements of the Royal Navy. I am indebted to many archivists and librarians in this establishment. Also in Germany I visited the *Deutsch Marine-Bund* in Wilhelmshaven. Captain Guenter Zietlow was extremely helpful in steering me to materials. In Westerland/Sylt I consulted the *U-Boot-Archiv* (now called *Traditions-archiv Unterseeboote*) maintained at the old Luftwaffe base on the island by Horst Bredow and his assistant, Rudolf Wieser. I exchanged some correspondence with Fleet Admiral Otto Kretschmer, who was most helpful, and spoke with Guenther Kuhnke, one of the World War II U-boat captains who lives near Wilhelmshaven. The photo librarian of the *Wilhelmshaven Zeitung* gave me a good deal of material. So did Gerd Kossack, now a Wilhelmshaven taxi driver, who was a prisoner of war in the

United States in World War II. Andrew Link and Sigrid Mattner of the Wilhelmshaven Public Library were also most helpful, and I owe a debt to a young lady named Hannah, at the front desk of Kaiser's Hotel in Wilhelmshaven for much assistance beyond the call of her duty.

I am also indebted to Anne-Marie Dussault and Claude Marcil of Emission Contrechamp of the Société Radio Canada, Ste. Foy, Quebec, for information about the German POW activities in Canada during the war.

Chapter Notes

Abbreviations: ASW, British Admiralty Anti-Submarine Warfare reports. These were issued monthly during the war.

Doenitz: *Twenty Years and Ten Days*. The memoirs of Admiral Karl Doenitz.

The Golden Horseshoe: The Golden Horseshoe, a biography of Otto Kretschmer, by Terence Robertson. London: Evans Brothers Ltd., 1955.

Walker: *Walker, R. N.* A biography of Captain Frederick John Walker, R.N., by Terence Robertson. London: Evans Brothers Ltd., 1956.

Cremer: *U-333*, by Peter Cremer. Berlin: Verlag Ullstein, 1982.

Churchill: The six-volume history *The Second World War*, by Winston H. Churchill. Boston: Houghton Mifflin Co., 1950. Referred to by vols. 1–6.

A Noble Proposal

The text of the London Submarine Agreement is printed in various diplomatic and military records. I found it in Admiral Doenitz's memoirs.

1

The material about Churchill and Pound comes from Churchill's vol. 1, *The Gathering Storm*, p. 422ff. Doenitz's message to his U-boat commanders is from *The Golden Horseshoe*, pp. 19–20, and his first war orders are from the same source, p. 24. The material on the sinking of the *Athenia* is contained in an interview with Captain James Cook and First Officer Copeland of the SS

Athenia by British naval intelligence, Sept. 1939. The German activities after Britain declared war are from an unpublished manuscript by the author, *Hitler's War.* Lemp's activities in the *U-30* are described well in Frank's *The Sea Wolves*. Doenitz's message on the existing orders for mercantile warfare is found in his memoirs. The account of the sinking of the *Royal Sceptre* is from the Admiralty report of Sept. 1939.

2

The report of the sinking of SS *Manaar* is from Admiralty reports. The account of the *Ark Royal* is contained in *The Life and Death of the Ark Royal,* Public Records file, Kew. The Admiralty report on the sinking of *U-27* is from ASW, Sept. 1939. Lemp's patrols in *U-30* are detailed in ASW report, March 1940.

3

The material on British intelligence comes from discussions with various British former naval officers regarding ONI intelligence techniques. The Doenitz war orders, copies captured from U-boats, are found in ASW report, April 1940. The details of Convoy KJF3 come from the interview of ONI with Captain C. E. Ratkins, Public Records Admiralty files. The material concerning Captain Edward Templeton Grayston of the *Karamea* comes from an interview with Captain Grayston, Admiralty files.

4

Lieutenant Rolf Dau's exploits in *U-42* are from ASW report, Nov. 1939. Much of the material for the period October to December 1939 can be found in *The Golden Horseshoe,* p, 29ff. Doenitz's concern with the torpedo failures is from his memoirs. The story of the sinking of the SS *Darino* is from the account of Chief Officer J. H. Casson of that ship, in Admiralty files.

5

Material on the sinking of *U-35* is from the ASW report, Dec. 1939. War activities in the North Sea is described in *The Golden Horseshoe* and by Doenitz. The attacks of the larger, oceangoing submarines on convoys are from ASW report, Feb. 1940.

6

The material on the British Cabinet meetings, the plans for Norway, and the activity in the Western Approaches is from the British Cabinet proceedings, Feb. 1940, the CAB file, Public Records, and also Doenitz. The sinking of *U-33* and other February U-boat activity is from the ASW report, March 1940. The account of the sinking of *U-63* is from ASW report, March 1940.

7

The story of *U-31* is contained in ASW report, Nov. 1940. The material on the German spring offensive is from Doenitz, Chapt. 5. The report on the sinking of *Arandora Star* is in the ADM files, Public Records. Description of U-boat headquarters and adulation of the captains is told in Cremer, Chapt. 3. Summer and fall 1940 U-boat activity can be found in *The Golden Horseshoe*, p. 49ff. *U-31* and *U-32* activity and sinking are from ASW report, Nov. 1940.

8

Italian submarine activity is described in *The Golden Horseshoe*, p. 67ff. Sinking of the Italian submarine *Durbo* is based on ASW report, Nov. 1940, which also contains the details of the sinking of the Italian submarine *Lafolé*. Doenitz's view on the Italian submarine effort is from his memoirs. The admiral was singularly harsh on the Italians, who did much more in the submarine war than he gave them credit for.

9

Material on the U-boat men is from talks with German U-boat personnel and propaganda leaflets collected by British naval intelligence, which paid a good deal of attention to the problems of German U-boat morale all during the war. Several reports and many documents and leaflets exist in the files of the Admiralty. January and February statistics are from the ASW for February and March 1940. The discussion of radio techniques is from a special report, "The Radio War," issued by ASW in March 1945. The long account of the sinking of Kretschmer, Schepke, and Prien within a few days comes from the ASW report for April 1941, and *The Golden Horseshoe*.

10

American participation in the Atlantic war, and April and May activity, is from reports of the British War Cabinet meetings, CAB files, Public Records, for April, May 1941. The sinking of *U-110,* ASW report, April 1941. The death of the *U-556* is from interrogation of Junior Officer aboard *U-556,* May 1941, War Office files, Public Records. July and August statistics are from U.S. naval records of U-boat sinkings in World War II. The story of the sinking of the *U-570* is from the files of the *Traditionsarchiv Unterseeboote* of Horst Bredow (formerly called *U-Boot-Archiv*) in Westerland/Sylt and the ASW report of Sept. 1941.

11

Material on the crew of *U-570* and on the prison camps is from Kretschmer's account in *The Golden Horseshoe,* War Office POW records, reports and articles in the files of the U-boat archives in Westerland. The official story of the escape and shooting of Lieutenant Berndt is still in the secret files of the British War Office and probably will not be released until after the year 2000, along with much other material about German POWs. The reason seems to be to protect the guilty, since Kretschmer and other Germans have spoken of bribing British guards, etc., in matters involving escapes and papers.

12

Kretschmer's meeting with Creasy is found in *The Golden Horseshoe,* preface by Admiral Sir George Creasy. The story of *U-111* is from ASW report, Nov. 1941, and the other sea war events of October and November are from ASW, Dec. 1941. The boatswain's mate account of *U-95* is from interrogation of unidentified boatswain's mate (POW 1067), War Office 208, and ASW, Jan. 1942.

13

The material for much of this chapter is from the ASW reports, Nov. 1941–Feb. 1942; Walker, p. 46ff; Account of Convoy HG 76, ADM files, Dec. 1941. The German U-boat commander's view of the sea war is from the broadcast of Lieutenant Bigalk over German Radio, Jan. 15, 1942, as reported in ASW monthly report, Feb. 1942.

14

December's events, U.S. Navy report of U-boats sunk, see Appendix. Description of U-boat types and capabilities from Horst Bredow, U-boat archives, Westerland. The account of *U-93* is from Opitz interview with British interrogators, WO files, Feb. 1942, and ASW report, March 1942. Material on Greger and *U-85* is pieced from the diary of Seaman Ungethuem, picked up by the USS *Roper* after the sinking, and in the U.S. Navy historical division files, the action report of USS *Roper,* for April 13, 14, 1942, and the report of the sinking of *U-85*, ASW, April 1942.

15

U-boat war, spring 1942, ASW report, May 1942. Account of Convoy HG 84, ASW report, July 1942. Also Walker, pp. 69–90. The sinking of *U-706* is contained in ASW, Aug. 1942, and in the U.S. Navy Eastern Sea Frontier war diary, July 1942. The Italian submarine activity is recorded in ASW report, Aug. 1942.

16

Account of the voyage of convoy ON 115, ASW report, Sept. 1942. Account of the sinking of *U-210*, ASW report, Oct. 1942. Account of the sinking of *U-379*, ASW, Sept. 1942.

17

Several accounts of the *pillenwerfer* appear in brief sections in the ASW in January and February 1943. Account of the sinking of *U-331*, ASW, Dec. 1942. Lieutenant von Tiesenhausen's letter of protest to the Allied authorities about the American attacks on his surrendered U-boat has been preserved in the ADM files. January 1943 activities, ASW monthly summary, Feb. 1943; Walker p. 82ff. Convoy YM 1, ASW monthly report, Feb. 1943.

18

Convoy HX 224 material, ASW monthly summary, March 1943, and account of Convoy HX 224. February U-boat activity, ASW summary, April 1943. The new German radar, special ASW report, "The Radio War," April 1945. Discussion with Rudolf Wieser, U-boat archives, Westerland/Sylt. U-boats damaged, specifically on heavy damage to U-boats in recent convoy attacks,

ASW report, April 1943. Changes in Doenitz's operations, ASW reports, April, May, June 1943.

19

Account of the sinking of the *U-506*, ASW report, Aug. 1943. "Information recently obtained..." quotation, ASW, Sept. 1943. Sinking of *U-513*, ASW account, Aug. 1943. Subsequent U-boat sinkings, and change in U-boat warfare, ASW reports, Sept., Oct., Nov. 1943, and diary of U.S. Navy Eastern Sea Frontier for the last quarter of 1943. This period marked the real end of the super-U-boat threat. Afterward, the U-boats continued to exact their toll, but there was no more chance that they could win the war for Germany, as had certainly been the case until the Atlantic air gap was closed and the escort carriers were brought forth in sufficient numbers to enable the formation of hunter-killer teams of close air-sea support. Sinking of the *U-340*, ASW, Nov. 1943.

20

The Cabinet and U-boat committee meetings of the last days of 1944 and early 1945 indicated how seriously worried were the highest British military and naval authorities about the renewed U-boat threat with the perfection of the schnorkel and the Type XXI and Type XXIII (large and small) submarines that could remain submerged for weeks. There really could not be that much grounds for worry because the Allied land forces were moving steadily, with the exception of the debacle at Christmastime 1944, when the American high command was caught at play by the Germans with their "do or die" offensive around Bastogne. But that offensive had to run out of steam very shortly, even had all the surrounded troops surrendered. The fact was that by Christmas 1944, the German war effort was finished. All the Germans were capable of doing from that point on was killing and creating mischief, but not of taking and holding territory. The U-boat war would continue to the bitter end, and some U-boat men still thought they had a chance, but the statistics say otherwise.

The March attacks of the U-boats are covered in the ASW monthly report, April 1945. The April U-boat activity is from ASW report, May 1945. That was the last real issue of the monthly Anti-Submarine Warfare report, and it gave the details on the surrender and the scuttling, and destruction of the German U-boat fleet by the Germans and the Allies. The end of the war finished the U-boats. In the course of the war, the Germans had sent 39,000 men to sea in these dangerous craft, and 28,000 of them had been lost. It was the highest mortality rate for the men of any service of any country.

Material about *U-1195* is from notes by Rudolf Wieser of the U-boat archives in Westerland. This was his U-boat, and he was one of the eighteen survivors who made it to the surface after the sinking.

Bibliography

Arnold-Forster, Mark. *The World At War.* New York: Stein and Day, 1973.

Bekker, Cajus. *Verdammte See.* Hamburg: Gerhard Stalling Verlag. English translation by Frank Ziegler. *Hitler's Naval War.* London: MacDonald and Jane's, 1974.

______. *Das Bildbuch der deutschen Kriegsmarine, 1939–1945.* Munich: Wilhelm Heyne Verlag, 1983.

Bloomfield, Howard V. L. *The Compact History of the United States Coast Guard.* New York: Hawthorn Books, 1966.

Brennecke, Jochen. *Haie im Paradies, der deutsche U-Boot-Krieg 1943–45 in Asiens Gewaessern.* Munich: Wilhelm Heyne Verlag, 1983.

______. *Die Wende im U-Boot-Krieg, ursachen und Folgen, 1939–1943.* Herford: Koehlers Verlagsgesellschaft, 1984.

Brustat-Naval, Fritz, und Teddy Suhren. *Nasses Eichenlaub, als Kommandant und F.d.U. im U-Boot-Krieg.* Herford: Koehlers Verlagsgesellschaft, 1983.

Bryant, Rear Admiral, Ben. *One Man Band, The Memoirs of a Submarine C.O.* London: Kimber and Co., 1958.

Buchheim, Lothat-Guenther. *The U-Boat.* Translated from the German by Denver and Helen Lindley. New York: Alfred A. Knopf, 1975.

______. *U-96, Szenen aus dem Sekrieg.* Munich: Albrecht Knaus Verlags, 1981.

Busch, Harald. *So War der UN-Boot Krieg.* English translation by L. P. R. Wilson, under the title *U-Boats at War.* New York: Ballantine Books, 1965.

Churchill, Winston S. *The Second World War.* 6 vols. Boston: Houghton Mifflin Co., 1948–53.

Cremer, Peter. *U-333*. Berlin: Verlag Ullstein, 1984.

Doenitz, Karl. *Zehn Jahre und Swanzig Tage*. Bonn: Athenaeum-Verlag Junker und Duennhaupt, K.G., 1958.

______. *The Conduct of the War At Sea*. Washington, D.C.: Division of Naval Intelligence, 1946.

Frank, Wolfgang. *The Sea Wolves*. English translation by Lt. Cdr. R. O. B. Long, RNVR. New York: Rinehart and Co., 1955.

Gallery, Rear Admiral, Daniel V. *Twenty Million Tons Under the Sea (U-505)*. New York: Warner Books, 1956.

Goebbels, Joseph. *The Goebbels Diaries*. Translated and edited by Fred Taylor. New York: G.P. Putnam's Sons, 1983.

Halstead, Ivor. *Heroes of the Atlantic*. New York: E.P. Dutton and Co., 1942.

Hezlet, Vice Admiral Sir Arthur. *The Submarine and Sea Power.* New York: Stein and Day, 1967.

Hinsley, F. H. *Hitler's Strategy.* Cambridge: Cambridge University Press, 1951.

His Majesty's Stationery Office. *The Battle of the Atlantic, Official Account of the Fight Against U-Boats*. London: HMSO, 1946.

Hoyt, Edwin P. *The Sea Wolves*. New York: Lancer Books, 1972.

______. *Submarines at War.* New York: Stein and Day, 1982.

Jones, R. V. *The Wizard War.* New York: Coward McCann & Geoghegen, 1978.

Kurowski, Franz. *Krieg unter Wasser.* Duesseldorf: Econ Verlag, 1979.

Lund, Paul, and Harry Ludlum. *Night of the U-Boats*. London: W. Foulsham and Co., Ltd., 1973.

MacIntyre, Captain Donald. *U-Boat Killer.* Annapolis: Naval Institute Press, 1976.

Mason, David. *U-Boat: The Secret Menace*. London: MacDonald & Co., 1968.

Middlebrook, Martin. *Convoy.* London: Allen Lane, Penguin Books, Ltd., 1976.

Morison, Samuel Eliot. *History of the United States Naval Operations in World War II*. 15 vols. Boston: Atlantic, Little Brown, 1948–62.

Noli, Jean. *Les Loups de l'Amiral*. Paris: Libraire Arthème Fayard, 1970. Translated by J. F. Bernard, published in the U.S. as

The Admiral's Wolf Pack. Garden City, N.Y.: Doubleday Inc., 1974.

Peillard, Leonce. *Geschichte des U-Bootkrieges 1939/1945*. Lagenfurt and Vienna: Verlag Buch und Welt, 1970.

Raeder, Grand Admiral, Erich. *Struggle for the Sea*. Translated by Edward Fitzgerald. London: William Kimber Ltd., 1959.

Reisenberg, Felix. *Sea War*. New York: Rinehart and Co., 1956.

Robertson, Terence. *The Golden Horseshoe*. London: Evans Brothers Ltd., 1955.

———. *R. N. Walker*. London: Evans Brothers, Ltd., 1956.

Rogge, Bernhard, with Wolfgang Frank. *Schiff 16*. Oldenburg: Gerhard Stalling Verlag, 1955.

Rohwer, Juergen. *Die-U-Boot Erfolge Der Achsenmachte 1939–1945, Bibliothek fuer Aeitgeschichte*. Munich: J. F. Lehmanns Verlag, 1968. English language version, translated by John A. Broadwin. Annapolis: Naval Institute Press, 1983.

Roscoe, Theodore. *United States Submarine Operations in World War II*. Annapolis: U.S. Naval Institute Press, 1949.

Roskill, Captain S.W., DSC, R.N. *History of the Second World War, United Kingdom Military Series. The War at Sea, 1939–45*. 4 vols. London: Her Majesty's Stationery Office, 1954.

Ruge, Admiral Friedrich. *Der Seekrieg. The German Navy's Story*. English translation by Commander M. G. Saunders, R.N. Annapolis: U.S. Naval Institute, 1957.

Schaefer, Heinz. *U-Boat 977*. New York: W. W. Norton and Co., 1952.

Shirer, William L. *The Rise and Fall of the Third Reich*. New York: Simon and Schuster, 1959.

Stevenson, William. *A Man Called Intrepid*. New York: Harcourt, Brace, Jovanovich, 1976.

Waters, John M. *Bloody Winter*. Princeton: Van Nostrand Co., 1967.

Watts, Anthony J. *The U-Boat Hunters*. London: MacDonald and Janes, 1976.

Werner, Herbert A. *Iron Coffins*. New York: Holt, Rinehart and Winston, 1969.

West, Nigel. *MI5*. New York: Stein and Day, 1982.

Index

WARNER TAKES YOU TO THE FRONT LINES.

- ☐ **SOME SURVIVED** by Manny Lawton
(H34-934, $3.95, USA) (H34-935, $4.95, Canada)
A World War II veteran and prisoner of war recounts the true story of the Bataan Death March—a harrowing journey through dust, agony and death at the hands of the Japanese.

- ☐ **BIRD** by S. L. A. Marshall
(H35-314, $3.95, USA) (H35-315, $4.95, Canada)
The brilliant account of the First Air Cavalry's heroic defense of the strategic Vietnam landing zone called "Bird."

- ☐ **FOX TWO** by Randy Cunningham with Jeff Ethell
(H35-458, $3.95, USA) (H35-459, $4.95, Canada)
A fighter pilot's birds-eye view of air combat in Vietnam, written by a decorated Navy jet commander.

Warner Books P.O. Box 690
New York, NY 10019

Please send me the books I have checked. I enclose a check or money order (not cash), plus 95¢ per order and 95¢ per copy to cover postage and handling.* (Allow 4-6 weeks for delivery.)

___Please send me your free mail order catalog. (If ordering only the catalog, include a large self-addressed, stamped envelope.)

Name ____________________

Address ____________________

City ____________ State ________ Zip ________

*New York and California residents add applicable sales tax. 389

From bestselling author Andrew Kaplan

☐ **DRAGONFIRE**

(A34-658, $4.50, U.S.A.) (A34-659, $5.50, Canada)

A lone American intelligence agent makes a suicidal journey through the hellish underbelly of Southeast Asia.

☐ **SCORPION**

(B73-622, $3.95, U.S.A.) (B34-432, $4.95, Canada)

A Vietnam veteran turned CIA-trained assassin is plunged into an intricate game of espionage when a Congressman's daughter is abducted.

☐ **HOUR OF THE ASSASSINS**

(A73-663, $3.95, U.S.A.) (A34-631, $4.95, Canada)

A CIA maverick is on the trail of notorious Nazi Josef Mengele—the key figure in a sinister plot to revive the Third Reich 30 years after World War II.

Warner Books P.O. Box 690
New York, NY 10019

Please send me the books I have checked. I enclose a check or money order (not cash), plus 95¢ per order and 95¢ per copy to cover postage and handling.* (Allow 4-6 weeks for delivery.)

___Please send me your free mail order catalog. (If ordering only the catalog, include a large self-addressed, stamped envelope.)

Name ______________________________

Address ______________________________

City ______________ State ______________ Zip ______________

*New York and California residents add applicable sales tax. 330